DAVID KLINGHOFFER

THE LORD WILL

GATHER ME IN

*My Journey to*

*Jewish Orthodoxy*

THE FREE PRESS

*New York London Toronto Sydney Singapore*

*f*P

THE FREE PRESS
A Division of Simon & Schuster Inc.
1230 Avenue of the Americas
New York, NY 10020

THE FREE PRESS and colophon are trademarks of Simon &
Schuster Inc.

*Designed by Pei Loi Koay*

Manufactured in the United States of America

10   9   8   7   6   5   4   3   2   1

Library of Congress Cataloging-in-Publication Data

Klinghoffer, David. 1965–
    The Lord will gather me in : my journey to Jewish Orthodoxy /
David Klinghoffer.
      p.  cm.
    ISBN 0-684-82341-1
    1. Klinghoffer, David. 1965–  .   2. Jews—United States
—Biography.   3. Jews—United States—Return to Orthodox Ju-
daism.   I. Title.
E184.37.K55   1999
973'.04924—dc21                         98-26387
                                                     CIP

*For my parents,*

*all of them*

*Should my father and mother abandon me,*

*the Lord will gather me in.*

PSALM 27:10

# CONTENTS

# INTRODUCTION

—

*A*s a five-year-old growing up in Southern California, I developed a preoccupation with a Swedish galleon that had sunk in Stockholm Harbor three centuries earlier. I turned five in 1970, which was the year of my first trip abroad. For a destination my Jewish parents could have done the predictable thing and taken me to Israel, but they didn't. Though my mother is dead, so I will never know for certain, I believe she wanted personally to escort me to Scandinavia. That year, following the advice of parenting manuals, she had told me that she and my father were not my "natural" parents. She said I had been adopted and that my natural mother was a Swedish woman.

I don't remember that conversation, but I do distinctly remember seeing the warship *Vasa*. The *Vasa* was ordered built in 1625 by the Swedish king Gustav Vasa as a sign to his opponents in the Thirty Years War that Sweden was not to be trifled with. Intended to be the largest ship ever built, she must have been magnificent to see, if you go in for this kind of thing. We picture ships of that period as sedate brownish crafts, but the *Vasa* looked more like something designed to parade down Fifth Avenue on Puerto Rican Day. Her dimensions, 228 feet long and 190 feet high at the mainmast, were covered in elaborate sculpture: devils, angels, lions, mermaids, monsters from Greek mythology, and unidentifiable creatures, all gilded or painted in gaudy colors. Unfortunately the splendor of the *Vasa* was not complemented by sound maritime engineering. Fifteen minutes after sailing in majesty on her maiden voyage in 1628, the *Vasa* encountered a squall, toppled over, and sank.

Anders Franzén, an underwater archaeologist, found her in 1956, largely intact, and Sweden resolved to raise her up from the mud and clay. The blackened oak pierced the surface of the waters in 1961. Thereafter the *Vasa* was preserved in a sort of aluminum greenhouse, floating on a pontoon, where she could be sprayed daily with polyethylene glycol to keep the wood from drying out.

With other tourists, my parents and I clambered along walkways opposite the *Vasa*'s double gun decks, enveloped by the rainforest-and-furniture-polish smell of the damp oak and preservative chemicals. We marveled at the giant, fearsome lion figurehead and the staring lion-head masks used to shield the gun ports. I imagine myself as I gazed wide-eyed at the towering black aftercastle, a little blond boy whose blood ancestors lived in Sweden at the time the *Vasa* sank. I brought home with me a cartoon picture book, *The Vasa Saga*, which portrayed the ship with a sleeping human face as it waited to be discovered by Anders Franzén, then an excited, curious expression as two giants from Swedish folklore lifted her up from the seabed on huge ropes, and a happy face as tourists gathered to admire her. It was my favorite book when I was a little boy, and I paged through it again and again. It entranced me.

We read in Genesis that at the start of Creation the Presence of God hovered upon the face of the waters. About that verse the medieval scholar Rashi comments that it was the Throne of Glory itself that was over the water. Similarly, in Psalm 29 King David imagines the Lord thundering across vast waters. But in our time, not least among modern secular Jews, it often seems that God's presence is submerged, sunk in mud and clay at the bottom of an ocean. Yet in individual lives He can frequently be observed rising through fathoms of dark water.

For much of my own life I had the sense of something hidden and secret, great and ancient and marvelous, approaching the daylight from below. The surface may have been broken, as if by the tip of the mast of a long-sunken ship, quite early on, maybe the night that I sought to ensure for myself that I really was a Jew, entering a bathroom in my parents' home with an old prayer book and a soap-cleansed razor blade to perform a do-it-yourself version of an ancient conversion rite. But the superstructure did not begin to emerge until later. At times it seemed that the thing that was rising might not hold together; its old timbers might split apart and fall back where they had come from. Always there was more to be revealed. There was more to come after each of my several conversions to Judaism. There was more to come after I waited, by the telephone in a Manhattan apartment, through the twenty-five hours of a Jewish Sabbath. I hoped that any moment the phone would ring and for the first time I would hear the voice of the Swedish woman my parents had told me about the year we saw the *Vasa.* God was not done rising in me then, either.

———

WHEN I WAS A BOY, an assumption prevailed about the future of American Jewry. My family belonged to the Reform movement, whose ideology rejects the millennia-old belief that Jews must observe the commandments in God's Torah. Secular, liberal, freed of the dogma and superstition my parents' generation associated with traditional Judaism, we all *knew* that Orthodoxy was dying and that we would bury it. Orthodoxy was for senior citizens and Reform for the young.

Today I am myself Orthodox. So are tens of thousands of other Jews in their twenties and thirties who grew up Reform, Conservative, or nothing at all. I live on New York City's Upper West Side, a neighborhood once associated with liberal, secular Jewishness in its most radical, alienated forms. From my window above West End Avenue I see religious Jews in skullcaps walking by at all hours. Young Jews. The vast prewar apartment buildings that line the avenue like the walls of a canyon form a vertical shtetl.

One Friday night before my thirtieth birthday I sought to attend the service for the Sabbath eve at a lovely weathered Romanesque synagogue on West 95th Street. It wasn't a holiday or a special Shabbat at all, but the crowd was so dense that I could barely squeeze in the front door. When prayers were through and the mass of Jews streamed out onto the street, I felt suddenly antique. Everyone seemed to be twenty-one years old.

I was struck not only by the average age of the group, but by the spiritual distance I knew many in the crowd had traveled. Often, at a Sabbath dinner or lunch at a friend's apartment on the West Side, I have looked around and realized that no one at the table grew up Orthodox. Several may not have been born Jewish at all. I have been at tables where everybody was a convert: a person born gentile who has accepted traditional Judaism.

The return of secular Jews to Orthodoxy has been called the *ba'al teshuvah* movement. In rabbinic literature a *ba'al teshuvah* is literally a "master of return" or "master of repentance." At Yom Kippur each year, every Jew is expected to give up his past year's sins and become a *ba'al teshuvah.* Another rabbinic term, *tinok sh'nishbah*, means a Jewish child who was stolen by bandits and raised by non-Jews in ignorance of his Jewish soul and his Jewish responsibilities, who therefore is considered innocent despite his failure to carry out those responsibilities. Though Jewish children are no longer stolen by bandits, that expression is sometimes applied to Jews who grew up bereft of any acquaintance with Judaism. But really there is no precise term for a person raised "secular" by Jews, who never knew he had been commanded by God to observe the teachings of the Torah, but who nevertheless comes to realize that God cares about what he does with his life, and reorders his commitments accordingly. So neither *ba'al teshu-*

*vah* nor *tinok sh'nishbah* gets across the astonishing newness of this development in Jewish history. But one must make do with the language available.

This is the story of one *ba'al teshuvah*, who is also a convert, and how he returned to Judaism though for twenty-six years he wasn't a Jew at all. What, from the secular liberal Jewish perspective, went wrong? Or if you prefer, what went right?

# Chapter 1

# EVIL SPEECH

*T*hough my father and mother gave me many things, there is one thing they could not give me because they had not been given it themselves. Thus my first encounter with Torah came as the kind of shock you get on reading one of those stories in the newspaper about a strange, rare animal that scientists have just discovered in a New Guinea forest. Yesterday it had been wandering around in that forest without your ever suspecting it, and now here it is on the breakfast table looking up from the cover of the "Science" section.

In eighth grade I happened to open a book I had been given by my maternal grandmother, Anna Bernstein, six years before for Hanukkah. The book was *To Be a Jew*, written in 1972 by Hayim Halevy Donin, an Orthodox rabbi in Detroit. It is about Jewish "law."

As I could not have told you then because I had never heard of that subject, Judaism rests on a foundation of teachings that are inaccurately called "law," a term that causes the unwary to sneeze as if they had sniffed some mere dusty jurisprudence, one that constricts the natural liveliness of people and stifles the attempt to achieve a state of spiritual union with God. But Halachah—the body of regulations intended to guide the behavior of Jews in everything from what words of blessing to say on relieving oneself to how to expiate sins—does not equal law. The word derives from the Hebrew root HLKH, meaning "walk" or "go." Jewish "law" is the way Jews have been taught to walk with God.

Donin addresses his account of Halachah to an audience possessing a modest level of Jewish learning. That was an advantage that I, like my parents and most other American Jews, did not have. So when I opened his book, I skipped all the parts about distinctively Jewish practices—festival days, prayer, food regulations—and landed as if by chance on a passage dealing with an activity I knew well. It concerned gossip and backbiting, the whole area of what Torah calls "evil speech."

In large American cities it is common to read newspaper stories about extreme viciousness by little boys: about, for example, some eleven-year-old boys who got hold of sawed-off shotguns, stuck up a bodega, and after all the money in the till had been surrendered, shot the cash register attendant to death. I'm not all that surprised by these stories. Boys, after all, will be wolves. When I was eleven years old in a well-to-do suburban town of horse trails and red-tile roofs, I was vicious in my own way, not quite like a wolf, but maybe like a koala: slow moving and pastoral, chewing meditatively on a leaf, but with sharp teeth and a nasty disposition. Some boys have hobbies such as playing soccer or sniffing glue. In company with another boy, Bennett Schneir, it was my hobby to make cruel fun of everyone I knew, usually but not always behind their backs. This began in the fourth grade when Bennett's parents moved to my hometown of Palos Verdes, a large hill that is also a peninsula in the southwest corner of Los Angeles County.

Writing about his childhood, C. S. Lewis recalled the delightful hours he spent with his older brother elaborating the history and geography of imaginary countries they called "Animal Land" and "India," full of colorful, charming inhabitants with their own system of parliamentary democracy. Bennett and I mapped out Mongoloid Apia, an imaginary planet, and talked about writing a book-length history of it (we never did). Far from the precocious humanism of Animal Land, Mongoloid Apia was devoted exclusively to mocking first our little brothers, both named Michael, then teachers, friends from Dapplegray Intermediate School, our friends' parents, even their pets. Everyone got his own "land" on Mongoloid Apia, with a theme tied to whatever we judged to be his most pathetic foible. For instance, Bennett and I were keen on making fun of people if they were poor—which, in our case, meant less than upper middle class. Somehow we got the idea into our heads that one boy's family was so impoverished that to feed themselves they were reduced to scouring the local beaches for grunions, which they kept in a bathtub. Thus: Grunion Land, where the citizens could afford no food but grunions.

Several boys we knew had unintentionally humorous fathers, who did odd things like blink a lot or collect comic books. For laughs we began making tape recordings, parodies of talk shows in which the boys and their fathers were hosts or guests, portrayed by Bennett and me. For each boy and his father Bennett and I had a distinct voice, a grotesque imitation of the boy's or father's real voice. We spent hours making tapes.

Which was why Rabbi Donin's book caught me by surprise. I remember reading the chapter headed "Laws Relating to Slander, Revenge, and Deceit" as I sat on the edge of my parents' bed, a feeling of horror growing in my stomach with each paragraph, as if by chance I had wandered into a grand jury room and it was me they were indicting.

I read: "The Torah states: 'You shall not go about as a tale bearer among your people' (Lev. 19:16). A tale bearer is one who goes about saying, 'I heard this and this about so and so.' Even if what he says is true, he still transgresses the commandment. Tale bearing is a great sin and can cause great bloodshed (literally or figuratively) and that is why this precept is immediately followed by the one, '. . . And you shall not stand idly by the blood of your neighbor.'" What's more, "There is an even greater sin that is included in the prohibition and this is an evil tongue. . . . This refers to one who goes about discrediting another telling uncomplimentary things about him *even if they are true.* One who speaks outright falsehoods is called a spreader of evil, malicious, and false reports. . . . He is the lowest of the low and is regarded as a 'moral leper.'"

It seemed that Rabbi Donin was writing specifically about me. I found his discussion devastating. Sitting on my parents' bed, I clutched *To Be a Jew* in two hands, my head lowered and my mouth slightly open.

There were many other ways in which my life differed from the model set forth by Rabbi Donin. But the rest of his chapters were on subjects that either had to do with adults (divorce, conjugal duties, birth control, and so on) or seemed as distant from Palos Verdes as Animal Land was from Mongoloid Apia. I must have glanced at the headings related to Jewish festivals, the Sabbath, kosher and nonkosher foods, and more arcane matters. I had heard little or nothing about most of these and so passed over all of them with a clear conscience. Or rather, almost all of them. One other chapter caught my eye. It was chapter 17, "Adoption and Conversion."

In 1965, the year I was born, 77,000 American children were adopted by adults biologically unrelated to them. Like many healthy, white children put up for adoption, I was adopted, or at least the formalities of my adoption had been completed, before I was born. In 1970 my mother told me that while she and my father loved me "more than anything in the world," the person who had in fact given birth to me was a young lady, concealed in vagueness, whose name my mother never mentioned. She had become pregnant but was unable, for unspecified reasons, to raise me as her own child. The only biographical details my mother included had to do with ethnicity: my birth mother was Swedish, and the man who got her pregnant was ethnically Irish. I didn't learn much more than this, but I must have questioned my mother on one point, for I knew that this young woman wasn't Jewish.

"We are your real parents," my mother told me more than once, and I got the point. Occasionally she would ask, "Do you ever think about your biological mother? Do you ever wonder about her?" This was in the same tone of voice in which once, when I was twelve and my brother Michael nine, she asked if we ever felt sexually attracted to other boys. I knew the answer she wanted to hear.

"No, Mom," I always said, "I never think about her." And I meant it.

Here in Rabbi Donin's book was another chapter apparently aimed straight at me. Rabin Donin divides his discussion into sections: "Adoption of a Jewish Child" and "Adoption and Conversion of a Non-Jewish Child." Under the former I found two pages of bulleted items using Hebrew terms and citing ancient sources that I knew nothing about, but the rabbi got his point across clearly enough: "Since Jewish law does not regard children as the property of parents, the notion of transferring title to the children to someone else through adoption simply does not exist. Jewish law regards the relationship between natural parents and their offspring to be irrevocable."

It comes as a shock to open a book almost at random and find it authoritatively stated that your parents are not your parents. And that was only the first page in Donin's treatment of the subject. Under "Adoption of a Non-Jewish Child," I read one of the most unexpected sentences of my reading life: "A child born to a non-Jewish mother, regardless of who the father is, has the status of a non-Jew according to Jewish law." Legal adoption makes no difference. Nor does giving your child a "Hebrew name" in addition to his secular one. A boy can be converted to Judaism, but the rite prescribed by Rabbi Donin clearly had never been acted out in my vicinity. It consists of two parts: a circumcision performed by a ritually trained *mohel*, "*with the intent of conversion*" and attended by a religious court of three learned men. This happens, as prescribed in the Book of Genesis, on the eighth day of the child's life. After the boy is a year old, his parents bring him to a ritual bath, a *mikvah*, where he is immersed, again in the presence of three learned men.

What shocked me initially might not be what you think. No identity crisis had grabbed hold of my eleven-year-old psyche. Rather, it was this: My parents were good Jewish people who didn't lie or cheat, but Rabbi Donin's book was the first time I had come across rigorously articulated rules of conduct, and his discussion of adoption was the first time I can recall hearing the term "Jew" defined with any seriousness, or in fact defined at all. That shock set off tremblings elsewhere in me that would, much later, change the way I understood myself and understood God.

Still, the question of what I was, Jew or non-Jew, entered my mind even then. What did I do about it? Nothing. I could have asked my mother (not really my father, a practical man who worked too hard as a dentist to go in for metaphysical speculation) if Rabbi Donin's statements were correct; but I didn't, for the same reason I never asked her anything about my biological parents. To take up that line of inquiry would have amounted to a tacit questioning of her identity as my mother. So I was left with this unsettling thought: If after reading Rabbi Donin's comments about "evil speech" I didn't know what kind of Jew I was, after reading his comments about adoption I began to feel I might not be a Jew at all.

Fortunately, children have a way of dealing with an assertion at variance with their experience of the world. Rather than accept it or reject it, as an adult would, they allow the troublesome claim to pass through their minds the way the body allows certain foods, like black pepper or NutraSweet, to pass through the body without digesting them. The difference between a child's mind and the digestive system is that while the latter has an opening at one end through which undigested material exits, the former doesn't.

What I had read did have one immediately discernible effect. For a couple of weeks, whenever Bennett and I would launch into one of our sessions of mockery and backbiting, Rabbi Donin's words came back to me. I couldn't imagine suddenly ceasing to talk about my friends behind their backs, one day out of nowhere announcing to Bennett that our good-natured fun "bordered on an evil tongue." But I could make a small compromise with myself.

I remember where that thought occurred to me. I was standing in the attendance office at Dapplegray Intermediate School. A girl was talking on the pay telephone by the door, and I was leaning on the counter where you would go to present your excuse, forged so as to appear to have been written by a parent or a doctor, for missing a class. Maybe after handing in such an excuse myself ("David could not attend first period today because our car broke down. . . ."), I had an attack of conscience. In any event I resolved that if Bennett initiated one of our sessions, I would go along with it. *But* I wouldn't start one myself.

And out of the attendance office I marched, fresh in my resolve to improve myself in this modest way. In Jewish thought, such a resolution is called *teshuvah*—repentance, literally a "return" to God. This act of *teshuvah*, solemnly entered into that day with Hayim Halevy Donin's admonitions sounding in my head, lasted, at the outside, about a month. Yet his claims about Judaism had shaken me, and though I quickly resumed old habits, I could never entirely shrug off what I had read. That peculiar animal from New Guinea had escaped from its newspaper photo and was itself now on my breakfast table, holding its ground.

# Chapter 2

# IN THE DESERT

*F*reud might have called my brush with Rabbi Donin's book a "return of the repressed," the breaking forth of unconscious thoughts and feelings previously trapped in the psyche's lower depths. Here, however, the psyche in question wasn't my own, but, broadly speaking, that of my family.

I know less about my mother's ancestors than about my father's, but the dynamic of Jewish return observed by the writer Michael Medved holds true of both. According to Medved, himself a *ba'al teshuvah*, you rarely find more than four consecutive generations of secular or Reform Jews. When a Jew breaks with traditional Judaism, his children or grandchildren either will intermarry and raise their own children as non-Jews or indifferent Jews, so that line of the family disappears from the people Israel—or they will return to the Judaism he thought he helped them escape. Thus the typical Reform Jew has an Orthodox predecessor no more than three generations back.

In 1958 my father was a dentist in the air force and my mother a speech therapist employed by the local Elks Club in Lancaster, California, a town in the Mojave Desert near Edwards Air Force Base. My father, a captain, worked in the dental clinic there. They met and seven months later were married. From Lancaster they relocated to Los Angeles County, which climatically speaking bears some resemblance to desert country; this fact is testified to by my reluctance even today to walk around my New York apartment barefoot, a habit of avoidance I picked up from the occasional scorpion we would find tottering around the kitchen floor of my childhood home. I take it as a metaphor that my parents met in a desert and proceeded to move to another desert, which is where I lived when I was adopted by them.

In Jewish tradition, a wilderness or desert has several meanings. The Sinai wilderness was the spot chosen by God to let the Jews as a people hear His voice. In Hebrew the words for "desert" and "word" share a common root, for in the desert one hears the Word of God.

Judaism also takes another, less positive view of the desert. It can signify spiritual emptiness. In his prophecy Isaiah hears a voice crying, "Prepare in the wilderness the way of the Lord, make straight in the desert a highway for our God." The desert is symbolically a location God does not customarily occupy or travel through, a land of waste as devoid of His life-giving presence as it is devoid of water—the emblem of a vain, errant Jewish society. Deserts oppress us with their sheer emptiness. I once had an oddly frightening experience driving through a desert, the Anza-Borrego, east of San Diego halfway to Mexicali. I hardly had a chance to appreciate its austere beauty, with the foothills of the Vallecito Mountains pushing up on either side of the narrow road and tiny yellow flowers the only living things in sight, because a feeling of dread rode along in the car with me. The emptiness of the yellow desert floor makes escape impossible. There is no place to escape to. The sensation wasn't alleviated by the frequent, enigmatic road

signs warning SUDDEN FLOODS. I was born into a spiritual desert,
the latter kind, as much as a geographical one.

My mother thought of herself as a Reform Jew. Her parents
were both *ba'alei teshuvah* in their way. Her mother, Anna Stein,
was born in what is now Poland but was then the Austro-Hungarian
empire, to a traveling violinist who took her to America as a baby
and left her and his wife in the Bronx while he and a small or-
chestra toured the southern United States. Anna wasn't raised in a
religious home, but then she met Samuel Bernstein at a dance in
New York in the 1920s. Sam worked as a shoe salesman at Macy's.
He was the son of pious parents, Polish Jews, a photo of whom
shows them looking very stern, she a large and impressive woman,
he with a white beard and wearing a black caftan and round brim-
less hat. But Sam was a modern young man. After he married
Anna he chose a home for them in the northernmost neighborhood of Manhattan, Inwood, where their neighbors were pre-
dominantly middle-class Irish. Sam dispensed with most of the
old-fashioned ways of his parents, but not all. Anna wanted her in-
laws to be able to eat at her table, so she learned to maintain a
kosher kitchen. She even lit Sabbath candles on Friday nights.

When I was a child, Sam and Anna were the only people I knew
who prayed. It was Anna's custom when she spoke on the telephone to sit in a chair by the kitchen door with the phone on her
lap and her eyes closed. She did not believe in long telephone conversations, since she disapproved of people who were "a lot of
talk." She made an exception, though, for conversations with God,
which she conducted sitting in that same chair with her eyes
closed. She had no need of the old black dial phone, which sat on
its stand, but instead simply whispered to Him.

I never knew Sam Bernstein to spend time in synagogues or observe the Sabbath. Yet every day, for at least the several years before his death, he said the traditional Jewish morning prayer
service, having affixed to his forehead and left arm a set of tefillin,
the leather straps and black leather boxes containing scriptural
passages on parchment, donned once a day by Orthodox men in
fulfillment of a biblical commandment. He had received the

tefillin half a century earlier as a bar mitzvah boy. I still have his *Standard Prayer Book,* published in 1915 and probably also a bar mitzvah gift, which he left so worn from use that its cover hangs from the rest of the book by lengths of black duct tape resembling tefillin straps.

I didn't associate my father's parents, Morton and Eleanor Klinghoffer, with prayer. Until recently in American Jewish history one generally found an inverse relationship between settledness in this country—the length of time the family has been here, their material prosperity—and spiritual intensity. My father's mother came from a well-established German Jewish family. Though she, like Morton, grew up in New Jersey, the family maintained its membership in Manhattan's swank Central Synagogue, a Reform house of worship designed to look like a Byzantine church. Eleanor was a formal woman who addressed her husband as "Klinghoffer." I have a sense that Morton, who distributed liquor wholesale, was more fun than his wife, his job requiring an ability to fraternize with the New Jersey tavern owners to whom he sold his product. But I didn't know either of them well.

Morton's father, Isaac, came from roots as Old World and pious as Sam Bernstein's parents. The Klinghoffer family in all its branches originated in a town called Drogobych, near Lvov, formerly part of the Austro-Hungarian empire, now Ukraine. (I am a distant cousin of the famous Leon Klinghoffer, whom Palestinian liberation fighters liberated from his wheelchair and launched over the side of the cruise ship *Achille Lauro* in 1985.) When Isaac left there, at age eighteen in 1890, the Jews in town divided ideologically down the lines that were then splitting East European Jewry: there were secular followers of the Jewish Enlightenment; mystical Hasids; and regular Orthodox Jews. Isaac's family—his father, Moses, grandfather Kalman, and great-grandfather Hersch Klinghoffer—fell into the last category. But while making his fortune as a Jersey City businessman in real estate and women's hats, he joined a Reform temple to suit his wife, Ada, and did not give his children an Orthodox education. In the Klinghoffer family, as in so many others, the spirituality of the Old World melted like snow into which handfuls of coarse salt have been thrown.

In this environment it was unlikely that my parents would receive anything like a serious Jewish education, and they didn't. So the idea of settling in a nonkosher locale didn't bother them in the least. Separately, after graduate school they made their way to Lancaster, a place definitely not known for a burgeoning Jewish population.

What our parents were like when they were young is a question that must fascinate many of us who grew up before the availability of videotape. Until a few years ago I could only speculate about my parents. Then a great-aunt happened to unearth three reel-to-reel tapes. After Paul and Carol got engaged they decided, rather than make a lot of expensive long-distance phone calls, to record their voices and send them across the country, in this way to introduce Carol to her future in-laws.

The first of the three tapes was recorded in December 1958. While his parents waited for rapturous tributes to Miss Carol Bernstein, my father recalls a trip to Knotts Berry Farm: "It's not as bad as you thought when you were out here. We had dinner at one of these restaurants [there] which was just very fair." There follow numerous inconsequential details: Christmas dinner at the hospital at Edwards Air Force Base, shopping for a ring at Fedco, my mother's qualities as a cook. "I got her one of those mixers, one of those GE mixers. She's been using it, to my advantage!" At last my mother can no longer contain herself. "What Paul is trying to say," she tells his parents, "is that we love each other. I know that I love him very much and I know he feels the same about me. He wouldn't tell you this, but I think perhaps I should."

I recognized a number of familiar qualities in my parents as they sounded back then. One was my father's shyness about discussing matters beyond the realm of observable facts. Another is the place of Judaism in their lives. It was there, but on the margins. "I told you how we met and everything," says my father, "at the, uh, Rosh Hashanah service, was it? Yeah." My mother talks about how much she wants her parents to meet Paul's parents. "However, I believe Paul told you that my grandfather recently passed away, and I think that my parents would like to wait the [Jewish] thirty-day mourning period before they make any plans." At the same time, she notes that she has just sent Christmas cards to Paul's aunts, "to Clara and Harold, and one to Lee and Violet."

After marrying, my parents settled on the Palos Verdes peninsula, a bucolic place overlooking Catalina Island on one side, the cargo ships and skyscraping cranes of Los Angeles Harbor on the other. From our backyard we could see the vast grid of Los Angeles itself, behind which stood the San Gabriel Mountains. Mt. Wilson was the tallest of them, our secular Mt. Olympus. If my parents had deliberately set out to find the spot most distant from and marginal to the great southwestern city's growing Jewish community, they could not have done a better job than to pick Palos Verdes. The closest thing to a leading religious denomination was perhaps a watery Presbyterianism. With its ocean cliffs and winding roads, cactus-dotted yellow hilltops and a slow-moving landslide that kept a large portion of the place depopulated by gradually tearing houses in half, this was quasi-desert country, with, fortunately, more than a few signs of life.

---

AS A VERY YOUNG CHILD, from about age six onward, I had a fascination with ruins. Any kind of ruins would do. I began telling adults that when I grew up I wanted to be "an aboveground archaeologist," since the dark places underneath ruins scared me off. I picked up the interest on a cruise my parents took me on in the Mediterranean. The cruise included stops in Israel, where I adored the Roman ruins at Caesarea, and at Ephesus, an ancient Greek city on the Turkish shore of the Aegean. In nineteenth-century England it was in vogue to debate the question, not *whether,* but *why* ruins are to be considered more beautiful than intact buildings. I think, though, that their appeal has little to do with beauty and more to do with some qualities they reflect in our lives. Ruins suggest to us what was in the past and what might have been in the present if the forces of chaos and general breakdown had not interfered. Ruins are also terribly poignant, doubly so now to me as I try to remember the first years of my life.

The beaches at the bottom of the cliffs at Palos Verdes are not frequented by bathers, since they are composed of tiny rocks that make it painful to walk around barefoot. Because these beaches are so poorly attended, flotsam accumulates there: masses of sea-weed, a rusted Century 21 real estate sign, a dead sea lion. My early recollections, like most everyone's, are basically flotsam, broken off from the clear recording my mind no doubt made of the events of my childhood as they happened—a recording that with the years has gone to ruins. Memories do that, even if, like me, you're still in your early thirties. I wonder what I thought about God when I was a little boy. That I can only guess, from picking here and there among debris, I find vaguely heartbreaking.

I remember an argument I had with a little neighbor girl, Tahare Barnes. Tahare's father was American and her mother was Iranian, but Tahare was being raised a Christian. She apparently had been instructed, somewhat confusedly, on the subject of Jesus. Sitting on our kitchen floor, we two kindergartners got into a shouting match over the question "Who is better, Jesus or God?" Loyally I took God's side, and she took Jesus'.

A midrash, or biblical interpolation, posits that at conception children possess great stores of knowledge. Jewish children in particular, whether their parents are deeply religious or avowedly secular, are said to hold in their minds the entire body of Torah. Before we are born, however, an angel touches us at the indentation on the upper lip just under the nose. Immediately we forget all we knew. Our task over a lifetime is to recover lost memories. But children instinctively know that God lives. It is only by the exertions of their parents, or sometimes just by drawing inferences from silence, that they are reduced to agnostics and the occasional atheist.

You would expect my mother to have been the one to instruct me about God, since my parents' taped communications from Lancaster show that she was the more likely of the two to broach delicate subjects. To the best of my ability to remember, that never happened. I did, however, receive confused hints. Outside the front door of our house, there was a cast-cement statue of Buddha, a few feet tall, though I had no notion that many people in Asia venerated him as the Enlightened One. Eventually the statue got pushed over and the Enlightened One's head was knocked off. In a similar syncretistic mode, my family observed Christmas one year—including, at my insistence, a real Christmas tree with fake snow on it. For one or two years we had an entirely artificial "Hanukkah bush," which my mother told me would be visited by a present-laden Santa Claus stand-in, "Hanukkah Charlie." At other times she could be an energetic purist in matters relating to Jewishness. When I was in second grade she became concerned that my class planned to put on a Christmas pageant but no Hanukkah pageant. So she wrote one for us, which we performed, with me in the improbable role of the warrior Judah Maccabee.

---

IF YOU VISITED our house today (my father still lives there) and entered the linoleum-tiled kitchen, you would see prominently displayed, above the radio and intercom, a large wooden sign designed to look antique. In a "ye olde-fashioned" typeface, it bears the warning "We Serve Kosher Food Only." This was untrue; but while my mother enjoyed making Cajun shrimp and didn't observe any other rules of maintaining a kosher kitchen, she intensely disliked pork. She would have no truck with the stuff and wouldn't even—unlike my father, brother, and me—eat it at restaurants. (I loved bacon, though I piously drew the line at ham.)

When I was growing up, the type of Jew who says, "Sorry, I don't eat pork," but then orders a shrimp cocktail was often encountered; but you don't meet many representatives of this philosophy anymore. The thinning of their ranks says something about the approach many other Jews took to Judaism. What sets pork apart from all other types of non-kosher food has nothing to do with Judaism and a lot to do with non-Jews.

Like our fellow Reform Jews, if they were ever told anything at all about the subject, we were informed that kashrut, the study of what makes food kosher or not, was an ingenious if now archaic ancestor of modern health diets. Somehow an ancient Hebrew Jane Brody figured out that pork was less healthy and more susceptible to contamination through bacteria or worms than beef or chicken and that low-fat, low-cholesterol fish was healthier than all of them. Thus pork was forbidden, while some beef, some chicken, and almost all fish were allowed. But nowadays, with modern methods of food storage and preparation, there is no need to worry about any of this, with the possible exception of high-cholesterol red meat. So go ahead, we were told, eat anything you like.

The problem with this piece of speculation, apart from its having no historical backing whatsoever, is that for all the ancient world, eating animal flesh of any kind was a risky venture. There was no refrigeration and no understanding of what bacteria are. Nor did the average person have to worry about cholesterol or fat content. He stood a relatively poor chance of living long enough to have a heart attack or a stroke.

Thus the twenty or so passages in the Torah dealing with food and its preparation have nothing to do with maintaining bodily health. These lay out a system defining forbidden animals and animal parts, conditions under which permitted animals become forbidden, forbidden methods of slaughtering permitted animals, forbidden food combinations, and conditions under which vessels permitted for food preparation become forbidden.

The subject of kashrut is enormously complicated, and rationalistic attempts to explain it all tend to be unconvincing. Professor Leon Kass, for instance, asserts that it reminds us of certain universal laws of nature and the organization of life on earth. But why we need kashrut to remind us of these laws when we have Leon Kass's book, which spells them out more clearly than the Bible, is left uncertain. The nineteenth-century German rabbi Samson Raphael Hirsch wrote that "even those commandments whose reason you believe you have understood, you should not fulfil because of this, for then you would be listening only to yourself, whereas you should listen to God." He nevertheless proceeded to offer one of the best explanations for kashrut.

In our time the boundary in the public mind separating men from animals fades to invisibility. The notion of "animal rights" is taken so seriously that we are not startled by a movie like *Twelve Monkeys*, about a group of animal rights activists apparently set to destroy the world's human population with a nuclear-strength virus, in retaliation for the mistreatment of animals. In Rabbi Hirsch's view, God wanted to set before us a constant reminder that men are not animals. Animals can eat anything they want. After all, they are incapable of exercising self-control. Man, on the other hand, is free, able to dominate his lower, animal instincts. "The body of man," wrote Hirsch, "should be the servant of his spirit." His spirit should be as bendable to his will, not as a wild animal or even a domesticated one, but as a plant. We therefore avoid the flesh of animals that are, you might say, too animalistic: frisky, headstrong, aggressive; but we are permitted animals that have the qualities of plants. The defining characteristics of the kosher barnyard resident is that, in the words of Deuteronomy and Leviticus, he "parts the hoof" and "chews the cud." That is, like cows and sheep and deer, he has cloven hooves and a system of four stomachs. Such an animal digests his food first in two stomachs, from which it is regurgitated, then passed through two more. Like plants, these creatures spend an inordinate amount of time simply absorbing food. Their cloven hooves are also better suited for standing around passively than for rousing themselves to battle with other animals: another plantlike quality.

In all this the pig doesn't stand out for special censure. He appears twice in the Torah, and then only as an example of a beast without the required anatomical features of four stomachs *and* cloven hooves, alongside "the camel, the hare, and the rock-badger." The harshest thing the Talmud has to say about pigs is a proverb to the effect that there is no point giving a pig a delicacy such as heart of palm, since the pig will just drag it back to his garbage pile. Why have some Jews chosen to reject pork and pork alone? The answer has to do with the history of the Jewish Diaspora. For some reason, gentiles who wanted to humiliate Jews fastened on the pig. As I Maccabees records, when the Greek king Antiochus Epiphanes decided to teach the Jews under his control to respect Greek culture, he enacted a number of reforms in Jerusalem. These included ordering "swine and other unclean beasts to be offered in sacrifice" at the Temple. Under the Inquisition in Spain and Portugal, Jews-turned-Christians were tortured to obtain evidence of backsliding by them and their ex-Jewish neighbors. One's refusal to eat pork was taken as a sure sign of "Judaizing" tendencies. "New Christians" were typically arrested on such charges as "refusing pork alleging medical reasons" or "preparing dishes using onions and garlic instead of lard." In medieval Germany, artists adopted the pig as an icon of everything they found hateful about Jews: the *Judensau*.

So when Jews like my mother refuse to eat pork, their concern is less to observe Halachah, which their liberal rabbis have told them is outdated and irrelevant, than to make a stand, in their own way, against anti-Semitism. My mother was a brave woman who didn't take guff from anyone. The sign over our kitchen radio was her way of putting anti-Semites on notice: "Don't tread on me."

The no-pork rule in our home reveals something else about the kind of Judaism I and many other young liberal American Jews grew up in. That is that, like most other Jewish mothers and fathers and their children, my parents did not think in terms of abstract notions of right and wrong, nor was that how they taught me to think. For them Jewishness was a matter of indelible identity, an identity that carried with it the obligation to assume an upright moral stance. They taught right behavior by their own examples, not by illuminating for me principles that could be expressed in words and applied generally.

In the increasingly unbuttoned decades of the sixties and seventies, Paul and Carol Klinghoffer remained staunchly buttoned.

My father was and is a devotedly ethical businessman, almost to a fault. He enjoyed investing the money he earned from dentistry, but a lack of ruthlessness often got in the way. So, for instance, he bought some houses in San Pedro, a few minutes from our house. After his tenants moved in they often failed to pay the rent, but my father was too kind to kick them out. One family that claimed indigence had a Rolls-Royce in the driveway.

I have known a few people who were born with a quality that might be considered either a defect or a perfection: a total lack of malice toward other human beings. I'm certainly not one of those people, but my father is. I have never heard him tell a mean-spirited joke or explain another person's failing as being connected to race, sex, or ethnicity. In fact, he did not and does not talk much at all about other people's failings. My parents didn't curse, tell off-color stories, or drink alcohol, except for a token quantity of wine if they held a dinner party. It would be hard to imagine a straighter married couple, including among Mormons.

Our home was almost Victorian, and this had a very definite educational effect on me. Psychologists observe that between the ages of seven and nine, children have a tendency to obsess about moral questions, but I doubt this happens in environments where the child's parents are not themselves moral people. In my case this stage took the form of a weird determination to tell the truth at all times.

Neither gregarious nor mischievous but, rather, stern and judgmental, a gray and somewhat boring child, with my light blond hair and tall, skinny frame, I think I must have suggested a Swedish Lutheran minister in training. The text of a "Student of the Month" award I received at Miraleste Elementary School commended me in the following terms: "Quiet, gets his work done, and doesn't bug people." So nobody in my fourth-grade class noticed when I suddenly became determined never to tell a lie and to volunteer the truth even if it wasn't asked for. Since I was "quiet" and "didn't bug" the other children, I had few opportunities to practice my truthfulness on them. But I did "get my work done," and this created problems. I began to feel that when I took tests or filled in the answers on a homework sheet, giving an incorrect answer was worse than merely inaccurate: it was a lie. I remember penciling in, then erasing, then penciling in and erasing again, a series of assignments on the American Revolution, oral hygiene, and the like.

This was neurotic and annoying. At home the problem became a true moral dilemma. I had the ambivalences about my parents that any normal nine-year-old does. Unlike other children, though, I felt compelled to reveal my true feelings. A question rose in my mind: Did I love my mother? One day I volunteered to her that I wasn't sure. Meanwhile, my mother being a very solidly built woman, I began to wonder if her heaviness embarrassed me. I concluded that it did and told her so—with predictably painful effects on her, given that despite her apparent self-confidence she was really a very sensitive person. These pointless confessions to my mother are probably among the most hurtful things I have done in my life.

So I had morals, but they bubbled up in my head in a confused way, a combination of instinct and lessons imperfectly learned from the examples set by my parents. Yet my intuition that there is truth and there is untruth, and that the difference between them should concern us, was a good one.

As a conceptual category, the Truth has come under fire lately. Influenced by the relativism emanating from the universities, Americans who consider themselves sophisticated increasingly doubt our right to call any assertion definitively "true." A given idea, we think, may be true for one culture but not for another, or for one time but not another. This trend was already under way in the early seventies, especially when it came to religion.

Whereas once the government was the only authority prevented from imposing beliefs, the culture as a whole was now subjected to the same limitation, and many parents had accepted it on themselves as well. This, the whole vexed question of commandments, was omitted entirely from my education. Of course, my teachers left us students with no doubt that we were expected to behave "well"; but why we should, and who said so apart from the teacher, the principal, and our parents, no one sought to clarify. My intuition told me that demands had been made on me not only by the administration of Miraleste Elementary and by my father and mother, but also by some other force in the world. But who or what was that? It didn't occur to me to wonder.

Lots of other people from secular backgrounds have had the identical vague sense that there is such a thing as commandments, actions that are right or wrong as a matter not of value, but of fact. We sense this, but in our untutored state we can't supply the details of the commandments: we are like men before the invention of the telescope who scanned the stars in the heavens but could only guess what details the tiny shining dots, obviously very far away, would reveal if magnified. So we guess, creating a diversity of secular moralities. Lately the dominant godless system of do's and don'ts has focused on what we eat, drink, and smoke. Secular Americans have their sin equivalents: eating fatty foods, drinking liquor, smoking cigarettes—especially smoking cigarettes. Though we tend to divide ourselves between those of us who possess faith and those who do not, the distinction is false. Everyone has faith; the question is, in what?

Along with any number of secular moralities, a version of the old, God-based morality was present in the environment around me as I grew up. It was modeled by my parents, as my father's ultra-decency in business and personal relations shows. I doubt I would have developed any preoccupation with truth telling if my parents had not been rigorously honest themselves. I can't remember an instance of either of them telling a lie. Why, however, you might reasonably ask, did they behave so high-mindedly?

Clearly you don't have to be religious to be moral. Some moral impulses seem almost to be coded in our blood, like those against incest and parricide. I assume that God presets them in us, though evolutionists would disagree. Other such impulses, not exactly instinctive, nevertheless persist even among the staunchest atheists. I mean, for instance, refined manners like those described by Emily Post, the essence of which is consideration for others. This might seem paradoxical. After all, if you think no authority exists that transcends human authority, I don't see any good reason to do anything in your life other than pursue your own interests as zealously as prudence dictates.

As far as I can tell, morality will permeate a society or a family when it has been absorbed, directly or indirectly, from one or two sources. The first, less reliable one is a perception of the natural order in the world. The problem with this notion, called natural law, is that nature has no right to compel our behavior. It possesses no quality of "ought." For example, it's certainly unnatural for men to fly. Many of us acknowledge this each time we say a prayer as our airplane takes off. Yet nobody thinks flying in a plane is morally problematic. So much for nature. The other source of moral impulses is Revelation, the will of heaven.

My parents did not philosophize about natural law, and religious faith had dimmed in their families decades earlier. Paul and Carol Klinghoffer did right not because they could give any convincing rationale for the strictures they obeyed, but merely because their parents had done so, as had their own—religious—parents. Like many other contemporary Americans, they believed vaguely in what is called "ethics"—morality that has been emptied of its old religious content, morality without God. Ethics is powered by the fumes of religion, in my parents' case the religion of their ancestors. Cut off from its source in Revelation, this kind of righteousness will eventually fade, like a cut flower.

In Europe, when the Austro-Hungarian empire still ruled over them, or later in America, some Klinghoffer and some Bernstein clipped the flower of their faith in Judaism from its stem, probably without realizing he had done it. Maybe they placed it between the pages of a heavy book, like the enormous old Hebrew Bible a great-aunt once showed me, my great-grandfather's Bible, with the name ISAAC KLINGHOFFER stamped in gold across the front. There were no flowers inside, but there were many clippings from the northern New Jersey newspapers. One, I remember, concerned a Jewish boy whose IQ set a world's record. The desiccated, brownish yellow clippings from the late 1920s required the most delicate handling if they were not to disintegrate in your hand. By the time of my birth the flowers belonging to the Kling-hoffer and Bernstein families had turned as brittle as that.

Which was why Rabbi Donin's book shocked me. The ethical environment in our home, as in most contemporary American Jewish homes, was not a living flower. Detached from its roots, it could no longer drink water from the earth. For most believers in a humanistic system that claims to define right and wrong behavior, "ethics" is simply in the air we breathe. People like that can no more explain the source of their ethics than they can (without consulting a science book) the source of air. The truth is, they receive their ethical principles from parents, friends, teachers, television commercials, billboard ads, art, architecture, pornography, the Op-Ed pages of *The New York Times:* helter-skelter, wherever. Rabbi Donin not only had definite ideas about right and wrong, transcendent ideas independent of what human beings say and think, which my intuition about Truth told me there must somewhere be; he could tell you Who handed those ideas down to us. He cited ancient texts. He said it was God.

Possibly, if I had not stumbled across that book, the flower I received from my parents would have crumbled into carbon dust. It might have done so anyway.

It is a curiosity that Jews raised in the godless secular world have frequently continued to identify themselves as Jews, though Judaism has no meaning for them. Some light was shed for me on this question by a sermon I heard once at the synagogue I now attend. In the Book of Exodus we meet Jethro, the father-in-law of Moses. Jethro was a Midianite and a pagan priest. When the tribes of Israel were released from their bondage in Egypt, he went to meet and dwell with them. The text says that he had "heard of all that God had done for Moses, and for Israel His people, how the Lord had brought Israel out of Egypt." Rabbi Jacob Schacter asked what exactly it was that Jethro "heard" that impressed him enough to send him out into the wilderness. In his commentary, Rashi states that Jethro had "heard" two things: about the attacks on the Israelites by the archetypally evil tribe called Amalek, and about the miracle in which God saved the Jews from Pharaoh's pursuing army by drowning the Egyptians in the Red Sea. From this, Rabbi Schacter extracted a contemporary meaning. Just as these two things—the hatred of the Jews by certain gentiles and the love of them by God—drew Jethro to his eventual decision to join the Israelites, Jews themselves historically have been drawn to Judaism and kept under its wings by two factors: the practical circumstance of living in an often hostile gentile world with the resulting need to stick together, and the spiritual circumstance of being a people in a unique relationship to God.

As the unwelcome status of pork in our home demonstrates, my parents, especially my mother, believed in Jews sticking together against the legions of non-Jews maliciously hoping to see you eat pig. My generation, however, was born into a world safer for Jews than the earth has ever been. I'm not sure this is an advantage, since our safety has not been universally complemented by a strong sense that God loves us and wants, as passionately as those now friendly gentiles with their proffered plates of pork, to have a relationship with us.

Like so many Jews in our century, I was given one concrete reason for being Jewish, namely the hostility of non-Jews, that was no longer a reason; along with a very desiccated understanding of the other, still relevant reason, namely God's desire to have a relationship with me. Equipped in this way, I went out into the world of adolescence, where two systems of thought—Judaism and humanistic "ethics"—did battle with each other to secure my devotion to one of them or the other. Like the struggle for California in the Mexican War, in which the Mexican and American armies kept showing up for battles from which the Mexican army tended to flee before anyone got off a shot, the struggle in my case between dried-up Judaism and vigorous humanism was unevenly matched. By the time of my bar mitzvah ceremony, when I was supposed to declare my loyalty to Judaism, with a minimum of violence and bloodshed it seemed the Mexicans had already been vanquished.

# Chapter 3

# KORACH'S REBELLION

*A*s a boy I believed in an invisible world populated by ghosts, unidentified flying objects, Sasquatch monsters, a Loch Ness monster, and squadrons of U.S. Air Force jets lost in the Bermuda triangle. I was a fan of Erich von Däniken's *Chariots of the Gods,* a book positing that millennia ago our planet was visited by "ancient astronauts" who might visit again. I purchased photo-illustrated paperbacks about the Bermuda triangle and Bigfoot. All that was supernatural; but nature's invisible world also fascinated me. As a five-year-old, on the same trip that I saw the *Vasa,* I stood amazed in the basement of an Oslo museum devoted to the Norwegian explorer Thor Heyerdahl's cross-Pacific *Kon Tiki* raft expedition. In this room had been constructed life-size models of the creatures that swam beneath *Kon Tiki,* behind glass and with deep-sea backdrops, so that the viewer felt he stood below the surface of the ocean, watching as a whale shark or a school of dolphins passed by.

When we look out over the ocean from the beach, we know that virtually a whole universe exists in front of but hidden from our eyes—and only yards from the familiar streets and buildings we spend our lives in, if you live near an ocean. My awe before the whale-shark diorama at the *Kon Tiki* museum, or the similar displays at the Los Angeles Maritime Museum, was a tribute to invisible Existence. I knew there must be something, in particular something divine, beyond the mundane reality we learned about at Miraleste Elementary and Dapplegray Intermediate.

I cannot prove to you that this implicit belief in God's existence was more firmly grounded in reality than the intuition that told me, if I ventured out of my tent at night on a Cub Scout camping trip, I might be confronted with one of the Bigfoot creatures said to haunt California forests. But children are born with an intuition that God lives, and certainly the world around me pointed independently to that conclusion. Next time you are at a natural history museum, look at the astonishing abstract designs on a 550-million-year-old snail shell from the Cambrian period, designs much more lovely than the ones, created by humans, at the art galleries across town. Especially if you grow up in California, the most beautiful place on earth, only a dunce could fail to notice the sheer, superfluous gorgeousness of creation. In its allegedly blind churning, the universe has brought forth beauty for no purpose other than to be beautiful. Who made such loveliness, evidently for His own contemplation?

I now have come to appreciate the word's superb contents, coupled with our (from a Darwinian point of view) entirely unnecessary ability to appreciate it all, as God's footsteps in the sand. That is why the Jewish prayer book, the siddur, prescribes a list of benedictions to be said, for example, on eating fruit, drinking wine, or seeing an unusually handsome person, a particularly gifted scholar, great mountains, the ocean, or any other sublime natural scene: "Blessed are You, Lord, our God, King of the universe, Who creates the fruit of the ground" or "the fruit of the earth," "Who has such in His universe," "Who makes the work of creation."

But appreciating creation is easy. What is expected of us in return?

———

OVER THREE DECADES I have contemplated a number of answers to that question. Though until fairly recently I associated the phrase "a relationship with God" mainly with Sunday-morning television preachers, I have in fact always wanted a relationship with Him. But in seeking one, I didn't start out as a tabula rasa. Like a new computer that comes with a "bundle" of mostly downmarket software already written on its hard disk, I embarked, though not meaning to, on my journey of religious exploration with a philosophy of God preinstalled. This was Reform Judaism.

Actually, while most of the people involved in it are Jews, to call the ideology of the Reform movement "Judaism" does violence to the history of the movement. Judaism has always existed within the framework of Halachah, which Reform insists can be disregarded. The Reform temple our family attended, Temple Beth Shalom, did not give the impression of an institution produced by a rebellion against Judaism, but it was just that.

From the time my family began attending Beth Shalom, in 1969, until long after I had passed through the temple's educational system, I never knew what Judaism really stood for. What does it stand for?

Historically the faith of Torah has asserted that the parameters of God's relationship with the Jews were revealed to them about 3,300 years ago at Mt. Sinai. That Revelation took place in two forms. From the Lord, Moses received Genesis, Exodus, Leviticus, Numbers, and Deuteronomy, but also an oral explanation of them, instructing the Jews on how these terse, enigmatic texts are to be understood and translated into a framework for communal and individual engagement with God. This tradition was passed from Moses to Joshua, who transmitted it to the elders of Israel, who passed it on to the prophets, and so on through a genealogy of sages ending with Rabbi Judah the Prince. Around 200 C.E. Rabbi Judah set down a condensation of oral Torah known to us as the Mishnah. But this work was almost as terse and mysterious as the written Torah it elaborated on. About three hundred years later, in Babylon, then the center of Jewish learning, a multivolume commentary was composed, elaborating on the Mishnah. This was the Talmud. Yet the Talmud requires explanation, too. Commentaries were duly written in medieval France, Germany, Spain, and elsewhere by authorities who had received the tradition from their fathers, who had received it from their fathers.

Only in our time did the word "tradition" absorb a sickly odor, thanks in no small part to the lyricist responsible for *Fiddler on the Roof.* Contrary to what that egregious musical asserts, "tradition" does not mean the mindless aping of our elders. Tradition means the transmission of data that originated at Sinai and is thus, as Torah sees it, the only reliable way we have available to know God's will.

This understanding of Judaism has been assailed by Jewish rebels many times. One sort of rebel hates divine authority and seeks to overthrow Torah altogether. With his campaign against the "illusion" of religion, Freud typifies this category of Jews, as does Marx.

But most Jewish rebels have resented not Judaism as a whole, but merely its tendency to keep them from entering desirable, gentile social circles. Thus the civil war in ancient Israel, in the time of the oppressor Antiochus Epiphanes, pitted assimilation-minded Hellenized Jews against defenders of the Torah. For Jews living in the Greek-dominated world of 175 B.C.E., social prestige and economic advancement were tied to one's ability to mix as an equal with the urbane, cosmopolitan Greek conquerors. A band of reformers arose, drawn mainly from the Jewish upper class and spurred on by the high priest Menelaus. In 167 B.C.E., backed by Antiochus, the reformers abolished Jewish law and introduced the worship of Olympian Zeus at the Temple in Jerusalem.

Like the reform movement in Judea circa 167 B.C.E., the Reform movement represented by your local Reform temple has its roots in social ambition, in this case among German Jews. The scholar I. Grunfeld identifies three stages in the early history of Reform. The first, naive stage was initiated in 1810 at Seesen, Westphalia, where a group of wealthy Jews opened the original Reform temple. The service was intended to simulate Christian prayer, complete with church bells. This was "merely an attempt to assimilate Judaism as much as possible to the Christian religion, the religious faith of the majority of the surrounding population," says Dr. Grunfeld. Reform temples appeared in Berlin in 1815 and Hamburg in 1818.

In early nineteenth-century Europe it had become chic for gentiles to visit traditional synagogues, where they snickered at the noisy, apparently disordered and primitive worship. For certain Jews this must have been humiliating. So when the Reformers set about designing religious facilities for themselves—to be called "temples" to underline the Reform assertion, contrary to the faith of Judaism, that no messianic Third Temple would ever be built in Jerusalem—they invented a Jewish church. Hebrew was edged out in favor of German; organs were introduced, though Jewish law prohibits the playing of musical instruments on the Sabbath; the liturgy was gutted. And followers of the movement were cut free from Halachah.

Later the theoreticians of Reform explained why the break with tradition was justifiable. At Frankfurt am Main, between 1833 and 1840, Michael Creizenach published his argument for jettisoning traditional practices. He differed from the leaders of the third stage of Reform's evolution in that he continued to assume the divine authority of both the written and oral Torahs. By 1839 Abraham Geiger had declared his opinion that neither Torah was the product of divine revelation. Another Reform leader, Samuel Holdheim, remarked that "in the Talmudic age, the Talmud was right. In my age, I am right." By this logic, Talmud study became an act hostile to Judaism, or Holdheimism. In Frankfurt am Main, an important testing ground for Reform in its struggle with Judaism, the Jewish Community Council enlisted the local police to make study of the Talmud and of the Bible in Hebrew a legal offense, punishable by a fine of fifty florins.

By 1880, 90 percent of American synagogues either had been transformed into temples or had started out that way. In the South, Reform rabbis sought to give the appearance of Christian clergymen, asking that they be addressed not as "Rabbi," but as "Dr.," "Reverend," or "Minister." Some wore black suits and white clerical collars, like Catholic and Episcopal priests. Yarmulkes and prayer shawls were banished, and some congregations met on the Christian Sabbath day instead of the Jewish one. In New York, Rabbi Judah Magnes of Temple Emanu-El, a synagogue built to resemble an art deco cathedral, boasted that "a prominent Christian lawyer of another city has told me that he entered this building at the beginning of a service on Sunday morning and did not discover that he was in a synagogue until a chance remark of the preacher betrayed it."

American Reformers produced declarations of independence from Halachah as audacious as those that had come out of Europe. In 1885 Reform rabbis gathered in Pittsburgh to formally state that any Torah law could be dismissed if it was "not adapted to the views and habits of modern civilization." Formerly, God through His Torah had been viewed as a force sitting in judgment of man; now man had set himself up in judgment of God.

———

NO ONE EVER explained any of this to us at Temple Beth Shalom. For me, as for most other children enrolled in Reform educational programs, Jewish ideas, whether traditional or reformed, floated on the margins of temple life. Immediately likable, our rabbi, Aaron Dinnerstein, was as quick with a gag as Johnny Carson and funnier, too. That sense of humor stood him in good stead with his audience of easygoing Reform Jews, who would have associated any serious talk about commandments, or about one's relationship to God, with Christianity.

Nevertheless, Rabbi Dinnerstein did use his humorous manner to sneak in lessons about Torah. One of the earliest memories I have is of a sermon he delivered on Rosh Hashanah. On that day each year, Jews read the biblical account of Abraham's near sacrifice of Isaac on Mt. Moriah, which tradition tells us happened at Rosh Hashanah. Just as Isaac was prepared to be offered as a burnt sacrifice by his father, so should we be willing to make the much smaller daily sacrifices God asks of us. And just as God saved Isaac before Abraham drew the knife across his throat, He will save us from death and reward us with eternal life. Reform ideology has distanced itself from traditional Jewish concepts like these: eternal life, daily sacrifice. So when Rabbi Dinnerstein told the story, so brutal to the modern ear, he eased its way with a joke. He had reached the awesome moment when God has called to Abraham and told him to offer a ram, caught by its horns in a nearby thicket of bushes, instead of Isaac. Looking up from the Torah scroll on the lectern, Rabbi Dinnerstein raised an eyebrow and said, "Now let me assure you this wasn't a Los Angeles Ram." Perhaps the Rams were having a difficult season that year. The audience laughed appreciatively.

In the life of a Reform child, Jewish education comes mainly through two channels: Hebrew school and camp. I escaped the latter for all but two summers. In Southern California the Jewish camps cluster in the Malibu hills. As a child my father had attended camps in Maine and spoke of them enthusiastically: places with Indian names where the children spent their days earnestly canoeing or sailing boats on the lake or engaged in handicrafts. But my first camp experience, after sixth grade, was the summer of 1976, and earnestness was out in Reform-oriented camps. What was in? At Camp JCA, which was Reform in spirit if not by formal affiliation, premature sexuality verging on homoeroticism.

My cabin at JCA fell under the custodianship of an obese counselor called Rolando, who our first night warned us in a jolly way that "after the lights go off I don't want to catch any of you finger-f———g each other." Oddly, Rolando was beloved by us in cabin six. We did not complain when, to punish us for some infraction, he would sit on the offending boy and make him smell his underarm. Despite such eccentricities, we considered ourselves lucky as compared with our chums in cabin seven, whose counselor reportedly offered them a deal: he would measure their penises, and the best-endowed boy was allowed to look at a copy of *Playboy*. I am quite sure nobody learned anything about Judaism at Camp JCA.

The next summer I joined several friends for a session at Camp Swig, near San Jose. Camp Swig was formally affiliated with the Union of American Hebrew Congregations, the synagogue branch of the Reform movement, and so had to take Judaism a little more seriously than JCA did.

Well, Judaism up to a point. There is a tendency among all the Jewish denominations to confuse enthusiasm for the state of Israel with the Jewish religion itself. My friends and I found ourselves housed in a surplus U.S. Army tent, next to a portable toilet but a mile from the nearest shower, which was supposed to conjure up the romance of kibbutz life. There was a fenced-in yard where barn animals were kept, and the children roughed it by eating peanut-butter-and-jelly sandwiches for lunch. For the experience of being a parachutist in the Israeli army, we were taken to a tree with a rope at the top running to the ground, which we slid down on an iron triangle. For the Zionist experience, we played a game in which we pretended to be Jews sneaking into Palestine in 1948. There was also musical entertainment. We sang and danced to Israeli folk tunes as well as to non-Jewish tunes like the Austrian "Cuckoo" song. The latter inspired some of us to give each other Nazi salutes, for which we received a severe dressing-down from our counselor.

In the course of my Reform education, Nazism is the single idea or form of behavior I can remember being told was absolutely evil. So it is ironic, or maybe not ironic, that among boys raised in the Reform movement I heard more cries of "Heil Hitler!" and saw more scribbled swastikas than in any other environment I have ever been in. Thus at Dapplegray there was a teacher Bennett Schneir and I regarded as excessively strict, so we decorated her photo in the school yearbook with a swastika armband. In the same yearbook I find a picture of the ladies who worked in the cafeteria; on the lapels of their white uniforms Bennett or I had penned in the letters "SS." When, in eighth grade, I enrolled in a post–bar mitzvah "Hebrew high school," my friend Jonathan Marks and I showed our contempt for the teacher, a well-meaning but ineffectual man, by standing and throwing Nazi salutes when he had his face to the blackboard. Among our non-Jewish peers, I saw no corresponding fascination with the Third Reich.

This was more than youthful rebelliousness. We knew very little about Nazism, but we sensed in it a certain thrilling seriousness, a passion to translate hard, demanding, unsentimental beliefs into actions, which was absent in Reform institutions.

What beliefs did the Reform movement stand for? A fog surrounds them in the minds of most Reform temple-goers, but when I visited Rabbi Dinnerstein in his study at the temple in 1995 to ask for some clarification of his views, he said something that crystallized Reform thinking for me. I asked him what he thought happened at Mt. Sinai. He answered that he wasn't sure but that he *didn't think it mattered that much.* From this blithe dismissal of the most crucial event in Jewish history, the rest of his religious outlook flowed naturally. Rabbi Dinnerstein believes that there are moral absolutes contained in the Torah. "I think keeping Shabbat is a bottom-line responsibility," he said. "But how I keep Shabbat, that's up for negotiation." As for responsibilities that are not "bottom line," the choice to obey the Torah or not "is based on what I find meaningful and relevant. The Reform movement interprets Jewish tradition to say that the Covenant allows for informed individual choice." In other words, Reform means doing what you want. Though the movement began as an internal rebellion against Judaism, these are not the fiery, decisive words of a revolutionary. Boys admire self-confidence and generally have a lower tolerance than their parents do for soupy, meaningless rhetoric. No wonder the symbols of Nazism appealed to us.

––––––

THE BULK OF our Reform education took place in Hebrew school, where for two hours after school twice a week, we prepared for our bar mitzvah ceremonies. This education was conducted by a series of indifferent Israelis. When not killing time by playing soporific film strips about olive farming on the slopes of Israel's Mt. Carmel, they managed to teach us as little about their native language as they did about Judaism. Oh, certain words stuck with me for years: *ken* ("yes"), *lo* ("no"), *celev* ("dog"), *hatool* ("cat"). In my Spanish classes at Dapplegray we learned conjugation and syntax, as well as vocabulary. In Hebrew school we learned only vocabulary, mostly of the kind that might be useful on a vacation in Israel, and practiced conversational exercises designed to mimic the speech of extremely dim residents of modern Tel Aviv or Haifa. Though Israeli Hebrew has more in common with biblical Hebrew than Elizabethan English does with modern English, the scraps of language we picked up did not help us understand the occasional paragraphs of Hebrew the Reform movement had refrained from excising from its bowdlerized version of the siddur. Alas, there are no dogs or cats in Jewish liturgy.

As for reading the Torah and comprehending what we read, there was no hope of that. We could pronounce the words. But if we wanted to understand them, we were obliged to turn to a translation. For the bar mitzvah occasion itself, all we needed to do was pronounce—though without the help of vowels, which do not appear in the Torah scroll—thirteen or so verses of text, along with the haftarah, a passage from one of the Bible's prophetic books. ("Now it's not called that because it's *half* as important as the Torah," joked Rabbi Dinnerstein.) Even this goal was not always met. Recently Jonathan (my friend from Hebrew high school) told me that "a couple of weeks before my bar mitzvah, my mother sat me down and tested me out on my portion. I knew nothing." Yet he counts his Reform schooling a success: "There are a lot of Israelis at my gym, and I can pick out words they say." Particularly, I suppose, if they are talking about their house pets.

Though a male Jew becomes a bar mitzvah, a "son of the commandment," at age thirteen, my own bar mitzvah was set for September 2, 1978, two months before my thirteenth birthday. Early that year, the boys in my Hebrew school class had begun to hound their parents to take them to Beverly Hills to buy a Pierre Cardin suit at Rudnick's on Beverly Drive. There the tailors outfitted us in tighter-fitting suits than would seem appropriate today. Unlucky was the boy who, taking off his jacket in order to dance the hora, hiked up his trousers an inch too far, causing a circumcised bulge to appear where it shouldn't have. My Rudnick's suit was sky blue.

Invitations went out, complete with a drawing of me by a local artist named Gemma, announcing that I would be "called to the Torah as a Bar Mitzvah," after which all would repair to the Golden Sails Inn on Pacific Coast Highway in Long Beach. Menus were prepared, promising in hand calligraphy a "Dinner of Celebration" featuring Cornish game hen, Carrots Vichy, Chablis wine, and peach Melba (all non-kosher, needless to say). According to the prevailing custom, copies of the invitation and menu were saved in order to be photographed, for my bar mitzvah album, stuck in a fern outside the temple's front door.

---

WHEN I TRY TO EXPLAIN why it is that I never took Reform Judaism seriously, I am drawn back to the bar mitzvah "circuit," as we called the series of parties for classmates that you got invited to as a thirteen-year-old and what that said about the meaning of Judaism. It is hard to imagine my fellow students sending their own children through the same Reform educational system. Non-Jews who grew up in other liberal religious denominations have also emerged disillusioned and for the same reasons. There seems to be something inherent in liberal religion that has tended to direct my generation in one of two directions: back to traditional faith or out the door of the temple or church marked "Exit," forever.

To understand the failure of Reform, it helps to understand the failure of its liberal Christian counterparts. So-called mainline Christianity and liberal Judaism are generally thought of as if one had nothing to do with the other, but the declining fortunes of both suggest that isn't true.

The numbers are not debatable. The fastest-growing sects in this country are typified by the Southern Baptists and the Mormons, whereas the mainline Christian groups—Episcopalians,

Congregationalists, Presbyterians, Methodists—have been bleeding young members since the mid-sixties, so that by the beginning of this decade they had experienced losses in membership ranging from a fifth to a third. The same applies to liberal Judaism. Though the Reform movement remains the largest body in Judaism, and frequently gains members through intermarriage (when a non-Jewish spouse can be prevailed on to sit through a nominal "conversion" to Judaism), the only Jewish denomination that has been able to hold on to its young people against intermarriage and assimilation is Orthodoxy. (The intermarriage rate among Reform Jews has reached 60 percent. Among Orthodox Jews it remains negligible; and along with very high birth rates, the influx of *ba'alei teshuvah* has added to the number of young Jews in the Orthodox community.)

If observers of the religious scene too frequently consider liberal Christianity in isolation from liberal Judaism, it is because they don't trouble to define liberal religion. To remedy the problem, here is a three-pronged definition, which will become clear from an account of an exemplary event of religious liberalism: my bar mitzvah.

Like other bar mitzvahs on the circuit, this consisted of three main parts—excluding the mass expenditure of cash and credit by my generous father. First came my reading of the Torah: a passage in Hebrew from Deuteronomy, including the famous injunction "Justice, justice, you shall pursue," of which I understood hardly a word.

Second came my bar mitzvah speech. In theory this is supposed to be the child's opportunity to deliver a few words in explanation of his Torah portion. But my Deuteronomical passage dealt with apparently mundane subjects like the need to establish courts of justice and uncomfortable ones like the obligation to root out apostates, Jewish men and women who "serve other gods and bow down to them." In its terse and unsentimental style, the Torah states that these idolatrous individuals are to be taken out and stoned. Such passages beg to be explained and sermonized upon, because they are obviously so important in the value system of the

Torah and because they seem so strangely primitive. But in the Reform movement, whatever is difficult or uncomfortable about Judaism is either ignored or explained away as an anachronism. For the distinctive message of the Torah, Reform tends to substitute the most respectable liberal opinions of our own day (that act of substitution itself being a form of idolatry, as the philosopher Will Herberg says).

My mother wrote quite a nice, typically Reform bar mitzvah speech for me. "It is the responsibility of each bar mitzvah student to interpret a section of the Torah," I said. "Each portion has a meaningful message." (I pronounced the last two words very distinctly, to take advantage of the alliteration.) In a total of five paragraphs, I breezed over the passage about stoning idolaters— "Of course, in modern society, this law is not observed because religious crimes are not punishable as they were in biblical days"—and proceeded to the "meaningful message," which had to do, as many a bar mitzvah speech did that year, with the plight of Soviet Jewry.

The Reform bar mitzvah follows a ritual of its own. All the other students on the circuit gave speeches demonstrating how little they had learned about Judaism, then received a certificate showing that in their honor the Jewish National Fund had planted two trees in the "Youth Woodland in Freedom Forest for Soviet Jewry" in Israel. They concluded with a second speech thanking everyone who had contributed to their Jewish education. The young man or woman was expected to thank his parents and teachers, make one joke, and if possible appear to become emotionally overwhelmed by the sheer drama of it all. Of my peers, Josh Labelle had the wittiest one-liner, having to do with horse racing. He apologized for the briefness of his thank-you speech, then explained that "I had to write this quickly because it was one hour before post time." If the bar mitzvah student had any close relatives who had died, he employed them as a throat-catching closer. I myself pretended to get choked up as I noted the absence of two departed grandparents.

Finally, the third and main part of a Reform bar mitzvah: the party. Around this time in the Los Angeles area, especially in Beverly Hills, the press would occasionally report on some Reform bar mitzvah party that so flagrantly violated the dictates of good taste that it became a news event. Who could forget the *Star Wars* bar mitzvah, held at the Los Angeles Memorial Coliseum, at which actors dressed as Darth Vader and C-3PO entertained the guests? In our own Jewish community, the customs were more modest, but not that much more. I myself was the proud center of a living tableau of all that was most embarrassing about the 1970s. My guests danced to "the hustle," led by two specially hired lady disco dancers in brown suede jumpsuits. When the guests weren't hustling, a professional cartoonist drew humorous caricatures as a party favor. He drew me riding a surfboard on a large wave, though I've never surfed.

The differences between this and a traditional bar mitzvah illuminate the differences between the liberal and traditional understandings of Judaism. An Orthodox boy reads a lengthy portion, usually a couple of chapters, from the Torah, and he understands all of it because he has been studying Hebrew as intensively as a Reform intermediate-school boy might study Spanish or German. He also gives a speech, elaborating on themes arising from the chapters he's just read whose relationship to Torah Judaism he has studied and understands. Then all adjourn to the synagogue social hall for pickled herring and shots of whiskey.

So we see in what directions liberal religion, including Reform Judaism, diverges from the tradition it comes out of. I mentioned a three-pronged definition:

First the matter of discipline and education. In traditional Judaism on turning thirteen, a boy should be able to read and understand the Hebrew Scriptures from which the system of Halachah derives, because on his thirteenth birthday the boy is suddenly responsible for carrying out that law. As a thirteen-year-old Reform boy, apart from sending thank-you letters for the many gifts I received, I was not asked to shoulder any responsibilities. For the most part, liberal religion, whether Jewish or Christian, eliminates the concept of a bar mitzvah, an individual on whom the responsibility falls to fulfill serious requirements imposed by God.

A comparison to liberal Christianity makes the point. A study in the ecumenical journal *First Things* lists some of the traditional Presbyterian standards of behavior that have fallen into desuetude: "Rules against worldly amusements and immodest dress went by the boards after World War One, standards of Sabbath observance were widely ignored by 1940, and in many congregations old norms concerning alcoholic beverages had become obsolete by the early 1950s." Among liberal Christians and Jews the most striking evolution in ideas about proper conduct involves homosexuality. All the liberal religious groups have begun to collapse in their once unanimous opposition to that activity. Rabbi Eric Yoffie, current head of the Reform movement's Union of American Hebrew Congregations, insists bewilderingly that sanctifying homosexual marriages is "consistent with Torah and tradition."

The first leg of my definition of liberal religion has to do with a watering down of moral requirements, and the second is not unrelated. It is the substitution of politics for morality. Notice that when the time came for me to comment on my Torah portion, I— or rather, my mother—chose to speak about a political issue: the mistreatment of Soviet Jews. "Social action" often seems to be the principal concern of Reform rabbis, as it does of liberal Christian leaders.

When explaining the ill fortunes of liberal denominations, conservatives often overemphasize this obsession with politics. According to these critics, parishioners in liberal churches resent the political declarations of their leaders. But at Temple Beth Shalom during the Reagan administration, when Rabbi Dinnerstein's sermons seemed to deal increasingly with the dangers of the arms race and the threat of nuclear winter, many of his congregants agreed with him. And anyway, while it received more attention than it should have done, politics played a relatively small role in the life of the temple.

Which leads me to the third part of my definition of liberal faith. For some decades now the attraction of these temples and churches has been religious only in part. Nor has it been political. It has been largely social. After all, the highlight of my bar mitzvah was the party. My parents' generation loves bar mitzvah parties, the *havurot* (groups of families that got together for outings to the zoo or the beach), the kiddush after services on Friday night (a benediction over wine and bread, and a little party afterward with coffee and cake). As an adult, I realize what a nice group of people attended Temple Beth Shalom. However, social enjoyment seemed to be the principal reason they went to temple; after all, they had not been seriously introduced by their rabbi to any other reason to do so. When a liberal religious body ceases to be concerned mainly with the dissemination of God's words, it can continue to function for a while as a social institution.

This helps explain why so many young Jews and Christians have dropped out of their parents' temples and churches. As other social organizations have discovered to their distress—fraternal organizations such as the Masons and the Shriners, do-good groups such as the American Jewish Committee and B'nai B'rith—young Americans today do not have time for them. We work too hard to spend Friday night at temple, Sunday morning at church, Wednesday night at the Moose Lodge—just to socialize. For that we can go to a health club and accomplish two objectives at once.

So from a strict marketing perspective, the liberal-religious strategy cannot work for long. The problem is a simple one of redundancy. Many nonreligious institutions in American life provide the benefits offered by liberal religion. The New Age movement promises the feeling of "spirituality"—without God. Want to make friends? Join a health club. A whole spectrum of political organizations provide the buzzing high of self-righteousness—without having to sit through an hour-long service and a lengthy sermon.

---

IF YOU COULD GO back in time to 1978 and plot my most likely spiritual trajectory, you would trace a line out the doors of the temple, past the fern, and into the empty expanses of undisguised secularism. Brought up to believe that Jewish institutions mainly serve the purpose of helping nice Jewish people meet other nice Jewish people and providing them with a sort of orally presented editorial page whenever they attend a temple service, I had no good reason to continue as a Reform Jew—or as a Jew.

What is the future of institutions like Temple Beth Shalom? The liberal project in religion has been tried before. In the Book of Numbers, we meet a curiously familiar character. While the Jews wandered in the wilderness, a Levite named Korach concluded that the authority to interpret God's will should not rest exclusively with Moses and Aaron. Let the people decide! So, with a group of followers, he rebelled. "All the congregation are holy," he reminded Moses and Aaron, "every one of them, and the Lord is among them; why then do you lift yourselves above the assembly of the Lord?" For their trouble, without even a moment to fret about "declining membership," Korach and his followers were swallowed up by a crack in the earth.

Writing on the topic of liberal Protestantism, columnist Don Feder quotes a Methodist theologian at Duke University. "God is killing mainline Protestantism in America," said the despondent mainliner, "and we . . . deserve it." That is excessively dramatic. I don't foresee any cracks opening up in the earth to swallow Temple Beth Shalom and its kindred institutions. Very slowly, liberal religion is killing itself.

# Chapter 4

# NEW LIFE

or a Jewish boy from my assimi-
lated background, the transition into quasi adulthood is marked
much less by his bar mitzvah ceremony than by entering high
school. At age thirteen I began as a student at Miraleste High
School, with a panoramic view east (hence the manufactured
Spanish name) over Los Angeles Harbor. Despite its suburban location and the prosperity of its citizens, Palos Verdes never attracted many Jews. Out of a freshman class of three hundred, I
was one of perhaps fifteen Jewish students. After school, many of
my classmates headed to CCD class at the local Catholic church,
Holy Trinity; others attended lunchtime meetings of the New
Life Club, an evangelizing Christian group. Of course, the Jews all
knew each other, including the handful who were so completely
assimilated that they didn't even attend a Reform temple.

Those of us who did attend had passed through our bar and bat mitzvahs. Before we were gone for good, Temple Beth Shalom felt obligated to impart a few words about the actual substance of Judaism. So in ninth grade I joined ten other kids from Beth Shalom as we prepared for confirmation, to be held on the festival of Shavuot. An invention of the Reform movement, the notion of "confirming" young Jews at age fifteen is borrowed from Christianity. A sort of Judaized first communion, it provides an excuse for remedial education, a last-ditch effort aimed at making up, to a very small extent, for all the material the typical student failed to learn for his bar mitzvah.

I do not remember being told that Shavuot commemorates the revelation of the Torah at Sinai. It does, though, and thus it would have been appropriate to use confirmation as a second opportunity for the young man or woman to publicly accept the contents of that revelation. Rabbi Dinnerstein taught the year-long class, and under the circumstances—the ideology in which he too had been educated and the minuscule demands a Reform rabbi can place on his congregants—he did his best.

When I went to visit him in 1995, Rabbi Dinnerstein kindly lent me his notes from the class. They are poignant. Only at this late date were we being instructed for the first time about elementary concepts of Halachah and the 613 commandments or mitzvot. The second class, for instance, posed the question "What is a Jew?" Later, in the course of one lecture and discussion, Rabbi Dinnerstein covered all ten major Jewish holidays and festivals: the study of a lifetime, sped past at high speed in two hours. On the back of some stationery from the Palm Springs Spa Hotel and Mineral Springs he reminded himself to ask us to identify our "favorite holidays. List all in order. Write: What are the major rlg. themes of all holidays?" This was almost on the order of being asked to identify our favorites stars in the Andromeda galaxy.

It was that same year, my sophomore year at Miraleste, that I met for the first time a man who viewed God's will not as an option, to be obeyed if we could find meaning in it, but as an obligation and a glory. Though William Hall taught Western civilization, he looked less like a high school teacher than a Welsh fisherman, with his big gray black beard, frameless octagonal eye-glasses, and "artisan" smock. At first it wasn't clear that Mr. Hall was a God-fearing man. Like many successful performers, he had a number of trademark phrases, gestures, and stunts that he used to get his students' attention. Afflicted by a clubbed foot, he would limp down the aisle, grinning and warning us that the examination he was about to hand out would be, in one of his favorite formulations, "hard as nails! I mean *nails!* Watch out!" And he knew that one way to interest high school students is by saying and doing anything that would offend their parents. Thus the thing William Hall's students remember most clearly from his class is what he did each year to a black leatherette Bible.

When the time came to discuss the rise of Christianity in the first century, Mr. Hall picked up a battered volume with the words "Holy Bible" in gold on the front over a small gold cross. "What's so special about this book?" he demanded. "I'll show you how important it is." At which he point he hurled the Bible like a Frisbee. It landed with a fat thump by the classroom door. All eyes locked on Mr. Hall or on the Holy Bible. "You're shocked," Mr. Hall announced, though we knew that already. "Why?"

A member of the Holy Trinity contingent piped up in a high, miffed voice: "It's a Bible!" To which Mr. Hall answered that what makes a Bible important is not the physical book itself, but the words inside. It was the first time I had heard an adult assert that the words of Scripture are "important."

Though his point was clear, I misconstrued him and arrived at a provisional conclusion that if he could show such disrespect for a Holy Bible with a cross on the front, he must be Jewish. The big rabbinical beard seemed a giveaway, as did his cracks at the expense of the squabbling popes of the Great Schism and his respectful comments about Jews and Judaism. As for the week-long series of lectures he devoted to the wonders of medieval cathedrals, especially Chartres—whose awesome "flyyy-yyying buttresses" he illustrated by lifting his arms heavenward as if he would himself take flight—I wrote this off as an eccentricity. It was no eccentricity. When the end of the year came, Mr. Hall at last admitted that he was in fact a devout Roman Catholic, with a family of six children to prove it.

After I had completed his elective class in comparative religion the following year, I was left in no doubt that Mr. Hall took God very seriously. Despite the Bible-tossing performance art, he turned out to be the most religiously earnest person I had ever met. He planted a seed in my head that would bear fruit, but only much later.

Don't blame the seed for its tardiness. For in the meantime there were other people assiduously trying to dig it up and replace it with another seed. With so much gardening going on at cross-purposes in my soul, no wonder the whole subject of religion was starting to make me nervous.

The summer after Western civilization with Mr. Hall, I met a girl from Long Beach called Sheryl Spencer. Sheryl was the first of a series of young women who for a while exerted more influence on my ideas about God than did any male. As Professor Richard Elliott Friedman has pointed out, the narrative of the Hebrew Bible begins with a woman helping to get a man expelled from Paradise and ends with another woman, Esther, playing the decisive role in saving the Jews of Persia from genocide. Too often men underestimate the degree to which women, though they hold few formal positions of power, especially in traditional churches and synagogues, shape our spiritual lives.

The last time I saw Sheryl was in 1985, my sophomore year in college, when I had come home to California for Christmas vacation and attempted unsuccessfully to renew an acquaintance that had ended four years earlier. Sheryl had just spent a week in the Fountain Valley Regional Hospital, where she underwent an operation to correct a problem with her spine. When I arrived at her parents' house to pick her up for an early dinner, she was still fiddling with a back brace. Her mother led me into the room where Sheryl was getting ready, and the scene I found on entering crystallized the attraction I still felt for her and the threat she posed. Sheryl was sitting beneath a skylight through which the afternoon California sun lit her shoulder-length blond hair so that she looked like a wingless angel. Not an Old Testament angel, either—but, quite distinctly, a New Testament one, as imagined, perhaps, by a nineteenth-century German or Scandinavian illustrator of popular Bibles.

I had met her on a month-long trip abroad for high school students, sponsored by a program under the charmingly pompous name People-to-People High School Student Ambassadors. The idea of People-to-People was to let American kids travel quickly over great distances and, at a few locales along the way, spend three or four days with surrogate families who would teach us the ways of their land. This particular People-to-People group traveled around the world in a month: from California to France and on to Egypt, Israel, China, and Japan. Sheryl was not only the first girl to kiss me, she was the first person to whisper in my ear that I was not meant to be a Jew at all, but a Christian.

At least judged by setting, it was an exotic first kiss. She and I had begun to get friendly in China. On a tour of Beijing, I had gotten a dust mote in my eye. Our Chinese guide asked to take a look—and then, without warning, proceeded to stick his tongue into my eyeball. It worked, the dust came out, and the incident also supplied the right note of appalled humor for me to start flirting with Sheryl. Or her with me. A few days later she and I were sitting in my hotel room when, as suddenly and unexpectedly as that Chinese guide with his mote-removing tongue, she leaned close to me and we were kissing. On the verge of starting her freshman year at California State University, Long Beach, Sheryl was (in my eyes) a woman of the world. Later that night, I ran exhilarated down the hotel stairs, feeling like a comic-book superhero.

On the flight to Japan, Sheryl began talking to me about Jesus. She had become a born-again evangelical Christian under the influence of a boyfriend: a dashing surfer who happened to be a son of the mayor of Long Beach. As she saw it, her newfound faith contained no doctrines except one: to be saved, you had to be born again.

"But I'm Jewish," I told her.

"You don't have to be," she said. "You could be born again."

Let me emphasize that Sheryl was a beautiful girl. She had a way of cocking her head and looking at me as if I were a beloved little boy who persisted in some childish error that, if he would only grow up a bit, he would surely abandon. I wanted very much to please her.

Instead I argued with her. Walking around Tokyo at night, we stood on a bridge over a diminutive canal, as romantic a spot as I could find—and argued about Christianity. Seated on a tatami mat in a hotel room, when my roommates had gone out and Sheryl and I were alone together—we argued about Christianity.

They were good-natured debates, though primitive. It didn't seem fair to me that to escape hell, you had be involved with a religious institution that didn't even exist everywhere in the world. What happened, I asked, to a person raised in the Chinese hinterlands who never met a Christian? Or what about people raised in other religions, like Judaism, who had been educated from earliest childhood to disregard Christianity? Her main answer to my questions was to cite Christian Scripture to the effect that if a man wishes to be saved, he must be born again. So our arguments went around in circles, which didn't displease me, since as we argued I could hold her hand and occasionally steal a kiss. It is hard to imagine a sweeter way to be proselytized.

When we got home to California, I looked for opportunities to argue with other people on the same subject. The following September I began to notice born-again Christians all around. The Campus Crusade for Christ and the New Life Club were active at Miraleste and, during lunchtime meetings in the classroom of a biology teacher, found an enthusiastic student audience. In the campus parking lot I saw a bumper sticker on a Toyota, "666— REFUSE THE MARK," alongside the other cars that advertised the spiritual progress of their owners. "I FOUND IT," read a Christian bumper stick ubiquitous in Southern California at the time.

Meanwhile a debate broke out around the question of whether rock music drove high school students to Satanism. Today we think of evangelical Christian activists as sophisticated operatives influencing public policy at the highest levels. But in 1981 it seemed that these people were mainly interested in exposing devil-worshiping heavy-metal bands. The bands encoded Satanic messages in their music, it was said, which could be heard if the albums were played in reverse. As an editor of the *Torreon*, our high school newspaper, I published letters to the editor examining the issue in detail. An anonymous "Concerned Mother" recommended the book *Satan's Music Exposed* and wrote of how in recent months she "had been greatly moved by the spirit of Christ" to "destroy anything in my home that even resembles Satan." Her daughters, unnamed Miraleste students, "even played some records backwards to see for themselves. It scared them!"

Something about "Concerned Mother" and those of my fellow students who shared her worries, something about students and other area residents who might choose to adorn their bumpers with Christian spiritual declarations, made me feel I must enter the conflict between born-again Christians and their detractors. The latter included the sorts of liberals who at the time were alarmed at Jerry Falwell's support of the newly elected President Reagan, which they said represented a grave threat to American liberty. I shared this view and published a page-long article in the *Torreon*, instructing my schoolmates to beware adult proselytizers from Campus Crusade and New Life. Pointing to "a wave of evangelical-fundamentalist morality currently sweeping Miraleste—a wave that threatens to engulf its followers in a torrent of bitterness and distrust," I warned of "McCarthyism," "heresy hunts," and "paranoia." Yet at Miraleste, where students with a reborn interest in God mostly wanted to strum guitars and sing about Jesus, the paranoia was all mine.

When I had a chance to argue with born-again Christians in person, I leapt at it. In comparison with Sheryl Spencer, I found a more sophisticated debating partner in Rita Chan, a girl in the Forensics Club, a quietly passionate reborn Christian whose parents had immigrated from China. In my father's elderly Cadillac on the way to public-speaking competitions, Rita would tell me about her New Life Club meetings and the earnest conversations about Jesus that went on at them. I presented her with my usual counterarguments—How did Rita explain hell? What happened to natives of the Chinese hinterlands? and so on—indulging myself, as I had with Sheryl, in that favorite absurdity heard from critics of biblical religion: the notion that human reason is so powerful an instrument that it can determine the lineaments of divine justice better than the Divinity Himself: "It seems unjust to me," I was essentially saying, "that God should order His world in such and such a way. Therefore, He doesn't."

Rita was kind enough not to point out my hubris but confined herself to the distinction between, as she put it, on the one hand, "knowing and experiencing God in a personal way," and on the other hand, "religion." "Having a personal relationship with Jesus Christ has given me so much joy and peace," she would say, smiling and looking directly into my eyes. "Because He's my Lord and Savior, I live for Him. He makes me who and what I am. I wish you could have a relationship like that with Him, instead of a 'religion.'" The more she talked about having "a relationship with Christ" and how much she thought I would benefit from one, the harder I fought her. For a "religion" was precisely what I had, if I had anything at all: a few abstract beliefs combined with a handful of dimly understood, ritualized cultural activities. Though I would not have admitted it at the time, to myself or anyone else, the poverty of my "religion" was obvious and Rita's comments ignited my combativeness because she had illuminated that poverty.

How could I have known that Torah-believing Jews regard themselves not as members of a "religion," but as a community in a unique relationship with God? Torah has no word for "religion" or for the conventional name of the Jewish religion, "Judaism." In a religion, human beings worship one or more gods. But speaking to Moses, who had asked His name, God called Himself by the formula *Ehyeh-Asher-Ehyeh* ("I Am That I Am" or "I Shall Be As I Shall Be"). Which is to say that God is not a god. Our Father is not *primus inter pares* among other divine persons. Even to call Him "God" suggests He can be fitted into a category designated by that word, that He is *a* something. In a similar way, Torah is simply *what it is,* not an item in a category, however exalted, but *the* terms of the relationship of God to the people Israel, the way of life He demands of us. When Torah becomes *a* mere religion it ceases to be Torah.

It is frequently observed that young Jews make up a disproportionate percentage of the members of certain cults and other evangelizing groups. This should come as no surprise, since modern Jews are fed a thinner version of their ancestral faith than any other statistically isolatable group is of their own. (A certain spiritual intensity, inborn among Jews, may also have something to do with it.) I myself might have ended up a New Lifer or a Jew for Jesus even before graduating high school, as a college friend of mine almost did. Two years after his Reform bar mitzvah, Matt Gilman found himself avidly reading a copy of the New Testament. He decided to get baptized and was on his way to a Presbyterian church when he was apprehended by his older brother, who talked him out of it.

I spent as much time as Matt did paging through a Bible, but it happened to be the Old Testament. The experiences that got me digging into my white leatherette Holy Scriptures, which I had received as a confirmation gift, took place on the campus of UCLA. The summer after high school my friend Bennett Schneir and I spent a semester there, ostensibly taking classes we had neglected to take in high school (physics in my case, calculus in his), though in fact we spent a great deal of time dozing away bright hot afternoons in our non-air-conditioned room in Sproul Hall. We eventually dropped out of our classes, but before that I attempted to improve my understanding of physics by purchasing a pointlessly elaborate Hewlett-Packard calculator at the student union. The calculator kept mysteriously malfunctioning, and I returned it twice for exchange. I should have wondered what interest fate had in sending me back and forth along Bruin Walk, the tree-lined pedestrian route leading to the main campus.

On my second trip to the electronics counter I noticed a tall bearded man in his thirties, standing on Bruin Walk next to a card table stacked with pamphlets, with a few students around, all of them evidently disagreeing with him about something. I stopped to listen, and it became evident that the man, called Sid, was a Jew for Jesus. He and I ended up talking for three-quarters of an hour. I began by telling him that rather than save souls, he should try to save lives, by doing charity work in some destitute Third World nation. Reasonably, Sid asked me why I thought it was so much more important to save lives than souls, since our lives will eventually end, while souls are immortal. An unsaved life can mean years of suffering or an early death, he admitted, but an unsaved soul can mean eternal suffering.

I abandoned that line of argument and asked him, in a truculent way, what made him think Jesus was the Messiah. Sid explained that he had once been like me. He wanted to disprove the scriptural citations that Christians use to demonstrate that the "Suffering Servant" in Isaiah's prophecy—who will "vindicate many, himself bearing the penalty of their guilt," who "bore the sin of many and interceded for their transgressions"—was Jesus Christ; that the "new covenant with Israel and Judah," by which God promised Jeremiah that He would "forgive their wrongdoing and remember their sin no more," was none other than Christianity. Instead he became convinced that Jesus was the Messiah.

Sweat broke out in my palms. A few responses popped into my mind—like, Wasn't the Messiah supposed to transform the world into a place of peace and harmony? Hadn't, in fact, the founding of the Christian Church resulted in a longer history of violence and persecution than any other single organization had ever caused? Sid explained that this was because the Church is a human vehicle for a divine end; and since humanity is inherently sinful, of course some nastiness had resulted. But he kept directing me back to Isaiah and Jeremiah.

By the time we parted I had forgotten about the defective calculator. Worried by my weak arguments for Judaism and returning to Sproul Hall for lunch, I narrated the conversation to Bennett, who had also received a Temple Beth Shalom religious education. He scoffed and assured me that Sid must be using some sort of deceptive Christian translation of the Bible. To allay my distress, he suggested that we drive out to the shabby Fairfax district of Los Angeles, with its population of Orthodox Jews, to find a Jewish book store that stocked books about the Messiah.

There was such a store, and the lady at the cash register, her hair covered in a snood, directed us to a shelf on messianic topics. What I needed was a defense of Judaism against Christianity, and I found it in a slim red paperback titled, without a hint of academic neutrality, *You Take Jesus, I'll Take God.* The book warned against the tactic among Christian missionaries of quoting scriptural passages out of context and then proceeded to take each of the missionaries' favorite citations and put them *into* context, mostly just by considering the verses immediately above and below. The "Suffering Servant" was identified by Isaiah himself not as any individual, but as some idealized remnant of the people Israel. And missionaries did indeed use cooked translations of the Hebrew. When, for example, Isaiah spoke of an *"almah"* who is "with child, and she will bear a son, and will call him Immanuel," Christians translated this word as "virgin" and connected it with the Virgin Mary; but *almah* simply meant "young woman." This relieved me. I even prepared an index card with abbreviated scriptural references and their explanations ("Isaiah 7:14, *almah* = young woman") in case I should encounter another missionary. The index card was a talisman for me. I put it in my wallet and carried it there for years afterward.

———

A "TALISMAN" AGAINST WHAT? As I said earlier, my angelic vision of Sheryl Spencer, luminescent under the skylight, represented a powerful attraction but also a threat. The shining yellow of her hair, combined with her vaguely Nordic appearance, signaled the danger. Though she was a more beautiful young woman than I was a handsome young man, we could have been brother and sister. It's a little acknowledged fact that lots of Jews are sensitive about Semitic looks and the contrast they present with "WASP" or, as I've heard it put many times, "Aryan" looks. "I'm told I don't look Jewish," they'll say with barely hidden pleasure;

or "Gee, he's awfully *ethnic* looking." In Jewish circles, Jews with fair skin and hair often seem to have a social advantage over the ones with more Arabic or even (those whose ancestors were raped by Russians) Oriental features. (Many dark-skinned American blacks feel something like that, a combination of envy and resentment, toward the more light-skinned members of their race, who are obviously the genetic legacy of mixing with white slave masters in centuries past.) When I was a little boy, my mother paid special, prideful attention to my blue-green eyes and blond hair (it's since gone to a sort of dirty-sand color) and conveyed to me that they were somehow more desirable as features than her own brown hair and brown eyes. In her mind, adopting me seemed to touch her with a little of that odd prestige Jews accord to the features idealized by Nazis. The result was that I associated non-Jewish, especially Nordic, looks with the biological disjunction between my parents and me. Sheryl made me think of my birth family, whoever they might be.

Judged by the definition of Jewishness I had found in Rabbi Donin's book, I was about as Jewish as Sheryl Spencer. She would have been less a symbol of this problem had she not been such a *Scandinavian* sort of angel. I don't remember thinking that Sheryl might look like my Swedish biological mother. But obviously that was very much a possibility. I believe that fact registered somewhere in my mind, if not at the conscious level. And if Sheryl was destined through her genetic heritage to be a born-again Christian, maybe I, with a similar heritage, shared her destiny.

But then again, maybe not. We enter now into the paradox of the adopted child.

Carol Klinghoffer sought to leave me with no doubt as to what I really was: a Jew and a true member of my father's family and her own, sharing their ancestors. When I was eight years old, my parents adopted another child, Michael. (There seemed to be no question of my mother having children herself; I didn't wonder why but accepted the fact implicitly, just as I never wondered why my mother could not fly through the air.) Healthy white American infants, available for adoption, had become so scarce that my parents were forced to look to foreign countries. Within a year we were driving to the airport to greet my new brother, a four-year-old Colombian. At the time my parents negotiated with the Catholic orphanage in Bogotá, they were told that Michael was the child of university professors who were Caucasian and who had died in a plane crash: every adoptive parent's dream, if he is adopting a four-year-old native of a Third World nation. But to look at Michael, with his broad nose, narrow eyes, and barrel chest, is to see instantly that he is an Indian, probably from a peasant family too destitute to raise him. He professes to remember nothing about his life before entering the orphanage.

Michael never truly thought of himself as a Jew. I certainly did think of myself as one. Yet even with an adopted child like me, if the child is not stupid and if he has not been given some superphysical, you might say supernatural, definition of his identity, then the question of this adoptee's body and *what he is*—Jew or Gentile? Caucasian or Indian?—will naturally intrude itself in his soul. Such a definition can be offered by a community whose religious faith transcends the physical world. But Paul and Carol Klinghoffer could not give me a supernatural community, because they did not belong to one themselves and never had. The Reform movement is a thing entirely of this world.

Some adoptees become obsessed with finding their "real parents." Others deny, with suspicious vehemence, that they have the least interest in knowing anything about, as I used to say, "the man and woman who conceived me." But often we can desire knowledge, and doubt things we think we know about ourselves, without consciously realizing it. My preoccupation with Christianity was the outward expression of a very real interest in understanding where my body had come from. I could not ignore that daughter faith of Judaism the way most Jews do. Back in a hidden space of my soul, I perceived it—with its emphasis on reaching out to the unbelieving and the uncommitted, the rootless and wandering— as my mother, looking for her son. She was a ghost with her arms extended to me. Jesus had his arms out toward me, too. From a certain angle, they were the same person.

However, I could not go out to meet them, because I already had a mother. To betray Judaism, even watery Reform Judaism, would be to betray her. So I was compelled to keep myself on guard.

A person who was raised by the man and woman who conceived him may not understand why a curiosity about where we come from bothers many adoptees so acutely. During the year of my confirmation class, my own curiosity took an additional unlikely form, along with my struggles against Christianity, that casts some light on the question. I was becoming intrigued by a certain quality for which I know only one, rather awkward term: authenticity.

People can be led to faith by a variety of odd and unexpected paths. Often the path appears to lead in a direction not approaching faith, but leading away from it. C. S. Lewis found his way to orthodox Christianity through an obsession with Wagner's music and Nordic mythology. He called this object of his affection "the Northernness." From his adoration of the gods he proceeded, over years and with an interlude of atheism, to an adoration of God. Authenticity was for me a more ridiculous means to the same end.

The word itself, "authenticity," entered my thinking around the time of our Temple Beth Shalom confirmation ceremony in May 1981. I believe it really was me, rather than my mother, who wrote the speech I gave from the pulpit for the occasion.

I declared that just as "a gazania or an oak tree" draws its life from the soil through its roots, "we, as young Jews, need to have roots in order to become effectual servants of God, as well as functional members of both our spiritual and secular communities." When a Jew becomes a bar mitzvah, "the root breaks the soil. At the confirmation, it is fully grown as we are confirmed as authentic Jews." What does a Jew receive through his roots if he wants to be "authentic"? "Our roots are not physical appendages; rather, they are our past. Our past not only gives us emotional strength, it also provides us with a firm foundation from which to base our actions." (My confirmation speech would have been enlivened if I'd asked Josh Labelle to supply me with a joke about horse racing.)

Jewish authenticity meant tracing roots from men and women of our time back to the Israel of history. During confirmation instruction, Rabbi Dinnerstein asked us to deliver a book report. I chose a book that had been published five years earlier and that exercised a peculiar fascination over me, Arthur Koestler's *The Thirteenth Tribe*. Famous for his anti-Communist writing, Koestler became convinced in later life that Eastern European Jews are not descended from the ancient Israelites.

While it had long been thought that the enormous population of Jews who lived in the kingdom of Poland-Lithuania by the seventeenth century had migrated there from France, Germany, and England, Koestler insisted that the medieval Jewish populations of those Western countries were too small to furnish so many migrants. Where did the Eastern Jews come from? Koestler pointed to the ancient Turkish empire of the Khazars. In the eighth century the Khazar aristocracy converted to Judaism, and a dubious legend persisted that the entire nation had followed suit. Koestler asserted that the Khazar people had done just that; and when they were driven out of their homeland four or five centuries later by Pecheneg and Mongol conquerors, the Khazar Jews fled to Eastern Europe to form the bulk of Jewry there.

Though I would not have been able to articulate this at the time, I liked the notion that not only I but many, if not most, born-Jewish Jews did not descend from Jews. To a small extent it soothed a tension I felt and quieted a doubt about my own gentile blood.

What I wanted was a personal history, a traceable line connecting the past, my own past, with the identity I presented to the world. It is one of the psychological prices of being an adoptee that the child, later the adult, feels himself to be an impostor. The adoptee has fallen, apparently by chance, into his identity. Any one of thousands of childless couples could have ended up as my "parents." What did I have in common with Paul and Carol Klinghoffer? What history did I share with them? Before the second day of my life, when Carol Klinghoffer brought me home from Santa

Monica Hospital, we had nothing more in common than the occupants of two cars that collide in an intersection.

It may be impossible to convey to anyone born with a history, received from his parents, the importance of a history like that to someone born without one. In a scattered fashion, the way birds build a nest from randomly encountered twigs and fallen pine needles, I began compiling a history of my own.

So, for example, when I was a ninth-grader my mother traveled with me to Ireland for a week-long bus tour. Did this have anything to do with the fragmentary information she had earlier imparted about my Irish American biological father? She didn't say. But I think she took me to Ireland for the same reason she took me to Sweden: so that I would know she and my father had not hesitated to show me the origins of my biological parents, precisely because they, Paul and Carol, were my *real parents*. I loved Ireland and especially whatever about it seemed very old, which is most of the place. When we got back to America, I would sit for hours listening to cassette tapes of the Chieftains, a group of Irish folk musicians. The flutes, fiddles, harps, and tin whistles gave me chills as I imagined ancient green hills. I had the sense that they were my hills.

Meanwhile, before the idea of pre-aged jeans and chinos had ever entered the mind of Ralph Lauren, I was determined to make my clothes look as old as possible: threadbare khakis, worn-out penny loafers repaired with duct tape, all-cotton Oxford shirts frayed at the collar from age. Such clothes—evoking traditions and even actual items of apparel handed down from father to son—charmed me to no end. I aged a pair of Sperry Top-siders by soaking them overnight in tap water mixed with table salt. After buying a pair of brand-new pants, I would not wear them outside the house until I had washed and tumble-dried them four or five times so as to impart at least a patina of age.

I became an aficionado of used-clothing stores. Accompanied by Bennett, I brought home used tuxedos, the top half of a formal U.S. Navy uniform complete with tails and brass buttons bearing elaborate American eagles, plaid pants circa 1960, a bowling shirt of the same era with the name "Ralph" embroidered on the breast. All these I wore to Miraleste, where, fortunately, strange outfits were not unusual. The students were more eccentric than the school's suburban California setting, and the high number of clubbable, preppy USC graduates among their parents, would suggest.

Yet for all this, my life as a consumer of antiquities had barely started. I had not yet begun to dream of the East Coast and its rich opportunities for a lineage-starved Jewish adoptee from California. There were fantasies of personal history I had not conceived of, and would not until I left California.

# Chapter 5

# LORD OF THE HANDKERCHIEF

*I*'m a Reform Jew," goes a comment I've heard in reference to one commandment or another, "so I don't have to keep kosher." Or, "I belong to the Conservative movement, so I can do whatever I want on Saturday morning." No one who says such a thing means in any way to deny his regard for the Jewish people and their folkways, or his hope of a shining future for his people. But to assertions like these, Will Herberg had a provocative reply. In his book *Judaism and Modern Man*, he argued that unless every Jew by birth, on existential grounds, simply by virtue of being a Jew, has the responsibility of living up to all the obligations entailed in the Covenant revealed at Sinai, then "Jewishness" has no meaning worthy of regard. If God and all the souls of Israel did not enter into an agreement at the foot of that mountain, then "the Jews" are merely an ethnic category, and a somewhat twisted one. For in that case only a "persistent and rather malignant delusion" can lead us to view the survival of the Jews per se, or their fate as a people (rather than as individuals), as a question of any weight or urgency. How important is it that a group of people continue, for the ages, to call themselves "Jews"? No more important than that a group of people call themselves "Sicilians" or "Croatians," "Italians" or "Indians."

Not many Jews actively deny the Covenant as a whole. Instead, as they have been taught to do by liberal rabbis, they minimize it: its obligatory nature and the scope of the obligations it entails. This was my own outlook as a high school student. And that makes it very hard to explain my decision to begin putting on my grandfather's tefillin.

That last sentence should have read "my decision to begin putting on tefillin in 1980" or "in 1981" or "1982." But the awkward truth is that of the first two major decisions I made to start enacting certain Jewish rituals, I don't remember precisely when either took place or what constituted my immediate motivation.

This is appropriate, in a way, since at the time I had gotten some ideas into my head about the illusion, as I saw it, that "motivations" mean anything at all. Come and observe, as the Talmud likes to say, the primitiveness of my thinking. I remember sitting in Mrs. Marion Hanson's junior-year English class and discussing ice cream. We had been reading Faulkner, and the issue of fate and free will had come up. Some girl was saying that she didn't feel under the influence of any such thing: she could choose vanilla ice cream if she wanted, or chocolate, whichever she might prefer. I raised my hand and pointed out that our tastes in even such a small matter as ice cream must be conditioned by something: physiological factors (taste buds delighting in chocolate), or education (what flavor did the girl's parents like?), or random associations (maybe chocolate was the flavor of the cake at a joyous birthday party). Otherwise how could we make such a choice at all? Mrs. Hanson's class had just read *The Sound and the Fury*. The book takes a fatalistic view of its characters' lives, summarized by the father of the doomed Compson family, who declares that man is "the sum of his climatic experiences."

Emboldened by the classroom debate, which I seemed to have won, I wrote a term paper explicating Faulkner's "determinism" and very quickly adopted it as my own belief. I still swore by blind fate the next year when I was applying to colleges. If you have never experienced real humiliation, look back at your college applications, especially the essay question calling for a summary of your personal philosophy of life in five hundred words or less. I still have the rough draft of mine for Harvard, in which I affirmed that "the choices we make that determine our actions and our beliefs, have, in turn, been determined by our environments, over which we have no control. Consequently, for me, there are no 'good' or 'evil' people, only people who are products of productive or non-productive environments."

Determinism is a philosophy that, in denying the freedom of men, must deny the sovereignty of God. Presumably if God lives, the incomprehensible source and ruler of the universe, nothing can stop Him from bestowing freedom on His creatures if He wants to do so. That's true even if, as religious predestinarians argue, there appears to be a contradiction between God's omnipotence and omniscience, and human freedom. Bridging paradoxes like that, high above the weak stream of human understanding, does not seem a task beyond His power. It's no coincidence that most people who share the opinion I held at the time, that it is archaic to describe people and deeds as good or evil, tend to think that belief in an omnipotent God is likewise hopelessly old-fashioned. Judgments of good and evil depend for their coherence on something that transcends human judgment and sets moral standards that can be violated but not abrogated. Otherwise it would indeed be high-handed to call a person evil.

―――

THE DISPROOF OF my determinism was in the commandment, the mitzvah, I was experimenting with most mornings. What in my environment could have suggested the idea of strapping on a pair of tefillin? True, I found this divine commandment described in Rabbi Donin's book, which had been given to me by my grandparents, who were part of my environment. And I had the necessary physical implements of the mitzvah, the tefillin themselves, because Sam Bernstein had died and left me his. But surely many another boy has found himself in possession of such a book and such a relic and never thought to do a thing with them.

Like every set of tefillin, a snaking mass of black leather straps attached to small black leather boxes, Sam's contained four passages from the Torah, written on rolled-up parchment, sealed in the boxes, and, in the case of the roll in the head-box, tied with a hair from a calf. In Exodus and Deuteronomy, God instructs the Jews to "bind" His words "for a sign upon your hand, and they shall be for frontlets between your eyes." But what are those things—a sign and frontlets? Obviously the author or Author assumed that readers would know what they are, either because the words were written after the practice of binding the sign and frontlets had already come into being, as unbelievers say, or because the words were explained simultaneously with their revelation. Either way, the mind swirls with possible interpretations. Maybe the Torah means the passage to be taken metaphorically, but as a metaphor for what? If we are supposed to understand the mitzvah literally—and the God of the Pentateuch tends to avoid the gassy poeticizing language of modern religious writers—we had better determine exactly what it is He wants us to bind to our bodies.

Fortunately, as Jewish tradition relates, God defined for Moses all the unfamiliar terms in His Torah. In the oral Torah Moses transmitted that explanation to his followers, who transmitted it to the rest of the Jews. The passages to be written on the rolled parchments are the passages that command the wearing of tefillin, including the first two paragraphs of the prayer *Sh'ma*, the fundamental statement of Jewish belief (Deuteronomy 6:4–9 and 11:13–21), "Hear, O Israel: The Lord our God, the Lord is One. And you shall love the Lord your God with all your heart, and with all your soul, and with all your might. . . ."

I did not love God with all my heart, soul, or might. Certainly that was not the reason I opened Sam Bernstein's worn red velvet tefillin bag. With the straps wrapped tightly around the boxes, tefillin in their bag remind you of testicles in a scrotum, as they are no doubt intended to do: tefillin are exclusively a male responsibility. So poking around in someone else's bag can seem an intrusive act. But I must have had the feeling that Sam wanted me to wear his tefillin. Though I can't tell you whether I was a high school freshman or sophomore at the time, I see myself sitting on my bed with Rabbi Donin's book laid out before me, following the diagram and instructions as carefully as I did a number of years later when I learned to tie a bow tie. Tefillin are worn preeminently for the daily morning recitation of the *Sh'ma* and the benedictions of the central prayer *Shemoneh Esrei.* In ancient times some Jewish men wore them all day long. But later it became clear that the prevailing spiritual condition, which is continually sinking, had sunk to a level where Jews could not for an entire day maintain the focus and purity of thought appropriate for wearing tefillin. For, as Rabbi Samson Raphael Hirsch explained, the practice "has the force of inscribing the Name of God" on one's own bare skin.

Perhaps it is that Name that gives tefillin their mysterious power for spiritual change. The Lubavitcher Hasidim know this. When proselytizing on university campuses, a Lubavitch emissary asks the young men as they walk by, "Are you Jewish? Are you Jewish?" If a student will admit this about himself, the emissary asks if he would like to try on a pair of tefillin and recite the *Sh'ma.* Usually there is a van or mobile home parked nearby where another Lubavitcher helps you strap on the tefillin and say the appropriate benedictions. They believe that the procedure sets off a chain reaction, leading secular Jewish men to seek out information about the faith of their great-grandparents. The fact that so many Lubavitchers grew up as unaffiliated Jews suggests the efficacy of this tactic. For Jewish women, lighting Sabbath candles is said to produce the same effect. I had never met a Lubavitcher, though, and neither had many of the other Jewish men I have known who began their journey toward God by affixing these peculiar ornaments to themselves.

Most mitzvot can be understood at a variety of levels, including allegory and symbol. Writing about the approach to Torah observance exemplified by Jewish mysticism, Gershom Scholem distinguishes these terms from one another: "If allegory can be defined as the representation of an expressible something by another expressible something, the mystical symbol is an expressible representation of something which lies beyond the sphere of expression and communication." Certainly tefillin operate at the level of allegory. Rabbi Hirsch explains that the word itself derives from the same root as the Hebrew verb "judge." The tefillin, he says, "tell you by their very name that they must achieve for you a submission of your inner self to God through the clarifying influence of a sound judgment of the ultimate values of life." Whatever William Faulkner wrote in his novels, we are not the playthings of some impersonal fate, "man the sum of his climatic experiences." We are free and entrusted with a mission: in the words of the *Sh'ma,* encased in the tefillin chamber, "to love the Lord your God, and to serve Him with all your heart and with all your soul."

The procedure by which a Jew puts on tefillin itself carries a meaning. He binds the arm first, then the head. Torah is a system of action that leads to belief. We tend to assume that it is somehow inauthentic to act on beliefs one does not entirely believe. The allegory of tefillin promises that if we merely begin to enact our obligations to God, we will come to believe. The details of correct action can be learned in due time. This is why we bind the arm (action), followed by the head (belief), and only then the hand, specifically the fingers (details), in a complex knot of black leather.

However, the key to the power of tefillin lies in their symbolism. Here we are forced to leave words behind. "In the mystical symbol," writes Scholem, "a reality which in itself has, for us, no form or shape becomes transparent and, as it were, visible, through the medium of another reality which clothes its content with visible and expressible meaning." The mitzvot are "represented as . . . the performance of a secret rite (or *mystery* in the sense in which the term was used by the Ancients). . . . Every mitzvah [becomes] an event of cosmic importance, an act which [has] a bearing upon the dynamics of the universe." And upon the soul.

It would be years before my grandfather's tefillin had worked their effect on me. I used to lay them on some mornings before school. Once the tefillin were in place, I would read the first paragraph of the *Sh'ma*. If anyone had asked me at the time why I was doing this, I don't know what I would have said. Perhaps I would have pointed to the pages in *To Be a Jew* that prescribed the daily wearing of tefillin. But unlike Hayim Halevy Donin, I did not believe in the status of mitzvot as divinely commanded actions. At the same time I felt that in laying tefillin, I was doing what I was supposed to be doing. Intended by whom, or Whom? I had no clear idea.

During my junior year in high school, laying tefillin was barely a habit. Sometimes I did it, sometimes not. I don't think I brought my tefillin with me the following summer for my second trip with the People-to-People High-School Student Ambassadors Program. Once again we were paired with families in a series of foreign countries as we raced through Europe for thirty days. The pairings were based on personal interests we students were asked to list before departing. Along with golf, among my interests I included "theology," which for me at that time still meant my hobby of bickering with Christians. So for our visit to Germany I stayed with the family of a Lutheran minister who lived near Munich and demonstrated his liberalism by putting up photographs of Martin Luther King Jr. around the house. I don't think we got around to discussing theology at all.

Yet in the sense of making mostly unsupported assertions about the true nature of God, theology was to assume a greater importance for me on my return from Europe. I never felt the need to read a book about the nature of God until that August of 1982.

Earlier that year, sickness had entered our home unannounced. My mother, a formidably healthy-looking forty-nine-year-old, had first been confined to a wheelchair that spring. On some wet tiles under the gatehouse outside our home, she'd slipped and twisted her ankle. The damage did not seem more serious than a severe sprain. Over several months afterward, however, she gradually lost the ability to carry weight on that leg. Her doctor sent her for physical therapy, but meanwhile she went from leaning on a cane when she walked to relying on a wheelchair and hardly walking at all. The pain in her leg became increasingly difficult to efface with pain relievers. Then it spread to her other leg.

While I was in Europe the mystery of her condition was resolved. The night our planeload of high school student ambassadors arrived at Los Angeles International, my father was there without my mother. "Mom still isn't feeling very well," he told me.

She was already asleep when we got home. The next morning I found her at the kitchen table, still in her bathrobe, dispiritedly spreading margarine on an English muffin. She could not stand up to kiss me hello. "I'm going to die," she said without stopping to introduce the subject, and began to cry. "I have cancer." Somehow her doctor had failed to notice the bone cancer that had colonized the interior cavities of her femur and tibia. Her "sprained ankle" had merely created a distraction while the invader got down to work.

Before August 1982 Carol Klinghoffer had been a woman as powerful and intimidating personally—to many people, though not to me—as she was physically dominating. In photographs taken at my bar mitzvah she appears at her zenith, in a long earth-colored gown, looking like an opera singer who could take on Wagner with ease. A year after the cancer was identified, she had been reduced to a wraith, all loose skin and bones. Thank God she never had to be confined to her bed. During a few months of remission she seemed almost normal, even happy, especially at the fact that she had taken off so much weight. She traveled extensively, to Australia with my father, to Japan by herself, to Israel and Germany with her mother.

No boy or young man should have to see such a mother transformed as my mother was, weeping over an English muffin and saying, "I'm going to die," in a voice that asked what it had never asked before: "Help me." Yet my mother's illness was not without its benefits for her—spiritually, I mean. The psychologist Viktor Frankl noted that incurable illness confronts a person "with the chance of achieving something through his own suffering." Having survived the Nazi death camps, Frankl could speak authoritatively about how "the way in which a man accepts his fate and all the suffering it entails, the way in which he takes up his cross, gives him ample opportunity—even under the most difficult circumstances—to add a deeper meaning to his life." He called his technique "logotherapy," based on the notion that neurosis develops from a lack of experienced meaning in life (*logos*), as derived from work, family, religion, or most any other worthy cause. Rather than finding life's true meaning, Frankl spoke of "adding" meaning—implying a variety of different life meanings, any one or more of which could be introduced into a person's thinking with equally healthful consequences. The *logos* becomes more or less a useful illusion. But it is difficult to believe in an illusion, no matter how useful. That's why you meet plenty of neurotics these days, but few devotees of logotherapy.

Still, Frankl was on to something. It never occurred to Freud that humans require meaning in their lives. In reality, suffering is a personally addressed invitation from the Source of All Meaning to discover Him at the moment we need Him most. My mother received this invitation and responded to it.

During the year after her diagnosis she kept a diary, mostly pegged to her travels. Though I don't remember hearing my mother talk much about God when I was growing up, it is obvious from the diary that He became for her a strongly felt presence. Much of the diary is prayer. The prayers of people in mortal danger are frequently imagined in sentimental terms, not least by Jews, who have a weakness for sentimentality while being well acquainted with premature death. Recently in the mail I received a fund-raising letter from the Holocaust Memorial Museum in Washington, claiming that the victims of Nazi Germany "in their darkest moments feared not so much their own deaths, but that they would be forgotten." I assure you that those who endure such extreme suffering are concerned "in their darkest moments" less with whether they will be memorialized with an expensive museum than with the sheer, brutal fact of impending death.

Certainly this was my mother's worry. She was terrified at the thought of dying, but often our terror of death is less of the final moment than of the terror that can precede it. We fear fear. So my mother prayed over and over again for the strength to face down her fears.

"Dear God," she writes, "please help me survive this test!"

"Help me, dear God, give me strength and let me rid myself of the cane. I need you, dearest God, please let me feel your love. Tonight depression again has filled my thoughts."

"How can I calm this turmoil inside me? Only God is my salvation."

And in May 1983, as her remission was drawing to a close, "I've begun to feel pains in my legs again. I pray it is nothing, but I fear the worst is returning and I'm uneasy and afraid."

My mother seems to have spent remarkably little time praying for mere survival. That amazes and awes me, given the tepidness of our spiritual life at Temple Beth Shalom, with its indifference to the question of whether the soul survives the body. Her main desire was to feel God's love. In some ways she remains in her diary the person I knew growing up, with her love of "beautiful things," shopping for opals in Melbourne, jade in Japan, a Mercedes in Germany. In other ways she is transformed. She has developed a relationship with God. She writes of her prayers for my father, that he will remarry if she dies before he does, and of her thanks to God for the life He has given her, "a precious gift." She can pray to him in this way because He has become a personal presence for her, not an abstract spiritual force, but a father. She feels "touched by God," and I have no doubt she was.

In Israel she visited Safed, a city that became the seat of Torah mysticism after the expulsion of the Jews from Spain. She visited "the old synagogues and the local museum for artists," finding the town "overpriced but interesting." As it happens, the rabbis who lived in Safed during the sixteenth century developed a theory about the experience she was having with her "beloved God."

Above all else, they taught, we must seek "adhesion" to God. The scholars of Safed elaborated on this idea in highly esoteric language, but my mother had grasped its essence: not in intellectual terms, but as an experience of closeness to the Lord. Praying and crying at the Western Wall of the Temple Mount in Jerusalem, she felt she had reached a "spiritual zenith." "I have felt the love of God," she wrote, "his nearness to me." In her own way, her soul adhered to Him.

As Viktor Frankl would put it, those of us who have not endured great suffering, but who are the family members of people who have suffered, also have the opportunity to achieve something. I believe my father and brother did so. My brother, Michael, still complains that we were not a close family; but cancer seemed to draw my father and brother closer to my mother. She became a different person for the year that included her remission; and in some ways the new Carol Klinghoffer suited her husband and younger son better than the old one. The cancer softened her, so that she less often came into conflict with Michael—who disliked school and vehemently disliked the pressure he felt from her to be as diligent a student as I was. She became, too, a sweeter wife to my father.

Before her illness, she and I had a better relationship than she ever did with Michael. But ours became more distant. Her neediness appalled me, never more so than one night when my father was out of town and my mother could not remember if she had taken her dose of cancer medicine. Whatever the medicine was, it had affected her memory and left her scared and weepy, in fear both of taking too much of it and of taking too little. I finally called her doctor at his home and he said not to worry, a double dose wouldn't hurt her. Only a few years earlier I had been the little boy who looked forward to being sick so he could stay home from school and be fussed over by his mother. The role reversal left me with a queasiness in the pit of my stomach, which comes back now as I remember that year.

Nor did my mother's sickness give me, as it gave to her, a more expansive sense of God's presence in the world. Perhaps it was my pretensions as a fatalist that drew my attention to a book that had been published the year before by Harold Kushner, a Conservative rabbi in Natick, Massachusetts. I guess I had already heard of Kushner's *When Bad Things Happen to Good People,* a best-seller, because the very day my mother told me she was going to die, I drove up to the Del Amo shopping mall in nearby Torrance and bought it.

An extremely compassionate man, Kushner, along with his wife, had been struck by an even more grievous loss than had my family. The Kushners' fourteen-year-old son had died of progeria, "rapid aging." In view of the Jewish belief in a God Who is perfectly righteous, perfectly loving, and all-powerful, the rabbi found himself unable to explain how this God had taken his son from him. So he dropped the part about God being all-powerful. It would not repay the effort to reconstruct Kushner's argument, but essentially he brought forward certain passages in the Book of Job to support his notion of a downsized Lord of the universe. This Divinity was like a very sympathetic radio talk-show host. You couldn't see Him, but He was present, in the way that radio waves are present all around us. You could talk to Him and imagine, through the words of the Bible, that He talked back. Like a disembodied Phil Donahue, He cared very deeply about His listening audience. When we cried, the Lord of the Handkerchief cried with us, plucking tissues from a Jupiter-size Kleenex box. However, He was unable to do much to help you, except for one thing. If you prayed to Him, he could give you emotional strength.

The gap between this view of God and the traditional one is particularly evident on the subject of illness, as reflected in the prayer for healing found in the ancient siddur. One of the benedictions of the prayer *Shemoneh Esrei* beseeches God for health and healing, beginning with a verse from Jeremiah: "Heal us, Lord—then we will be healed; save us—then we will be saved." The distinction is between a Creator Who, if He wills it, can save us from anything; and a Comforter Who can visit us at the hospital.

But I was looking for a way to understand the doom that appeared to await my mother, and the kindly voice of Rabbi Kushner was the only voice I was prepared to hear. I read the book with great appreciation and passed it on to my mother, who I am pretty sure did not read it. That is for the best. The next year, as a college freshman, I had a Latin teacher who without warning succumbed to cancer. While she lay dying in a hospital, I wrote her a long letter expressing my admiration for Rabbi Kushner's theology and promising her that while God couldn't help her with the cancer, He surely felt very sad on her behalf. Meanwhile the logical, terrifying conclusion of Kushnerism did not occur to me: that any God Who is powerless to save us in life can hardly save us after death. So if Professor Gordon was any type of a Christian, with an expectation of life after death, I'm sure that she paid no attention to my smug letter. Otherwise, I hope her family threw it out before she had a chance to read it.

––––––

THAT I HELD this emasculating opinion of God makes it all the harder to explain my decision to go into my bathroom one night with a razor blade and my grandfather's siddur. If God really isn't the transcendent, omnipotent Source of All Being, He is in no position to ask a boy to do to himself what I did.

I know this happened before I started college, either my junior year or my senior year at Miraleste—in other words, before or after my mother became sick. As with the tefillin, I am unable to say for certain when it happened. Maybe it had something to do with my mother, maybe it was due to the sheer internal logic represented by her father's tefillin.

Laying tefillin is an act of admission: admitting our responsibility to abide by God's will, in mind and body. From the moment I began experimenting with tefillin, I had unwittingly begun the very long process of admitting my responsibility to obey the Lord. Torah in its practical aspect is not called Halachah, "the Way," for nothing: it is a path that, if we agree to follow it, leads in a certain direction.

But immediately I was confronted with a problem of definition. The Torah tradition that specifies the responsibilities of a Jew de-

nied that I was a Jew at all. But that wasn't what my parents or
Rabbi Dinnerstein had told me. For once, I wanted a clear answer
to the question: What am I?

One day after school, when neither of my parents was around, I
picked up the kitchen telephone and dialed a Lubavitcher rabbi. I
had had a few encounters with Hasidim, none that left me feeling
at all attracted to these ultra-Orthodox Jews in their costumes of
black suit, white shirt, no tie, and black fedora, the ensemble giving the impression of bearded undertakers for the Mafia. Among
secular and Reform Jews, however, there persists an unarticulated
hunch that Hasidim (of whom Lubavitchers are the best-known
sect) are the most authentically Jewish Jews. At least before the
imbroglio in which Lubavitchers began proclaiming to the world
that their dying rebbe was the long-awaited King Messiah, a large
portion of the most generous financial contributions to Lubavitch
institutions came from nonobservant Jews. Most Reform homes
have on their walls at least one painting of Hasidim dancing,
beards and frock coats flying, most likely purchased on a trip to Israel. Our home had one picture of Hasidim dancing and another
of them sitting at a long table arguing over a page of Talmud. Especially outside of New York City, where you don't encounter live
specimens very often, Jews are glad that Hasidim exist, perpetually dancing or arguing or whatever exactly they do with their
time. While we ourselves marry gentiles and bid our children
farewell as they exit the Jewish people, thanks to the Hasidim we
know there will always be Jews. This comforting thought goes a
long way toward explaining the money secular Jews are willing to
part with to support Lubavitchers. They are our excuse, and well
worth the expense.

Therefore when I decided to ask a Jewish authority if I was a
Jew or not, I naturally turned to the local Lubavitch rabbi. To act
as his emissary in the South Bay area, the Lubavitch rebbe had
sent this man to Lomita, a nearby town centered on a strip of Pacific Coast Highway lined with cheap motels, liquor stores, and
Cantonese restaurants, containing even fewer Jews than did Palos

Verdes. One afternoon I called his office. A woman picked up the phone and I asked to speak with the rabbi, not knowing his name.

Briefly I told him my story: that I was adopted, that my birth parents were non-Jews, that my adoptive parents were Jewish, and I considered myself Jewish. But was I really?

The rabbi replied in a businesslike fashion. Did I know, he asked, if I had been circumcised by a *mohel*, a man specially trained in the Torah laws of circumcision, or by a doctor? It happened at the hospital, I said, so probably a doctor. And was I, he asked, ever immersed in a *mikvah*, a ritual pool of water? No. Then, he said, that meant I had never been converted to Judaism and therefore I was not a Jew.

He knew what I was going to ask next. I could become a Jew, he said, but there were certain preconditions. Did my parents observe the Sabbath or keep a kosher home? No. They would have to do both, he said. And that was just the beginning. I would have to learn about Judaism from an Orthodox rabbi. This could take years. But if I persisted, I could someday undergo a conversion to Judaism.

I asked what that consisted of. Two things, he said. A male who has already been circumcised must undergo a "symbolic circumcision," where a drop of blood is taken from the tip of the penis, after which a benediction is said. Then the convert is immersed in a *mikvah*, followed by another benediction. When he comes out, he is a Jew.

At this point we had been on the phone for about ten minutes. There was nothing more to say, so the rabbi hung up.

That night my mother made dinner and we ate with my father and brother. I didn't mention the conversation, but it was on my mind. The demands the rabbi said I would have to make on my parents were out of the question. But as for the "symbolic circumcision" and the dip in a bath, couldn't I skip the rest and do that, which seemed to be the essential part, by myself?

Fighting off squeamishness, I concluded that with a sharp enough knife, I could indeed convert myself. The next day after school I stopped at the Save-On drugstore in San Pedro and bought a razor blade.

The ritual of conversion is very old, its origins recorded in Exodus. When the Israelites stood at the foot of Mt. Sinai, Moses needed, in effect, to convert them en masse to Judaism, which he did through animal sacrifices on their behalf. "Early in the morning, he set up an altar at the foot of the mountain. . . . He designated some young men among the Israelites, and they offered burnt offerings and sacrificed bulls as offerings of well-being to the Lord. Moses took one part of blood and put it in basins, and the other part of the blood he dashed against the altar." The Talmud states that it was a regulation imposed at Sinai that there can be no sacrifice performed for a person who has not been ritually immersed in a *mikvah*. Meanwhile, in the Book of Joshua, it is noted that "all the people who came out of Egypt had been circumcised." So, says the tradition, the rite of conversion comprises three distinct elements: immersion, animal sacrifice, and (for males) circumcision. Of course, this three-part ritual was not set in motion until the would-be convert had accepted on himself the responsibilities entailed in the Torah. When there was a Temple in Jerusalem, converts would present themselves to the priests with two birds in hand—or less frequently, if they could afford it, with cattle. The birds would be killed by pinching their heads off, the blood dashed against the altar. After the Second Temple was destroyed in 70 C.E., this gory element had to be discontinued (though some rabbis maintain that after the Messiah appears and the Third Temple is built, converts will need to offer their sacrifices retroactively). Immersion and circumcision remained obligatory, predicated on the convert's first having undertaken the way of Torah.

My self-conversion was accomplished with no ado at all. Sam Bernstein's siddur contained the blessing to be recited over a circumcision. I soaped up the razor blade with a bar of Irish Spring, rinsed and dried it, and got into the bathtub. If you have ever tried cutting yourself, you know that it takes a little time to work up the necessary gumption. Naturally some parts of the body are easier to cut than others. After a couple of failed passes, which did not hurt nearly as much as I expected, a very small bead of red appeared. "Blessed are you," I read out quietly from the siddur, first in English, then sounding it out in Hebrew, "Lord our God, King of the Universe, who has sanctified us by his commandments and commanded us regarding circumcision. *Baruch attah Hashem, Elokeinu, Melech Haolam, asher kidishanu b'mitzvotav v'tzivanu al ha milah.*"

I then filled the bathtub with lukewarm water, took off my clothes, stepped in, lay down, and pressed my back to the floor of the tub so that the water covered my face for a moment. When I had done this, I got up, dried off, and drained the bath.

I was now a Jew, I thought.

I did not feel appreciably different, but then no one had told me I should expect to receive some exciting burst of spiritual energy like Christians on TV evangelical shows. My life as a Jew went on pretty much as before. I continued to put on tefillin for a while. I continued to go to high school. I continued to be interested in girls.

The summer after my second People-to-People High-School Student Ambassador trip, I got my first real girlfriend: Traci Lander, a student at Rolling Hills High School, whose family belonged to a Conservative synagogue. Starting with our junior-year prom, Traci and I dated steadily into our first year of college. I remember driving her to Temple Beth Shalom for services on a few occasions, but in general having a girl to entertain took my mind off spiritual pursuits. I quit laying tefillin.

There was, of course, an additional factor perpetually in the background of my last year in high school and constantly threatening to break into the foreground. My mother was now, without question, dying. In July the pain recommenced throbbing up and down her legs, across her ribs and shoulders. She was depressed, needless to say, a condition that was not helped by the medicine she was taking to fight pain, a substance derived from morphine. Since her doctor believed that the tumors in her bones were being fed by estrogen, she went into Torrance Memorial Medical Center to have her ovaries and pituitary glands removed.

In August I started my freshman year at Brown University. She had been too sick to drive with me to the airport and cried on the couch in the TV room as I waited for a shuttle van to pick me up. The last time I saw my mother was that October when she and my father visited me in Providence.

She had briefly recovered the ability to walk and drive but otherwise remained the ghost she had become in the past year. Around the house I grew up in we still have photographs of her from that time. I hate to look at them. By that point, it was as if Carol Klinghoffer had already died, only to have her place taken by a sick, elderly relative over whom the apprehension of doom clearly hung. She, my father, and I tried to pretend that we were like any other freshman's family, taking in the sights of a Rhode Island autumn. But none of us enjoyed it. Rabbi Kushner's teachings no longer provided any protection from the feeling any boy must experience at seeing his mother walking dead before his eyes.

From Providence my mother flew with my father to New York City, "to say good-bye," as her mother later interpreted the visit. On the plane ride back to California she began to feel very ill and, on arrival, went straight to Torrance Memorial. There, on October 25, 1983, she died.

| *Chapter 6* |

# UNDER GLASS

death properly mourned is a
comfort to mourners, or so I'm told. Judaism prescribes a regimen
of practices to be followed by those who have experienced the
death of loved one, none of which my family was familiar with.
So, not surprisingly, after my mother died I never entirely felt that
we had paid proper tribute to her. What is proper tribute? The
Torah begins and end with acts of loving-kindness performed by
God. In Genesis He makes clothing for Adam and Eve, and in
Deuteronomy He buries Moses in the earth. These two gestures
have in common their concern for human dignity. A person walking around naked in public is an affront to that soul's own dignity,
as is a dead body that has not been covered in the ground. When
the time came to bury my mother, we chose not a traditional Jewish cemetery, but Hillside Memorial Park, an L.A. landmark with
its famous sarcophagus of Al Jolson overlooking the San Diego

Freeway. There, mostly secular and Reform Jews are entombed aboveground in a concrete necropolis of vaults piled one on top of the other. When my father and I toured the facility, I noticed a line of ants climbing up a wall of vaults. A man representing Hillside was showing us around and I asked him what those ants were doing there. "Don't look at that," he told me.

After the funeral, rather than sit shivah, the customary practice of staying at home to receive guests for the week after a family member's death, we immediately went about our business—even, in my case, visiting an amusement park, Knott's Berry Farm, three days later for Halloween night, my birthday. Park employees had gotten dressed up as zombies, mummies, and other unburied corpses and prowled around the roller-coaster rides, scaring customers, who screamed in delight. I never cried for my mother's death, which seems vaguely ungrateful of me as a son. A week later I resumed my freshman year of college.

American universities once organized their educational priorities according to the advice of Psalm 111: "The beginning of wisdom is fear of the Lord [*yirat Hashem*]. All who practice [His commandments] gain sound understanding." In Hebrew, the word loosely translated as "fear," *yirah*, is related by its grammatical root to the verb "to see." *Yirat Hashem* does not mean to live in terror of God, but rather to conduct yourself in accordance with the knowledge that at all times He is watching us—or, conversely, to behave as you would if you saw Him at all times in front of you. My college, Brown, began its existence as a center for the moral education of God-fearing Baptists—as Harvard did for Puritans, Yale for Congregationalists, Princeton for Presbyterians, Columbia for Anglicans. Since 1770 Brown has held its graduation in the First Baptist Meeting House, at the bottom of College Hill. But long before I arrived the administrators in University Hall had ceased to take the school's Latin motto—*In Deo Speramus*, "In God We Hope"—with any seriousness. On most American campuses, faith had been defeated by secularism, driven in a humiliating retreat into the Theology Department, which was renamed the Department of Religious Studies. Religion was considered no longer a living source of truth, but the mere object of academic study, like a dried-out butterfly under glass, to be poked at by specialists.

I enrolled at Brown as a secular Jew and a political liberal. I brought my Birkenstock sandals, and one of my first destinations during orientation week was a meeting of Democratic Socialists of America.

Though many liberals believe in God, the fact that they do so is a tribute to the mind's ability to embrace two or more contradictory ideas at once. Philosophically speaking, liberalism and secularism are brother and sister, both starting from the assumption that we humans, not God, are sovereign over our lives. We, not He, define right and wrong. So once you begin to be liberated from liberalism, it's easier to escape from secularism. My own left liberalism was even shallower than my secularism. The typical high school student rebels against his parents by having sex, drinking booze, smoking dope, or sniffing cocaine. I was too much of a mama's boy for any of that, so I expressed my independence in political terms. My parents were moderate Democrats living among conservative Republicans; in 1980 and 1984 Ronald Reagan swept Palos Verdes by more than 80 percent. When I was a high school student, calling myself a "socialist" and bewailing the presidency of Ronald Reagan had been my only rebellious acts. By adopting political opinions to go along with my Birkenstocks, I could dismay my parents, my friends' parents, and many of my classmates, while remaining safely within the limits of the law and the dictates of good health. As for sex, it never occurred to me that was an option. When, after graduation, Bennett casually mentioned that some of our own Miraleste classmates had engaged in intercourse, I thought he was kidding.

At Brown, to my disappointment, I was no longer the sole campus leftist. The campus swarmed with political "nonconformists," who failed to see that on College Hill there was no one to shock: heterodoxy at the plush high schools most had graduated from had become orthodoxy at a plush college, and the former individualists rushed to enforce this orthodoxy. During my freshman year the

issues provoking the highest levels of manufactured student in-
dignation were CIA recruiting on campus, apartheid, and nuclear
weapons. This last concern attracted national attention when some
students, pretending to be hysterically afraid of what violence the
evil Reagan administration might provoke from the Soviet Union,
started demanding that Brown Health Services stock suicide pills
in case of a nuclear attack on Providence.

I still wanted to be different, and very quickly I was transformed: from a shallow Bolshevik to a shallow Republican. At the
start of my freshman year, to the disgust of my lacrosse-playing
roommate, I had decorated the cinder-block walls of our room in
Emery Hall with a big poster of Marx and a small red banner
bearing a hammer and sickle. The following summer I traveled to
Dallas as a "youth delegate" to the 1984 Republican convention.
The sudden metamorphosis did not strike me as odd.

This was because I had absorbed more of the Brown ethos than
I realized, in both politics and religion. At Brown, as at most of the
Ivy League colleges, political opinions are valued possessions, con-
ferring prestige as much as food from a luxurious restaurant
might, or clothing from an elite designer. Opinions are recognized
as high status by a sort of demographic calculation. My classmates
at Brown defined the elite as people who hold certain opinions in
line with those prevalent in their immediate surroundings (liberal), but at odds with the opinions of the majority of people in
the country at large (conservative). I happened to assume the reverse: the elite person is in conflict with his near neighbors,
though maybe in accord with the rest of the nation. I was not
more thoughtful than my fellow students. I wanted to possess status opinions as much as they did. That's why I started calling myself a "conservative."

———

BUT RELIGIOUSLY, I remained a liberal. The religion I practiced
at the time could not have been much more secular. It hardly qual-
ified as Judaism. For instance, though I had joined the rugby team,
I decided to miss the game against Yale in order to roll out of bed

at 11:30 A.M. and head for Sayles Hall to attend Yom Kippur services, which had begun hours before. This was my supreme act of religious devotion for the year.

This arid thing was the Judaism that, in the main intellectual endeavor of my college years, I sought to defend in terms acceptable to secular thinking. I was one of those college students who went through a period, embarrassing to me as an adult, of calling myself an "existentialist" and subsequently a "Nietzschean." As a freshman, I took a philosophy class where I read books by Kierkegaard, Sartre, Camus, and Nietzsche. The next year it was Hume, Feuerbach, and more Nietzsche. When I look back now on the papers I wrote for those classes, I realize I was struggling to create an excuse for affirming some basic religious and moral tenets, while at the same time adhering to the most fiercely simple-minded type of religious skepticism.

Warning: What follows is the sort of potted philosophy that college freshmen are famous for. Still, a potted philosophy is better than no philosophy; and I see now that, in my naive way, I was groping for answers to real, in fact ultimate, questions. My skepticism came from Camus and Hume. Camus's *The Myth of Sisyphus* set forth the problem of that characteristically modern creature, the "absurd man." This person wants to know the fundamental truths underlying his existence, notably the truth about God and about the nature of right and wrong, but realizes that there can be no such knowledge. Combining this posture with Kierkegaard's idea of the "Knight of Faith"—who, like Abraham when he agreed to sacrifice his own son, confronts man's inability to understand God but continues to accept His will without question—I came up with a theory I called an "amoral ethics." This was an ethical posture that recognized that there can be no coherent moral code that does not come from God: unless there is a Supreme Being behind that code, it doesn't make sense to talk about things I "ought" or "ought not" to do. At the same time, Camus had written that "the absurd does not liberate; it binds. It does not authorize all actions. 'Everything is permitted' does not mean that nothing is forbidden." I proposed a criterion for an "absurd" ethical code: the criterion was one's own happiness. In effect, as I understood it, this would lead to an ethical code vaguely like the one associated with God-centered religious systems. "Sins" such as murder, theft, lying, and cheating lead to unhappiness for the person who commits them and were thus forbidden.

I doubt that I actually read all of David Hume's *Dialogues Concerning Natural Religion,* in which among other things he bats down the old-fashioned rationalistic proof for the existence of God: the so-called cosmological argument, which traces the existence of the universe through a series of intermediate causes back to its ultimate cause, which must be the Deity Himself. But I absorbed its skepticism, which I applied to Hume himself. This very reasonable philosopher expected all the propositions he believed in to be rationally justifiable—all except one. Hume accepted nothing on faith except for the necessity to accept nothing on faith. Why the exception? How, I wanted to know, can we rationally justify the superiority of truth over falsehood? We can't.

The skeptic needs some other guide to help him choose his beliefs. Again, my pleasure principle dashed to the rescue: Believe whatever makes you happiest. If the belief system that gives you the most pleasure and comfort is some form of traditional God-centered religious faith, well, go for it!

I had cribbed this sort of analysis from Nietzsche. His *Beyond Good and Evil* was a book that I came back to again and again as a college student. In its first three pages he has already lined up against the wall and shot the philosophical "prejudice" in which falsehood is rejected in favor of truth. "We asked about the *value* of this will [to know the truth]. Suppose we want truth; *why not rather* untruth? and uncertainty? even ignorance?" Nietzsche despised the New Testament and its "slavish" moral outlook and approved of the Hebrew Bible to the extent that it could be used as a stick to beat Christianity. He certainly did not mean his writings to be employed in defense of religious belief. Yet he had written, "The falseness of a judgment is for us not necessarily an objection to a judgment. . . . The question is to what extent it is life-promoting, life-preserving, species-preserving, perhaps species-cultivating." It seemed to me that religious belief, however false, was more "life-promoting" than any system that had issued from Nietzsche's philosophy, such as Nazism or the nihilistic academic pose you heard a lot about at Brown: deconstructionism. I am the only person I know of who came to Orthodox Judaism via Friedrich Nietzsche.

FOR GIVING ME a first slight inkling that traditional religion is indeed "life-promoting," I thank my first friend at Brown, Danny Warshay. An earnest, frizzy-haired kid from a suburb of Cleveland, Danny had grown up in a typical Conservative synagogue. Nevertheless he had become a *ba'al teshuvah*.

One Saturday morning in his junior year of high school, a friend had invited Danny to drive with him to a decrepit old shul in downtown Cleveland. The old men in attendance welcomed him and showered him with honors: he was asked to say the benediction before the reading of the Torah, to carry the Torah from its ark and, at the conclusion of the reading, put it away. They asked him to come back regularly to help them form a minyan, a prayer quorum of ten men, for the seven A.M. weekday services. He agreed but was nervous when they offered to show him how to lay tefillin and lead the men in their morning prayers. The old men loved Danny, and he loved them. Meanwhile the tefillin had begun to perform their magic.

I met Danny as a group of freshmen walked across campus for dinner at the "Ratty" (as Brown students call the Refectory) a night or two into our first year. Somehow we got onto the subject of the old men at the shul in Cleveland and how he had decided, on their inspiration, to do unthinkable things. He had begun observing Shabbat, which for him meant praying in shul on Friday night and not doing schoolwork on Saturday. And he had started keeping kosher, which for him meant eating vegetarian when kosher meat wasn't available.

Danny took me to the Hillel House, where I had my first encounter with other religiously earnest Jews. At any college the Hillel almost certainly will have a reputation as the main gathering spot for Jewish nerds. Our own Hillel, a white barnlike structure on Brown Street, was a comfortable refuge for Jewish freshmen like me who wanted to make friends and thought they would have an easier time doing it in a Jewish setting.

The friends I made weren't exactly Orthodox. Before services on Friday nights, a few of the women would smoke marijuana to ensure that they arrived in a carefree mood; after all, it was the Sabbath, a day of peace. Some were "Orthodox for Shabbat"— meaning that they observed a selection of Jewish laws from Friday night until Saturday afternoon. Others who explicitly identified themselves as fully Orthodox had certain quirks. One of the leaders of the Orthodox minyan dated a gentile girl. There was even a bisexual who maintained a boyfriend and girlfriend simultaneously, both Jewish.

My only college romance was with a somewhat irregular Orthodox girl. As a sophomore I had developed a flirtatious friendship with Ketura Persellin—whose real name was Kathleen. Raised barely Reform in Texas, she had as a high school student lived for a year in England, where she fell in love with an Orthodox boy. She then spent a year in Israel, where she exchanged her English name for a Hebrew one and became a *ba'alat teshuvah.* For me there was something irresistibly exotic about her. A girl who addressed groups of us as "y'all" and scorned the liberal Judaism we had both grown up in, she enjoyed shocking me with her left-wing political opinions and had become enamored of Brown's most chic academic discipline, "semiotics," the nihilistic, obscurantist "science of signs." The word is interchangeable with "deconstructionism," which comes down to the proposition that all texts employ meanings only by a self-referential system of language construction. In practice that means it's impossible to make authoritative judgments: mainly about the meaning of a "text," but also about the superiority of one book over another, or in fact the truth of any statement concerning literature, politics, history, religion, or any other important subject. Yet in her spiritual life Ketura had committed herself to a religious system devoted to making precisely such judgments.

I was charmed by the contradictions she encompassed, no less than by her adorable freckled face. We would be sitting in a diner called Louis's, the surrounding air thickened by fumes of stuff frying in lard, with her latest incomprehensible semiotics paper between us—about Lacan or Foucault or some other dead Frenchman. While I joked about how impossible I found it to understand her jargon-heavy writing, she would delightedly sneer at the nonkosher food in front of me. "Even the coffee here is *trefe* [nonkosher]," she liked to say. It was partly my envy of her commitment and partly a simple desire to have an excuse to spend time with her that motivated me to try out Orthodox prayer.

I had never participated in a traditional Jewish prayer service. The Brown Hillel included Reform, Conservative, and Orthodox minyanim. While the Reform kids met in a spacious street-level parlor, and the Conservatives in the high-ceilinged upstairs dining hall, the Orthodox were confined to a room like a walk-in closet. I couldn't understand their prayers, which were in Hebrew, any more than I did the papers Ketura wrote for her semiotics classes. Even more annoying was the breakneck speed of the prayers. The Friday night service prescribed in the siddur was, I thought, unnecessarily long. To get through it, the students seemed to race the way you'd race through brushing your teeth if you were late for a morning class. I could never tell what part of the service the prayer leader had reached at any given moment. The Orthodox students all knew each other and, except for Ketura, showed no interest in helping me understand their worship. Their conversations were punctuated with a jargon of words in Hebrew or Yiddish, I didn't know which. In their presence I felt unwelcome and incompetent.

As a second best, from the perspective of wooing Ketura, I settled on the Conservative minyan. This was more or less the same liturgy, but edited and translated into English here and there. Halfway through my sophomore year I had figured out the order of the prayers, so that on one occasion I led part of the service myself. Because the Conservative philosophy encourages some experimentation with liturgy, I stopped in the middle and pompously harangued the students on the importance of *kavannah*, or intentionality, in prayer—a word I had recently learned. The Orthodox, I said, prayed as if they were brushing their teeth. It happened that Ketura was sitting in the room. Infuriated by my disrespect, she stormed out.

Yet I also perceived that the Orthodox minyan had something in its loud, spirited worship that I hadn't come across before. An analogy can be drawn to art. An art critic I know says that he first came to appreciate abstract painting one day when he was visiting a gallery with some mediocre specimens on the wall. By chance he had a postcard in his pocket with a picture by Jackson Pollock on the front. He put the one up next to the other, and the difference struck him instantly. The Pollock had a "buzz" to it of energy and crackling life. The other painting was flat, dead. At that moment he realized he could develop the ability to distinguish good art from bad.

Orthodox prayer buzzed. When Ketura and her friends sang the sixteenth-century mystical hymn *"L'chah Dodi"* ("Come, My Beloved"), intended to welcome the Sabbath personified as an ecstatically awaited bride—the speed of their singing was less that of the late-waking student brushing his teeth than that of an eager groom running to meet his new wife. The prayers issuing from the Conservative minyan whined like an impatient child or moaned like an ailing cat.

It's an odd fact that my spiritual evolution was prodded on in the beginning by my inclination to sin: that is, by resentment of the Orthodox students, by envy of them, and by lust for Ketura. Probably the strongest of these was envy. I had entered what I took to be my sophomore slump. "I'm not excited about anything," I complained in a letter to a friend in California. "I have few real convictions. Ugg!" The justification for belief I had tried to work out in my college papers had not, in fact, led to belief; and the obvious sincerity of Ketura's religious friends heightened my awareness of this. I wanted to *feel something*. In addition, as a young man whose pride in himself depended on intellectual accomplishment more than any other kind, I was embarrassed at my ignorance of Judaism's basic texts and my inability to understand its holy language. I wanted to *know something*, too.

That's why I resolved to read some of the Bible. Apart from the prophetic passages I needed to fend off Christian proselytizers, I had never really done that. So I took a class on the Old Testament, taught by a likable professor, Henry Waring. My interest was still in Jewish apologetics—as in thinking up textual arguments to refute Christians—and I wrote a long paper about Isaiah's "Suffering Servant." I didn't learn much from Professor Waring's slow-moving lectures, which mostly seemed to lead up to their subject without ever arriving there, but I did feel comforted by the so-called higher criticism that was the working assumption of all biblical studies at Brown.

This criticism was "higher" in that it sought to explain in what order and at what time ancient human authors had jotted down the Holy Scriptures, to be edited and "redacted" by other humans. Pioneered by an unbelieving Jew, Baruch Spinoza, and perfected by a nineteenth-century German, Julius Wellhausen, with his Documentary Hypothesis, this approach began with the assumption that God could not have dictated the entire Pentateuch. The rest followed naturally. Any apparent contradictions in the text—as between the two accounts of creation in Genesis—did not, as a traditionalist would say, carry meaning precisely by the technique of *apparent* contradiction; instead they resulted from the imperfect sewing together of prose fragments written by fallible old Jews.

I liked the posture of the higher criticism because it allowed me to read the Bible without feeling that it required me to do anything I didn't want to do or to believe anything I would feel embarrassed to profess openly. I could just explain away anything I found unattractive as the mere opinions of human beings. This was a useful defense not only against Christians, but against the Orthodox Jews at Hillel. The latter I perceived as fundamentalists no less than the former, eager to impose all kinds of biblical commandments on me—like wearing tefillin more regularly than I did, or keeping kosher, or observing the Sabbath. In short, there was no *yirat Hashem* in Professor Waring's class, and that was fine by me. Most of the classes I was signing up for had at least some indirect bearing on religion: classical Greek, armed with which I hoped to read the New Testament in the original and debunk the Gospels; Latin, with its liturgical associations; Professor Waring's class; "Philosophy 70: Classical Philosophy of Religion." All these left me safe, it seemed, from the grasp of the Deity. As I put it in a letter to Jesus College, Brown's sister institution at Cambridge University, where I wanted to spend junior year: "My interest in religion is mainly academic." (Jesus College wasn't impressed and wrote back to say it couldn't accommodate me.)

Around this time Ketura asked me what plans I had for Passover. I had none. "Why don't you try spending Pesach with an Orthodox family?" she suggested. This was possible through arrangements Hillel offered to make, putting Brown students together with local Jewish people willing to have us at their seder table. The turning points in a person's life often do not seem that way when he is actually experiencing them. Only when he looks back does he see that an apparently chance encounter with a person, place, or event nudged him in a certain direction. I requested an Orthodox family and got a Lubavitch one.

I was greeted by the couple's seven noisy children, who climbed over each other, the furniture, and the guests throughout the evening. The seder itself consisted of the father and another guest, a visitor in his twenties from Brooklyn who studied in a Lubavitch yeshiva, reading aloud in Hebrew from the Haggadah, the text of the seder. When the time came to eat matzah, the yeshiva student, named something like Yitzchak Greenbaum, pulled out a plastic-coated card about a foot square. He told us that we had to eat a precisely defined amount of matzah in a set, brief period of time. To guarantee that we ate the right amount, we could measure our matzah against the plastic-coated card, which showed in red ink an outline of the correct amount. To insure that he did not take too long eating it, Yitzchak forced the matzah against his rapidly gnawing teeth, so that with unleavened crumbs spreading out across his chest and the table in front of him, he resembled a large black-hatted beaver. It didn't impress me as a very uplifting seder.

There is a misconception prevalent among Jews of all religious dispositions: that God invented Passover as a holiday for children, to educate them about the formative experience of the Jewish people, the Exodus from Egypt. So what adults do at the seder doesn't really matter. But the truth is that God instituted the festival of Passover to help all Jews, adults and otherwise, remember something more profound and difficult than the liberation of some slaves from an ancient Middle Eastern country.

One of the constant refrains of the Torah is that it was God "who brought you out of the Land of Egypt to be your God." On this line as it appears in Leviticus 22:33, Rashi comments that God released the Jews from slavery on the condition that they accept Him as their God. Another exegete, the thirteenth-century Spanish rabbi Moshe ben Nachman, puts this a little bit differently. We are obliged to "sanctify His Name [by observing the commandments] because we are His servants whom He has redeemed from Egypt." Must Jews obey God only because He is God? No, also because He withdrew them from the rule of one king, Pharaoh, and set them under His own rule.

The Jews might have rejected that rule. But instead they knowingly accepted God's covenant with them, calling out at the foot of Mt. Sinai, "Everything that the Lord has said, we will do and we will obey." (Another translation of that last phrase is "we will do and we will understand": that is, even before understanding the Torah, we will fulfill its commandments.) The day before he died, Moses told the assembled Israelites, "Not with you alone do I seal this covenant and this imprecation, but with whoever is here, standing with us today before the Lord, our God, and with whoever is not here with us today." This means that the souls of all Jews, living and not yet born, were somehow mystically present in the wilderness and agreed to abide by the covenant.

When Carl Jung postulated a form of memory that belonged not to an individual, but to a race, ethnicity, or folk, he could have had that verse from Deuteronomy in mind. If it is true that all Jews possess a stored-away idea in their souls' attic—of standing at Mt. Sinai in thunder and lightning, hearing God's voice, and crying out their willingness to do and to obey—then the Jewish festivals (Passover, Shavuot, and Sukkot) are times set aside by God for His people to reawaken those memories. Judaism, says Will Herberg, "is historical religion, above all in the sense that the believer must himself appropriate it in his own life as his own history"— because it *is* his own history.

The first time I heard this idea was from Yitzchak. The seder was not a complete wash. He had noticed that I understood little of the Haggadah, and after dinner he tried to explain it to me. "So," he said at one point, "any Jew, anyone born to a Jewish mother, was there, present at Mt. Sinai."

My ears pricked up at that. Nervously I broached the subject of my adoption and self-conversion, which I described. He seemed impressed but explained, as I guess I had anticipated, that my efforts did not add up to what I had intended. An authentic conversion, he said, is witnessed by a court of three religious authorities. The pool of water is not a bathtub, but a *mikvah*, a pool of a certain size containing at least a minimum volume of natural water, for instance rainwater or river water. And this rite can't be performed at all until the would-be convert has agreed to abide by the mitzvot described in the Torah. Until and unless I had made that commitment, I could not be considered a Jew, said Yitzchak.

He said it with such authority, in his quiet way, that it did not occur to me to doubt that what he said was true. It was important, he added, to take these details seriously. "After all, we're talking about eternity." Then he brightened. "I'm not sure what God has in store for you, but I've got a feeling that someday you may become a convert. Your self-conversion, that wasn't kosher, but it suggests something about your *neshamah*. Do you know what a *neshamah* is?" I didn't. "It's your soul. Every soul contains a spark from God. All the sparks belonging to all the Jews who would ever live were present at Mt. Sinai. All the converts who would ever live were there, too. When one of these sparks is born in the body of a gentile, it seeks to return to God."

Another way of saying this is that *all* Jews are in a sense converts. At Mt. Sinai, the gathered *neshamot* accepted the Torah and its obligations. The children and children's children of the Jews physically present at the mountain did not and do not require immersion and sacrifice (though the males must, of course, be circumcised) to be considered Jews. Souls who entered the Jewish people through gentile mothers do require immersion, sacrifice (in the future), and circumcision.

---

THAT WAS THE FIRST TIME the thought had entered my mind that God might have a plan for my soul, as he does for the soul of every Jew and non-Jew.

Without my realizing it, the encounter changed the way I thought about Torah and its relevance to my life. Before Passover of 1985, my plan for the following summer was to spend it in New York City, taking an intensive course in German at Columbia University. I had hit on the idea of getting a Ph.D. in religious studies, and a faculty adviser had mentioned that knowing some German would help when I applied to graduate school. Now I was making the transition from thinking about faith as a dead butterfly under glass to feeling it as a living force in the universe that I needed to come to grips with. I decided to spend the summer not at Columbia, but at the Jewish Theological Seminary, where rabbis of the Conservative movement in Judaism are ordained. There I would study not German, but Hebrew. I had also resolved to have myself converted to Judaism—again.

# Chapter 7

# THE ROSE GOLDSTEIN ROOM

*N*ot long ago I was leafing through my worn-out, coverless copy of the New English Bible, which I bought for Professor Waring's class. Under one page from the Book of Hosea, a footnote explained that the prophet's reference to the "knowledge of God" really meant, not knowledge in the sense of facts perceived through reason and observation, but "the experience of God in obedience and surrender, resulting in a close personal relationship." From the word "relationship" down into the lower margin I had drawn a serpentine mark in ballpoint pen ink, at the end of which I had written "ridiculous."

It struck me as absurd and vaguely Christian to think a person could have a "personal relationship" with the Lord. Bumper stickers you see on the road throughout the United States proclaim JESUS IS MY BEST FRIEND or WHAT A FRIEND I HAVE IN JESUS, but the God I had worked out in my philosophy courses wasn't about to get into close personal contact with anyone. He wasn't about to do anything at all, such as make demands or offer salvation.

Faith in a God that anemic has a difficult time holding most people's attention, as the disappearing membership of liberal churches suggests. That is why a few words from Yitzchak Greenbaum could, within a week's time, inspire me to change my plans for the coming summer. Yitzchak believed that God was real and that He might have plans for me. The idea was electrifying. I needed to find out more about Judaism.

It was the most obvious gap in my Jewish education, though hardly the most profound, that I could pronounce Hebrew but not understand it. So I decided to try to correct that lack first. I found a course in the language at the Jewish Theological Seminary (JTS) and sent in my registration form.

I did this with some nervousness. My concentration adviser in the Comparative Literature Department was, I knew, active in a local Conservative synagogue. I had gone to visit him to make sure he thought the Hebrew program at JTS was academically solid. An extremely irascible man, Professor Ira Liebman was not the type to hold back his opinion. The education would be good enough, he thought. Then, taking into account my aspiration to study religion in graduate school, he offered some further advice. Leaning a couple of inches in my direction and fixing his eyes on me, he said in a half whisper: "Don't tell them you're Jewish. You don't look Jewish. They won't figure it out. Say you're a lapsed Episcopalian or something like that. Whatever you do, don't let them get their goddamn hands on your soul!"

This ought to have shocked me, coming as it did from a man who strongly identified as a Conservative Jew. But I was still under the spell of secularism and accepted unquestioningly its assumption that the fear of God is not the beginning but the end of wisdom. It seemed reasonable to me that if the Jews at JTS "got their hands on my soul," I would become a right-wing religious fanatic like them.

THE TERM "CONSERVATIVE MOVEMENT" confuses people, who assume there is something conservative about it. The movement's theological school, JTS, was founded in New York in 1887 as a more traditional-minded alternative to the American Reform seminary, Hebrew Union College. The rabbis who started JTS sought to "conserve" Torah law while integrating religiously observant Jews into the secular world and the best of that world into Jewish culture. At first, rabbis and laymen who were themselves fully loyal to the Torah regarded JTS as an organization in line with Torah Judaism.

However, in 1950 a revolution took place. That year the movement's Rabbinical Assembly voted to allow Conservative Jews to drive to the synagogue on Shabbat. The significance of that would be hard to understate.

What had divided the Conservatives from the Reformers wasn't so much the reverence felt by either for the Pentateuch, the Five Books of Moses, but rather for oral Torah, the Talmud, and other rabbinic literature. The leaders of the Conservative movement remained loyal to the oral Torah until 1950. The written Torah sketches, among other matters, the outline of Sabbath observance. The oral Torah provides the details. On the Sabbath, Jews commemorate God's creation of the world by refraining from creative work, thus acknowledging that whatever we create we do so because God alone gave us the requisite power, knowledge, and raw materials. According to the oral Torah, some labors forbidden on Shabbat include creating fire, as in an automobile engine, and traveling long distances. For a Jew, driving a car on Shabbat should be an impossibility.

But the Rabbinical Assembly had a problem. Following World War II, with the suburbanization of American Jewry, it was becoming a challenge to convince Conservative Jews that they must live close enough to shul to walk there on Shabbat. As the Conservative rabbis wrote in their responsum on the subject, they were familiar with "the realities of modern life." "Large segments of the population," they knew, "regard riding to the locale of their activities—economic, social, recreational and religious—as a normal feature of modern life." They concluded that "the positive values involved in the participation in public worship on the Sabbath outweigh the negative values of refraining from riding in an automobile." In deference to their congregants, who were also their employers, the rabbis compromised.

There followed many other compromises, with the result that Conservative Halachah died by a hundred small cuts, along with Conservative religious observance. Conservative Jews who follow even the trimmed-back Conservative version of Halachah are as rare as bald eagles. As a Conservative rabbi, Stephen C. Lerner, plainly put it in 1979, "we have been or are becoming a clerical movement. We have no observant laity." Among American Conservative Jews whose families have been in America for four generations, nearly 10 percent attend a synagogue at least once a month (as compared with 2.5 percent of Reform Jews). Though Conservative rabbis may hope their congregants fulfill such bottom-line responsibilities as keeping kosher, wearing tefillin at daily prayer, observing the Sabbath, and maintaining "family purity" (married couples must separate from each other sexually for a period each month), realistically they do not expect observance in any of these areas. The responsum in favor of driving on Shabbat confirmed a hunch many laymen had about their spiritual leaders: the rabbis did not really think the oral Torah was from God. So why should anyone else?

Professor Liebman needn't have worried about my soul getting snatched. Despite its address on Broadway in Morningside Heights, at the edge of Harlem, JTS seemed a paragon of unthreatening suburban conventionality. Within its tall bland neo-Georgian walls, I was as safe from Jewish proselytization as I was from the crime rates of two blocks north. Ketura and I drove down from Providence. She deposited me at the Mathilde Schechter Residence Hall, which looked like a run-down European hotel but inside was all garishly painted walls and plastic furniture. Like the building itself, most of the rooms, kitchens, and recreational areas were named for someone, typically a donor to the seminary. Suburban Jews love to name things after their relatives and themselves and emboss the name on a fake-bronze wall plaque. I occupied a narrow dorm room entitled "The Rose Goldstein Room."

The material surroundings suggested a 1970s Reform or Conservative temple, in Nassau County or the San Fernando Valley, but the people around me recalled a different but equally unlikely environment. Most were studying to be rabbis, but there was nothing especially rabbinical about them. JTS functions as a school for college graduates interested in pursuing Judaism as a profession, and its denizens reminded me of the graduate students at any other university.

The young rabbis-in-training I met were smart, a bit cynical, a little nerdy, with no apparent awe for the holy texts they were studying. Many had a grad student look: the men with a trimmed beard, off-brand jeans, T-shirt (usually blue, I'm not sure why), and a slight paunch. Sometimes I had a hard time telling one seminarian from another: not surprising because many had been friends for years, since they'd attended the same Conservative summer camps. In fact, among the small number of its most devoted young adherents, Conservative Judaism at the time seemed like an extension of summer camp: T-shirts, shorts, sandals, particular Jewish songs sung to particular tunes, a certain incestuous atmosphere combined with an everyone-round-the-campfire! bonhomie.

If I had to say exactly what kind of secular grad students the seminarians reminded me of, I would say graduate students in political science. After all, the Conservative movement thinks of itself in political terms: as the ideological midpoint between two extremes. Instinctively the students and faculty broke down into factions: traditionalists, feminists, radicals, campaigners for the inclusion of open, practicing homosexuals in Jewish leadership, and so on. The two major divisions, traditionalists and feminists, found they couldn't even pray together and insisted on separate minyanim: one with a partition between men and women as called for by Halachah and hated by the feminists; and one without, called the "egalitarian" minyan. They also tended to see the rest of American Jews as a conglomeration of ideological parties. While waiting to use a pay phone, I overheard a couple of young scholars discussing their experience at an Israel Day Parade. They were talking about the attendance: how many secular Jews had been present, how many from JTS, and how many "Orthos"—an abbreviation used in the same spirit of rivalry and jockeying for status as when Republicans refer to their opponents as "libs" (liberals) and "Dems" (Democrats).

There was not much to transcend politics at JTS because the Transcendent was itself in less than abundant supply. Like moderates in other fields, Conservative rabbis want to have it both ways: to be perceived as faithful to religious texts and yet also modern and enlightened, with a proper appreciation for the contributions of biblical criticism to our understanding of Torah. No one can say with perfect confidence exactly what Conservative authorities believe anymore about anything, but generally they hold that while Torah, in its written and oral components, comes from God, the specific content of the Revelation at Sinai has been fiddled around with over the centuries by various scribes, editors, and other busybodies. It can be fiddled around with by us today.

It's easy to see the appeal of Conservative Judaism. I very much felt it myself. Its early leaders offered a Judaism that held fast to most details of Halachah. And you can make a plausible argument for a Torah-based Judaism, which, compared to Orthodoxy, merely is on a somewhat faster evolutionary track. So the Conservative Rabbinical Assembly voted to allow breaking of Sabbath laws; but hadn't the consensus of Orthodox rabbis also allowed Halachah to change with the times? Consider three examples of the way Judaism has historically dealt with women.

Having multiple wives was once condoned, but a millennium ago Rabbi Gershom of Mainz, Germany, banned it. (He reasoned that although Jews had largely abandoned polygamy a thousand years earlier, the fact that it was still technically legal gave Christians an occasion to denounce Judaism as immoral.) A couple of centuries ago, Jewish women learned about Torah at home from their parents but received no formal Jewish education. Now even the ultra-Orthodox approve of such schooling. Meanwhile, in most traditional European communities, it once would have been considered inappropriate for a woman to work outside the home for a man other than her husband. Lately, among the ultra-Orthodox the practice has spread to send women out to work while their husbands sit and learn Torah together. (The most exceptional scholars were always encouraged to devote themselves entirely to study, and in the past they could do so because the richest merchants married their daughters to the brightest yeshiva boys. The father-in-law would then support the couple financially. Now even many of the duller students set themselves up as full-time scholars and, without a wealthy father-in-law, must depend on their wives for an income.) So religious practice does in fact change.

However, the changes in Orthodox practice were unlike the ones adopted by Conservatism. None of the former permitted actions that violated basic principles of Torah law. For instance, it had never been *forbidden* for a woman to work outside the home. Instead, the wisdom of Torah saw it as contrary to her interests. (Many contemporary American women, frantic in pursuit of career and family satisfaction, have come to feel similarly.) While the Conservative movement retained the broad outline of Torah practice, basic principles were indeed drastically reformed—like those of not creating fire and not traveling on Shabbat. And where such principles were kept safe from reinterpretation, Halachah came to be treated the way jaywalking laws are in many big cities: while the law remains on the books, a cop would receive looks of shock and outrage if he insisted that pedestrians obey it.

But more important than plausibility, Conservativism has the attraction of warding off the appearance of fundamentalism. Jews whose great-grandparents came to America as tradesmen and merchants, whose parents entered the ranks of the professional class as doctors and lawyers, who ourselves graduated from tony Ivy League colleges—Jews like me find that biblical fundamen-

talism lacks a certain cachet that we value. To be precise, "fundamentalism" doesn't accurately describe traditional Judaism because real fundamentalists think that to know God's will, all you
need is faith and a Bible. The idea of an oral tradition, without
which the Bible can't be understood, strongly disagrees. (In rejecting the oral tradition, Reform Judaism is intellectually closer to
the fundamentalist approach.) But socially, "fundamentalism"
hits exactly the right note. Well-heeled Americans, Jewish and
non-Jewish, tend to view those of their fellow citizens who take
the Bible too seriously as bit of an embarrasment. The way the
term is used, a fundamentalist is distinguished as much by class
characteristics (big hair, excessive makeup, unfashionable clothing, funny accent) as by religious ones. In this spirit, until the *ba'al
teshuvah* movement surfaced, urbane Jews regarded their Orthodox brethren as country cousins. You couldn't invite such people to
a cocktail party, and if you saw them at your favorite department
store, you'd probably have to reconsider where you shop. American
Jews of my parents' generation loved America and wanted to be
part of it, in every way, and at the highest social levels they could
manage. Fundamentalism in religion was like synthetic fabrics in
clothing: it marked you across the forehead in big black letters,
LOW CLASS.

Yet these same Jews also loved being Jewish, and many felt that
the Reform movement essentially had adopted another religion.
What to do? Conservatism offered a solution to the problem. You
could remain faithful to traditional Judaism in theory, but wear it
lightly, like a lovely antique silk scarf thrown around a woman's
shoulders. Warm-butter phrases like "our rich heritage" and "our
wonderful religious inheritance" are often heard from Conservative rabbis, as if Judaism were a priceless old family heirloom but
nothing more transcendent than that, the words "rich" and "wonderful" hinting that if the "heritage" were less charming and delightful, we could justifiably cast it off.

Alas, without a belief in the integrity of the Torah, Judaism is
drained of much of its power to fire our souls. The "moderate"
perspective, located halfway between the Reform and Orthodox

extremes, presents certain problems of internal coherence and smells of backroom compromise. I have touched on the content of Conservative belief. By way of explaining why this form of Judaism generally fails to ignite Jewish souls, I will elaborate a little.

The Conservative perspective includes the following beliefs: 1) God revealed His will to the Jews at Mt. Sinai; 2) Revelation probably included some of but not the whole Pentateuch as we have it today; 3) one or more redactors brought the text to its present form; 4) the Revelation might have included some of but certainly not all the legal, mystical, philosophical, and narrative material in the oral Torah; 5) therefore, since the content of the Torah's teachings is unfixed and uncertain, rabbis in our own time are empowered to take the best parts and leave the outdated ones.

The oral Torah is the key to understanding what can be dissatisfying about this. Begin by considering why there must be an oral Torah at all. Many of the verses that describe specific *halachot*, requirements of Torah law, have an unnerving quality in common: it is apparent that they make assumptions about what the reader knows, assumptions that would have been unjustified at the first moment of the theophany, God's appearance at Sinai. For instance, God has a marked tendency to say things like "You may slaughter from your cattle and your flocks that the Lord has given you, as I have commanded you" (Deut. 12:21)—without, at least in the text, having commanded that method.

Or He will set the date of one of the three pilgrimage festivals, Shavuot, by instructing the Israelites to celebrate it after Passover, fifty days "from the day after the Shabbat." But "Shabbat" has two meanings in the Pentateuch. It means a day on which we cease from our labor: either the day observed from Friday night to Saturday night or a festival day. So which is it? If Saturday, which one? There are fifty-two in a year. The oral tradition informs us that Shabbat here refers to the first day of Passover. The text doesn't say, but it expects us to know which is called for.

At a less technical level, God uses phrases to describe major concepts whose definitions are agreed on today, but which at Sinai itself would have been mysterious to their audience. So He instructs the Israelites that on Yom Kippur "you shall afflict your souls." The Talmud says this commandment means that on the Day of Atonement, Jews are to abstain from food, drink, sex, and bathing, and this is the practice accepted by Jews everywhere. But what in the world could that have meant to the Israelites to whom it was directed more than a thousand years before the Talmud was composed? "Afflict our souls"? How? With the bright light of the individual conscience? With whips? Or take the unelaborated prohibition against *melachah* on the Sabbath. What is *melachah*? It is translated as "work," but what does *that* mean? Again the oral tradition steps in with an extensive explanation. When Moses brought before God an Israelite who had gone out to gather wood on Shabbat, Moses took for granted that the Israelite knew he was sinning. The question put to God by Moses wasn't, Has this man done *melachah*? but, rather, Obviously this man has done *melachah*, so what do we do with him? The Israelites were expected to know that gathering wood counted as *melachah*. But would that have been obvious without an explanation contemporaneous with the giving of the Pentateuch? Not to me.

The Torah cannot be understood without the oral tradition. It seems unlikely that God would reveal a largely inscrutable string of words and expect the Jews to order their lives according to it. The Torah tells us it was revealed in the Sinai wilderness, and rabbinic tradition attests to this. It would seem, then, that two possibilities exist: either 1) the Torah really was accompanied by an explanation; or 2) its account of its origin is a fraud. If we cannot trust either the Torah or the rabbinic tradition on such a basic question as where Torah comes from, it would be naive to trust either on anything at all.

Conservative rabbis, in theory, agree that the Revelation included an oral Torah. They do not agree that the tradition as it has come down to us is on all points identical with the true oral Torah. That, along with their stipulation that the written Torah we possess is not necessarily the same text given to Moses at Sinai, is their compromise with modernity. Unfortunately for the spiritual life of

JTS and its graduates, there is a tension inherent to Judaism that makes this compromise untenable.

For either we accept that in the Sinai wilderness God gave the Pentateuch to Moses in its familiar form, exactly, or we do not. If not, that leaves two possibilities: 1) no God has issued any special directive to the Jews; or 2) if He did, then over thousands of years, through messing around by scribes and "redactors," the content of the Revelation has become uncertain. If 1), then obviously we have no business worshiping the God of Moses. If 2), then God is not the Being Who has been advertised to most of us from childhood. What kind of Almighty Lord of the Universe is powerless to keep His Revelation intact, free of human errors, for a mere 3,300 years? Such errors would testify to God's falling short of omnipotence. After all, in the Bible He seems to care passionately about the details of religious observance. If there are errors of transmission in the Torah, we can't confidently say we know what those details are. Any one, as we find it in Scripture, could be a goof or an interpolation by some ancient scribe. In other words: No Torah? No God. If you believe that the God of Moses lives, there is no coherent option but to accept that He revealed the Pentateuch at Sinai.

If you accept *that*, I cannot think of a coherent alternative to accepting that the written Torah was accompanied by an oral Torah and that through tradition we also possess an accurate record of that Revelation. For the reasons just outlined, it is incoherent to believe an Almighty Lord unable to preserve intact an orally transmitted revelation. If God gave the written Torah, he also gave the oral Torah. If he gave both, then we possess them today in precisely the form He wishes, namely their true form. If the oral Torah cannot be trusted, then God never gave the Jews the written Torah, either. In short: No oral Torah? No God.

I realize this sounds rather stark. The assumption that Scripture is full of mistakes, fudgings, and interpolations by humans is impressed so deeply on us by our modernist educations that it takes some effort to free ourselves of the notion. Plain misunderstanding also makes it hard to believe in scriptural inerrancy. Contrary to what a lot of people think, such inerrancy does not mean the Bible can be perused like a newspaper, where every word means what it seems to mean. The oral Torah would exclude, for instance, a naive reading of Genesis 1. In any event, no one should be faulted for being unready to see the matter as I've presented it.

But you don't have to be able to articulate what is incoherent about Conservative Judaism, as I certainly could not at the time, to feel that there is something problematic about its approach to Torah. Having stood at Sinai, Jews intuit more than we consciously understand. The choice we are given is between Torah—both Torahs—and the void. In seeking its middle ground and denying this tension, Conservatism balances on a wire strung up at a dismaying height. On one side is Torah. On the other is a precipice and then nothing.

As I learned from talking with JTS students, their teachers were unprepared to keep them from falling over that precipice. I met one female rabbinical student, a sexy Californian in tight Levi's jeans, who said she wasn't sure if God exists. Over the course of her education she hoped to find out whether He does or not. However, since she had arrived in New York, her doubts had increased, thanks in part to the chilly, academic attitude her teachers took toward Jewish texts. She hoped to regain her belief. If she did, she planned to accept a pulpit at a Conservative shul. If not, she would take a job in Jewish education, teaching Jewish children—what?

I came into contact with two teachers. One was our young Israeli Hebrew instructor, called Dubi. We spent four hours a day in a classroom upstairs in the main seminary building, and at the end of the summer I was able to write a letter to Ketura in Hebrew, composed of sentiments like "How are you? I am fine. New York is hot in the summer." But as at Temple Beth Shalom, the emphasis was on modern Hebrew: how to say "cookies," "ice cream," "coffee," "pen," "pencil," so as to be understood by a Tel Aviv storekeeper. The seminary offered no instruction in biblical Hebrew. Another JTS scholar I encountered was the summer school dean, who told me kindly that if I wanted a class to help me read the Bible in Hebrew, I could go to the Christian institution across Broadway, Union Theological Seminary.

I had come to New York in the hope of finding a holy atmosphere that would provide an easy, obvious route not only to learning more about Judaism, but to having myself converted. JTS was not the place I expected, and no opportunity arose. However, the seminary was not entirely devoid of Jewish spirit. If the Reform movement acts as the door through which Jews exit Judaism, its Conservative counterpart is often the door through which they enter.

Jewish community leaders are famous for fretting about how to interest Jews in the faith of their ancestors, but the most effective way to draw Jews to Torah is never discussed. Jews need to hear other Jews speak about God in a way our leaders are unaccustomed to speaking of Him: as a real, living force in our lives. It was among Ketura and her friends that I first heard God spoken of that way by Jews. And I heard some more of this at JTS, from a group of religious Conservative undergraduates who happened to be around for the summer. They were students either at neighboring Columbia or in a program that brought undergraduates to the seminary, where they also took classes through the Columbia School of General Studies.

These young men and women had an earnestness the rabbinical students lacked. My encounters with them were brief—a burly, bearish Columbia senior who had invited me to a couple of Shabbat lunches, a JTS-Columbia sophomore who lived upstairs from the Rose Goldstein Room—but influential. The name of the latter student was, I think, Danny. (In my experience, earnest Conservative youths are disproportionately named "Danny.") I remember walking up Amsterdam Avenue on a humid afternoon as he sought to convince me to give up shaving with a razor.

The topic had arisen because in that rough neighborhood no full-service drugstore had plucked up the nerve to open for business. I asked Danny where I could buy a straight razor and he hesitated in a funny way. "Are you sure that's what you want?" he asked, as if I had mentioned a desire to buy some crack cocaine from one of the dealers who patrolled the avenue. Danny then introduced me to a Torah law the reason for which is mysterious and can only be speculated about.

In Leviticus, God instructs the Jews to do something that must have seemed queer to their pagan neighbors: "You shall not round off the edge of your scalp and you shall not destroy the edge of your beard." What does it mean to "round off the edge of your scalp" and "destroy the edge of your beard"? The oral tradition can be summarized to the effect that Jewish men are forbidden to remove the hair from their sideburn areas so as to form a straight hairline above the ear; and from shaving the beard with a razor; however, cutting it with scissors or an electric razor (which operates on the scissors principle of blade against blade rather than blade against skin) is permitted.

Danny, who was clean-shaven, did not enter into the various exegeses offered by rabbis over the centuries concerning this peculiar mitzvah. According to Herodotus, priests of the god Dionysus cut their hair in precisely the way forbidden by the Torah. Samson Raphael Hirsch observed that the proscribed haircut removes "the externally visible division between the frontal part of the head and the rear part of it, coinciding with the cerebrum and the cerebellum respectively." The former is the seat of the uniquely human functions of the brain, the latter of its animal functions. So the priests of Dionysus, chief party god of Greek mythology, represent the failure to carefully distinguish between animals and humans. Secularists never tire of telling us that humans are "just animals," with the implication that little more can be expected of us morally than can be expected of pigs or monkeys. God instructs us to reject that kind of thinking—quite concretely, in the way we tend our bodies and cut our hair.

As for the electric shaver, it does not "destroy" the hair, as a razor does, but only trims it back. (As anybody who uses one knows, it is impossible to get a really close shave even with the most expensive model.) When a man forgoes destroying the hair along the edge of his face, he acknowledges that the body he inhabits is not his property but belongs to God.

Danny wanted to communicate to me the repugnance he felt at the idea of shaving with a razor or cutting off his sideburns. He said, "I mean, putting a sharp naked blade up against your face, your neck? It just seems barbaric, doesn't it?" With those last six words, he had said it all.

Later in the day, when I found a Love's discount store, I remembered what Danny had said. His image of the "sharp, naked blade up against your face" had found its way to the bottom of my stomach, where it was uncurling. As I stood at the rack holding disposable razors, I felt just briefly the kind of intestinal uneasiness I had felt on contemplating the idea of putting another sharp, naked blade against the skin of another part of my anatomy a few years before. What the hell, I thought, and bought a Remington electric instead.

It didn't last: Remington at the time made a lousy shaver, and within a couple of months I had gone back to disposable straight razors. Yet in putting aside, however briefly, the "barbaric" custom of swiping a naked blade across my face every morning, I had acknowledged God. And actions, I repeat, lead in time to belief.

In its outward manifestations, Jewish spiritual return can appear to take the shape of a series of acts in which the Jew accepts on himself apparently random habits of discipline. I distinctly remember the last time I attended a movie on the Sabbath and the last time I slept with a gentile girl. The summer I spent at JTS wasn't the last time I used a straight razor, but it was the last time I knowingly ate nonkosher beef or chicken.

How did that happen? The influence of my other earnest Conservative friend, Danny Warshay, played a part. As a freshman, he made something of a show of refraining from eating nonkosher meat. While everyone groused about the food in the Emery-Woolley dining hall, Danny complained about the lack of tasty vegetarian dishes to such an extent that a classmate was inspired to doctor some photocopied paintings of Jesus on the cross. Danny's face was substituted for Jesus', under the heading "The Martyrdom of St. Danny of Cleveland," with captions such as "O Father in Heaven, not the squash almondine again!"

Still, I was moved by both Dannys' commitment to Torah observance. I had a vague notion that there was something inconsistent about calling myself a Jew, more or less believing in God, and at the same time ignoring the demands that, since ancient times, other Jews had insisted God made on them. My thoughts on the subject did not penetrate any deeper than that. Yet somehow this was sufficient to motivate me, one night at an Ethiopian restaurant called Zula on Amsterdam and 122nd Street, to decide that my excellent meal of spicy chicken and sourbread pancakes would be my last taste of nonkosher meat. I left the restaurant and never felt the strong desire for those foods again.

There is an irony in the fact that Jews in the process of returning to Judaism often pick kashrut as the first new mitzvah they undertake. That has something do with the practical consideration that one can more or less go about his business as before—eating at restaurants and choosing prepared foods in the supermarket—while leaving out of his diet foods like pork and shellfish, and even while maintaining a strictly vegetarian regimen. Keeping some semblance of kashrut is easier than observing Shabbat, but kashrut makes a radical, even alarming, claim.

When we are dealing with types of meat not by definition prohibited to Jews (such as chicken, turkey, and beef), kashrut is governed by two main criteria: 1) whether the animal has been properly slaughtered; and 2) whether its blood has then been fully drained from the lifeless body. Consider the second criterion. One often hears the assertion, generally made by liberal Jews who retain some affection for the religion, that Judaism rescued the world from the monstrous notion of human sacrifice. However, just what is so bad about sacrificing humans to God? He made our bodies. Why can He not ask for them back?

One often hears, too, that Judaism differs from Christianity in that it rejects the idea that God will accept one person's sacrifice of himself in return for annulling the sacrifice that should have been required of another person. That idea underlies the salvational theory used to explicate the crucifixion of Jesus: "He died for our sins," Christians say. Doesn't Judaism maintain that a person must himself pay the price required of him?

In fact, in Torah human lives and animals ones *are* sacrificed in behalf of others. The priestly caste that ran the Temple in Jerusalem was not originally meant to serve in that role. When God liberated the Israelites from Egypt, He decreed that all the firstborn in that land should die, but then exempted the firstborn of Israel. Thus, in a special way not shared by their brethren, the first-born sons of the Israelites belonged to God. The Lord had intended to make *them* and their descendants His hereditary priests; but after the episode of the Golden Calf, in which the firstborn participated in constructing an idol but the tribe of Levi did not, He reconsidered. God took the descendants of Moses' brother, Aaron the Levite, as His priests—to sacrifice their lives to Him, as it were—in place of the firstborn.

Similarly, when the Temple stood in Jerusalem the Jews offered sacrifices in substitution for their own lives. If a Jew had sinned or received a material or spiritual blessing of some kind, he owed a payment to God. Since nothing he possessed could adequately repay this debt, he really owed God his life. In substitution for such a payment, God allowed him to offer sacrifices at the Temple in the form of animals, grain, and wine. But the sacrifice that overshadowed all the others was that of animal blood. In Leviticus, God instructs Moses on this point: "The soul of the flesh is in the blood; and I have given it to you upon the altar to make atonements for your souls; for it is the blood that makes atonement for the soul." Therefore, says God, "whatsoever man of the house of Israel . . . that eats any manner of blood, then I will set My face against the soul that eats of the blood, and will cut him off from among his people." As Rashi comments on this verse, "Let there come one soul and make atonement for another soul."

There is no longer a Temple in Jerusalem, but the principle still applies. By rights, we literally should have to offer our own lives to God. The Lord did not abolish the logic of human sacrifice, just the practice of it. It is the view of Torah that in atonement for his sins, each Jew owes to God at very least the blood in the animals he eats. We can no longer offer it on the altar; but as a token of our atonement, we can and must refrain from eating it. So when a kosher animal is slaughtered according to the rules of kashrut, its blood must be extracted and disposed of.

This second criterion of kashrut, the extraction of blood, alludes to animal and, in a sense, human sacrifice. What could be more upsetting to the modern sensibility than that? The first criterion, the proper method of slaughter, makes what is in fact probably a more disturbing claim.

The method used both in the Temple on animals being prepared for sacrifice and in kosher slaughtering today involves cutting the esophagus with a single, quick stroke of the knife. The knife must be perfect, the stroke uninterrupted. The results are bloody and, despite what one hears from some Jews who wish to find a modern-sounding rationale for Torah laws, it is not at all clear that this form of slaughter is kinder and gentler than all other forms. Rabbi Daniel Lapin thinks that the bloodiness and *intimacy* of the act of slaughter is part of the point. The experience reinforces two important Torah lessons. First, a human is not an animal: it is all right, even sacred, to kill an animal. Second, violence has consequences. There is a horror inherent in kosher slaughtering that has a salutary effect: it drives home the relationship of violence to bloody death. Which is why Rabbi Lapin, half-jokingly, says he would like to see American schoolchildren given mandatory instruction in animal sacrifice.

What's disturbing is this: It would be one thing if this method of slaughter could be found in the written Torah. But as I have already said, it can't be found there. It comes to us entirely through the oral Torah. That fact is hard for anyone, and especially a Jew, to accept.

The people Israel really are "stiff-necked," as the Bible repeatedly notes. Jews tend disproportionately to be intellectuals, or pseudointellectuals, and they have a strong inclination to believe they can figure things out for themselves. To this attitude kosher

slaughter delivers a rebuke. There are matters of central importance to God, it says, that cannot be discovered by the mere application of our intelligence to the text of the Torah. If Jews want to
be loyal to the will of their Creator, they need to do more than
ponder the Bible. They need to listen closely to the ancient, transmitted words of the Sages. They must place faith not only in God,
but in human teachers.

In the dietary laws, that is, God calls for a double sacrifice.
These laws ask us not only to sacrifice animal blood as a substitute
for our own blood, which by itself is an offensive notion to the
modern intellect. Still more troubling is the sacrifice that kashrut
insists we make of that prideful intellect itself: we must accept
that rabbis and other expert Jewish scholars have access to a source
of revelation in which most of us have not been initiated.

It may be a good thing that most *ba'alei teshuvah* have little
inkling of the deeper significance of the mitzvot they begin to observe. If I had, I might never have quit eating *trefe* meat. My pride
was still riding tall in the saddle; and the idea that I would accept
any rabbi's word for anything would have seemed an absurdity.

But like many Jews, I didn't know all this. I just started keeping
kosher as a token of wanting to follow more of the Torah's path a
little more closely than I had done previously. By the time I left
JTS in August, I knew a few hundred Hebrew words and some
rules of grammar. At the beginning of my junior year, I wanted to
learn more about Judaism. In Professor Waring's class, I had read
much of the Old Testament. I was now ready, I felt, to study the
Talmud.

Anyone who has attempted to "read" as much as a paragraph of
that multivolume work will know what nonsense this was. The
Talmud takes the form of debates among rabbis who sought to
precisely define the oral tradition. It cannot be read, however, like
the transcript of a debate in Congress. It must be decoded. The
Talmud was recorded in a preliterate time when information was
committed mainly to memory, not to paper. Thus to ease memo-
rization, the rabbinical opinions that make up its text have been
crystallized and shortened to such a degree that to make sense of

any of it, the student requires a teacher sitting by his side to eluci-date each verse. That teacher has had the text explained to *him* by his own teacher, who had it explained to him by *his* teacher, and so on back through the millennia.

I knew nothing of this, either, and—no doubt thanks to my inattentiveness as a student—still knew little of it by the time I had completed Professor Jacob Neusner's class, "Judaism in Late Antiquity." This involved reading books about the Talmud but glancing at an actual page of it only briefly. When years later I finally examined one of these and had it explained to me, I was surprised at its complexity: extract of Mishnah followed by commentary that forms the bulk of the work, surrounded in the wide margins by the medieval exegeses of Rashi on one side and his followers on the other, with smaller notes by later rabbis in the most distant margins. Professor Neusner's method of teaching consisted of evaluating the Talmud thematically rather than ask-ing the student to grapple with the text itself. Traditional scholar-ship emphasizes such grappling because each word is regarded as revelation in need of clarification.

Jacob Neusner, a brilliantly prolific writer who happened to be an ordained Conservative rabbi, correctly would reject the idea that, as a professor, he was obliged at the same time to play the part of a rabbi. It was his role, he might say, to subject rabbinical teach-ings to the cool gaze of modern scholarship. In that respect his was an approach representative of JTS.

Judge the tree by the fruit it bears. Conservative Judaism is a Judaism best suited for college professors. See its fruit: blame me for this, not Professor Neusner, but it isn't entirely a coincidence that in his class I thought up ideas that were closer to real blas-phemy than anything I have thought up since. Using quotations from the Talmud I had found in other books, stripped from con-text, I wrote papers denouncing "rabbinic Judaism" as a "slave re-ligion": the rabbis, I thought, refused to accept responsibility for imposing their own views on the people. The oral Torah was the result: a lie designed to disguise what the rabbis were too wimpy to admit was a bald play for power. In another paper I asserted that the traditions about the Messiah recorded in the Talmud were put there, by those sneaky rabbis again, in order to fend off the incipient belief among some Jews that the Messiah had already come in the form of Jesus of Nazareth.

As the subject of that paper suggests, I remained as caught up in the challenge I felt from Christianity as I had been in high school. In another class that year I studied the New Testament and kept an eye out for the arguments St. Paul advanced against the eternality of the Torah. In my wallet I still carried the card with references to the Hebrew prophets and their hints about the Messiah, which came in handy for arguing with evangelical Christian preachers who visited Brown and held forth on the college green.

I was still defending myself against God, against the idea of a relationship with Him, whatever form men said He took. In fact, I had made little spiritual progress since I had been a student in William Hall's Western civilization class six years earlier. I had met a few committed Jews, and this had benefited me, but their influence was mainly on the surface of my life. What would happen when I began to meet committed Christians? What would happen when I was forced to leave the protective womb of Brown and confront the world, without God?

# Chapter 8

# THE HEART OF THE MATTER

*I*f this were a novel, I would be at fault for neglecting to clarify the motivation of the main character. Because we read novels and see movies, we become accustomed to thinking in terms of this concept, motivation. We take it to mean that any course of action will be executed with the intention of bringing about certain results. But the return of an individual to God does not necessarily submit to that sort of analysis.

Judaism asserts that man possesses a free will, that, in the words of the Talmud, "Everything is the hand of Heaven except the fear [that hard-to-translate *yirah*] of Heaven." In other words, God controls the world, but we have it in our power to decide whether we will acknowledge His control and act accordingly. This suggests that had someone asked why, in fits and starts, I had undertaken part of a commandment here, another part of a different commandment there, I should have been able to give a coherent answer. But I could not have done so. Sometimes the power of *yi-rah* acts on us without our knowing it.

When I graduated from Brown and drove to New York to work as an editorial assistant at *National Review,* the conservative opinion magazine, I was still keeping kosher, in my way. Once in a while I would put on tefillin. But otherwise my spiritual life was submerged under the cares of my daily life. I had other things on my mind, which I would have said were independent of my relationship, or lack of a relationship, with God. But they were not independent.

What was on my mind? I mention the following absurd episode only because it was the start of a growing intuition I had, in that first year out of college, that I was dying.

I was not one of those kids at Miraleste who experimented with drugs or alcohol. In college I tried marijuana only once. After college, during the Christmas break we took at *National Review* the first year I was there, I went home to California for a week. A college classmate, living in Los Angeles, had discovered that he enjoyed cocaine, and one night in his apartment we sniffed a lot of it. It was my first and last cocaine high. No one could have failed to enjoy the first few hours, the sensation that you are the most fascinating person in the world, that you possess many brilliant insights that pour forth with breaks only to half listen to your companion, who is under the identical impression about himself. The hard part is coming down. For me it was simply terror. The basketball player Len Bias had died of cocaine intoxication the previous year, and for seven hours I lay on a couch, expecting that any moment the same thing would happen to me.

How I wished I had never sniffed that cocaine. My vacation was scheduled to end the next day. I took an overnight flight into Kennedy Airport and was at my desk the next morning, but I wasn't the same calm person I had been when I'd sat there a week earlier. Anxiety had descended on me as never before. I kept expecting my pulse to shoot back up to whatever rate it had reached under the influence of the drug.

It was "Magazine Monday" at *NR*, the day every other week

when the magazine's editor, William F. Buckley Jr., led the editorial meeting. At the end of the day, he and the senior editors would walk to a grottolike Italian restaurant, Nicola Paone's. By the end of this particular Monday, I was eager to go home to my apartment in Brooklyn. But at four P.M. the executive editor cheerfully poked her head through my office door to invite me to dinner with the senior editors: a treat.

Throughout the meal I had my hands under the table, taking my pulse, waiting for it to shoot up. *NR*'s publisher, William Rusher, described a fatal heart attack that had befallen a contributor to the magazine at a surprisingly early age. Bill Buckley must have noticed me go pale, because he kindly asked if I was jet-lagged and suggested that jet-lag remedies, pep pills, could be bought over the counter. The mere idea of such a thing made my pulse race with fear. I had to get out of there.

"Actually," I said, "I'd better go home and go to sleep. Right now." I got up and left.

For weeks my heart was continually on my mind. I went to a cardiologist, who told me I had higher blood pressure than a young man should have. On his recommendation I took hypertension medicine for several years, until another doctor guessed that my blood pressure at the time had something to do with my anxiety at the possibility of having high blood pressure. At Brown I had become a regular at University Health Services, mainly in connection with assorted skin complaints. Now I began to visit the doctors of New York City. Two cardiologists. Two neurologists, when I started getting headaches in the morning. A dermatologist, when blue patches began to appear on my fingers at night. (Dr. Stein was puzzled, until it occurred to me that the patches came from the ink in a cheaply printed novel I was reading.)

Gradually the headaches went away. My pulse seemed normal. And I began to accept that there was nothing seriously wrong with me.

Meanwhile I had moved to Manhattan. As I will explain later, where I chose to live says as much about my motivation as a *ba'al teshuvah* as does my hypochondria. I wanted to live in an old building.

My fondness for anything antique had persisted after high school. In Providence I got to know the used-clothing shops along Thayer Street and bought large quantities of new clothes that looked old: wrinkled cotton Oxford shirts of the kind that became chic five years later and baggy cardigan sweaters and baggy khaki pants, likewise ahead of their time, which friends said reminded them of their grandfathers. It was my great hope, realized when I was a senior, to live in Brown's second-oldest dormitory, Slater Hall, on the college green next to the pre–Revolutionary War administration building, University Hall. When my classmate David Lipsky and I decided to find a place together in Manhattan, I sought out the most antique building we could afford and found it on 19th Street in Chelsea: a sepulchral tenement blackened with soot.

But despite my pleasure at these physical surroundings, my fear of death by sudden heart attack returned in a fury. I do not blame William Buckley for the coincidence of his being present at both the apparent beginning and the true beginning of my years of hypochondria.

Another treat: Bill Buckley had invited me and another assistant editor for an overnight trip on his sailboat, out across the Long Island Sound from the Buckleys' home in Connecticut. We anchored in a little indentation on the north coast of Long Island— after which, really living it up, the other editorial assistant and I did more drinking and cigar smoking than was prudent. Though I learned how to drink liquor at *National Review,* at this point I had not yet learned. Then we all went to sleep. At about four A.M. the liquor woke me up. Something was wrong, I could tell, and what it was occurred to me in a moment: my heart was beating as fast as it had the night I took that cocaine. I walked out on the deck of the boat and imagined myself waking Bill Buckley to tell him I was having a heart attack. I waited for the chest pains signaling cardiac arrest, but they didn't come. As I had the night at Paone's, I felt a strong desire to get out of there and retreat to my apartment, but this time I couldn't. Finally I calmed down.

In weeks to come I found myself persistently waking up, night after night around four A.M., with an odd, anxious feeling. I would take my pulse, which of course was racing. It was another "night panic," as I came to think of these experiences.

Back I went to the cardiologist, Dr. Robbins, who fitted me with a Holter Monitor, a device somewhat larger than a Sony Walkman that automatically measured my heart's activities over twenty-four hours. But the doctor could find no abnormalities. I would call him at his home at ten or eleven at night.

"My heart's really beating fast. Maybe a hundred beats per minute."

"Why don't you have a drink and relax?" he would say.

By this time I had purchased a sphygmomanometer (a blood pressure pump and cuff), and David Lipsky would come home after a date and find me at the kitchen table with a stethoscope in my ears and the sphygmomanometer before me, measuring my blood pressure. "Shhh, I can't hear," I would tell him if he tried to talk too loudly as I was doing this. At *National Review* I would close the door to my office and, while puzzled co-workers wondered what I could be up to, take the sphygmomanometer out of a desk drawer and measure my blood pressure. When the subscription clerk mentioned he had heard that pain in the left arm could signal the onset of cardiac arrest, that very night I began to feel twinges in my left arm.

Finally Dr. Robbins gently asked if I had considered seeking professional assistance from a doctor other than a cardiologist, neurologist, or dermatologist. I took his advice and began seeing a psychiatrist named Dr. O'Brien. At first this helped a lot, and I continued to see a psychiatrist or psychologist, in whatever city I lived in, for the next seven years, longer than I had worn braces in high school: an achievement.

----

SEEKING THE ASSURANCE of one doctor after another that I was healthy, chasing after antique authenticity, I was suffering from a definite restlessness of the soul. Soon my hunger for security and roots found a new object. The idea struck me that, if I wanted, I could find my birth mother.

In the beginning this was pretty much all I did: I was visiting my father in California, and he had taken my brother and me for brunch in nearby San Pedro. "Dad," I found myself saying over plates of Belgian waffles, "I was wondering. Do you knowing anything about the woman who gave birth to me?" The question had just come out, before I had a chance to feel any nervousness about asking. I was surprised to hear myself say it, because the truth is I had not been wondering about my birth mother. But I was suddenly glad I had asked and excited to hear his answer.

That I had asked did not appear to surprise my father; from his reaction, you might have thought I was asking what he knew about the man who did his taxes. It was the first time I heard her name. "Well, she was called Harriet Lund. She was from Sweden. Your mother and I met her a couple of times for lunch at the Hamburger Hamlet in Westwood," he said, naming a restaurant I had been to many times in high school. "But we didn't know her too well. I think she had a master's degree in child psychology or something like that. She worked at—I think it was called the Kennedy Child Study Center at St. John's Hospital up in Santa Monica." She had been about twenty-seven at the time, unmarried, and had come to the United States from Sweden a few years earlier. He remembered hearing that she had gone back there.

Trying to conceal my excitement at this sudden, unexpected venting of information, I pressed for details. She was a "very attractive" woman, he thought. He and my mother had met Harriet Lund for lunch in order to size each other up, the meeting having been arranged by a Beverly Hills attorney named Anthony Carsola, who specialized in adoption.

"What about," I began hesitantly, "the man who got her pregnant?"

"Well, we didn't meet him," said my father. "I think he worked with Harriet, there at the Kennedy Child Study Center." Swedish too? I asked. Or Irish American, as I thought my mother had mentioned? No, said my father, he had understood that the man was an

American of German descent. And that was all. My father had told me everything he knew, or remembered, or wished to remember.

I will not say I was transformed by this conversation. When we got back to the house I wrote the name of my birth mother on a slip of paper, so as not to forget it. And I walked down Palos Verdes Drive to see Bennett Schneir, who was visiting his own parents for a day or two. I immediately told him what I had learned and wondered aloud whether I might call this Kennedy Child Study Center and find out if she still worked there or, if not, where she had gone after 1965. I could then travel to wherever she was and just *look* at her. Maybe, I imagined, I would knock on her door, say my car had broken down, and ask to use her phone to call the Triple A.

Shortly afterward I went back to the East Coast and forgot all about calling the Kennedy Child Study Center.

————

IT REMAINS TO MAKE CLEAR what any of these matters— heart fears, old things, the idea of learning about my birth mother—has to do with the others.

At the time these subjects were on my mind, I was not alone in pondering them. This is not to say that other people were concerned about my personal history or about my birth mother; they were concerned about their own. In my old preoccupation with authenticity I had company. A professor in England, David Lowenthal, recently published a book whose title summarizes a trend in global culture: *Possessed by the Past.* As Lowenthal argues, people the world over have become obsessed with what he calls "heritage" but can also be called authenticity: not history, exactly, but the past in such manifestations as can be put to use fulfilling very present-day needs.

Authenticity and heritage can take the form of the sublime or the ridiculous, but they gravitate to the ridiculous. Shoppers in the late eighties and early nineties constantly came across articles of clothing or other personal or household items marketed as "authentic." This meant new items that had been designed to look either ragged and old or like items sold decades ago but preserved in mint condition: "fossil authentic" wristwatches, old-fashioned "authentic chinos" from Dockers based on a model worn by soldiers in World War Two, Ralph Lauren khaki pants labeled "Authentic Dry Goods," J. Crew denim shirts described in the catalog as "like shirts from old photos," clothing from the Gap in "classic" styles labeled "Authentic" and "Traditional," "distressed" blue jeans simulating years of wear, "distressed" jewelry from Donna Karan intended to look like military dog tags that survived World War One, and other miscellaneous stuff like copper candle sticks from the Pottery Barn patinaed in green as if from decades of use.

In film, the mid-1990s were notable for the popularity of precisely researched costume dramas—Merchant-Ivory knockoffs, multiple renditions of Jane Austen novels, *Little Women, Restoration, Jane Eyre,* and so on—in which, a *New York Times* critic noted, "grand homes, furnishings, costumes, and hair styles take leading roles. . . . You don't doubt for an instant that each place setting is correct to the decade, if not the year." In the performance of classical music, a movement toward the use of original instruments has been in force for thirty years or so. In architecture and building design, new is out and old is decidedly in. The latest skyscraper to be built in Manhattan, the Four Seasons Hotel, gives the impression of an art deco tomb. Meanwhile actual old buildings, which in previous decades had been modernized, were being restored to their original appearance, sometimes with lovely results, such as the dinosaur galleries at New York's American Museum of Natural History, in which all the architectural details of the elaborate original design were revealed after being hidden for decades under plaster walls and lowered ceilings. Old buildings that have not been tampered with have lately come under the stewardship of conservationists determined to see that the structures never will be altered or, heaven forbid, torn down. Those seeking to fill new or old buildings with new furniture increasingly turn to copying styles of a century ago, as in the revival of the Arts and Crafts style that flourished originally at the turn of the century.

We are like Major-General Stanley in *The Pirates of Penzance,* a social climber who bought an ancient estate, including a chapel with tombs. Showing off the "family" chapel, he boasts: "In this chapel are ancestors: you cannot deny that. With the estate, I bought the chapel and its contents. I don't know whose ancestors they *were,* but I know whose ancestors they *are.*" He is, he asserts, their "descendant by purchase."

It is not only other people's history that we have been seeking. It is also our own history. By 1988, the year I am writing about now, I had made only minimal attempts to find out about my biological heritage. Compared with a lot of other people, I was behind the curve. Authenticity has to do not only with jeans, but with genes.

As David Lowenthal notes, in previous decades and centuries the interest in discovering and documenting one's ancestors was confined to elderly aunts and blue-blooded aristocrats. Since the 1970s, that interest has been democratized. Visit your local branch of the National Archives, where microfilmed U.S. Census documents are kept, and you will see microfilm machines crowded with men and women of all ages, races, and ethnicities. Online bulletin boards devoted to genealogy likewise overflow with folks seeking the history of their blood. "All at once heritage is everywhere," writes Lowenthal. "Millions now hunt their roots, protect beloved scenes, cherish mementos, and generally dote on the past."

The 1970s also saw the beginning of another back-to-roots movement: among adults who as children had been adopted by families unrelated to them by blood. My blossoming interest in finding my birth mother was an interest shared by thousands of other adoptees. According to Betty Jean Lifton, a writer and an adoptee, before 1975 there was no history of "reunions" between birth parents and adopted children. Today, David Lowenthal estimates, almost half of adoptees attempt to locate their natural parents. He quotes one twenty-eight-year-old: "To feel that I'm *authentic,* I need to be like every other human being who knows where he came from and where he belongs." Recently the adoptee-return phenomenon has spun off a movement among people who grew up knowing their birth mother but not their birth father, the latter having merely donated his sperm through a sperm bank or other anonymous medium. *The New York Times Magazine* devoted a cover story to sperm donors who are being tracked down by their biological children.

———

CLEARLY SOMETHING HAS CHANGED in the atmosphere of American life to cause so many of us to long for "heritage" and "authenticity," but what? An answer is hinted at by a verse in Psalms. The concept of heritage entered Western thinking in the Bible. In Psalm 16 it is understood as a gift from God: the "goodly heritage" for which David thanked the Lord. Of course, other ancient peoples were familiar with the idea of a heritage in the sense of an inheritance of material goods left by a father ordinarily to his sons. However, the heritage that was most important to the Jews of the Bible consisted not of gold and silver, but of something metaphysical: namely the Covenant between God and the Jews. Knowledge of this Covenant was passed from parents to children. Parents taught Torah to their children, who taught it to their children. Both parents participated in this act of intergenerational transmission; but as in many other areas, Judaism assumes a division of labor.

Traditional Jews lay great stress on the idea that the status of a Jew as a Jew is passed from mother to children; but the father has an equally important role. In the Pentateuch, God instructs Moses to conduct censuses of the Israelites "according to their fathers' household." These were censuses by tribe, and tribal status was determined by a child's father. Commenting on Numbers 26:2 and citing the Talmud, Rashi states that "by the tribe of their father they shall trace their genealogy, and not by [that of] the mother." In the wilderness, the Jews encamped according to which of the tribes of Israel they belonged to. When they entered the Land of Israel, each tribe was assigned to a portion of it. So tribal membership was significant, but what does it mean?

As Rabbi Daniel Lapin points out, the Hebrew word for male,

*zachor,* shares a root with the Hebrew word for memory, *zachar.* Whereas the nation of Israel as a whole is defined by race, the tribe signifies culture and, more important, history. A mother conveys race; and for reasons of His own, God determined that a father should convey history, memory. In *Mishneh Torah,* his codification of Jewish law, Maimonides considers this idea important enough to allude to it in the first chapter, second sentence, of his division "Torah Study": "A father is obligated to teach his son Torah. . . . A woman is not obligated to teach her son." The principal content of Jewish memory is the Covenant, standing at Mt. Sinai and receiving the two Torahs from God. When a Jew compiles his genealogy, he counts the links in the chain connecting him to Sinai.

The relationship between all this and the authenticity/heritage movement should be coming clear. Obviously most of the hundreds of thousands of roots seekers in America are gentiles, but the underlying principles of Torah do not apply only to Jews. When the Torah establishes the connection of genealogy, especially patrilineal genealogy, to the memory of revelation, this has a universal significance. All people receive their knowledge of God from their parents, who received it from their parents, who received it from their parents. It may sound like a stretch to say that those of us who have lately found ourselves with a craving for roots are really in search of something else: namely, God. Surely, though, the hunger for authenticity, like a hunger for food or water, arises from a lack of *something.* What do we lack that our great-grandparents possessed in abundance?

When we recall the past thirty or forty years under the perspective of world history, it becomes apparent that we have experienced no truly unprecedented changes—except for one. Since the 1950s God has been banished from public life. In the United States the change has been vivid. By Supreme Court fiat, children may not pray in public schools. Crèches are forbidden on public land. In many places landlords are forbidden to bring their religious convictions to bear in choosing tenants and must rent to anyone who can pay regardless of the sexual lifestyle he intends to carry on in the rented apartment. Employees are fired for displaying pictures of Jesus or quotations from the Bible above their desks at work.

Such legal reformations, or deformations, mirror an evolution in the rules of polite public discourse. God and religion are rarely depicted in the news and entertainment media except as objects of doubt and scorn. In other areas, such as politics and academia, public figures who purport to be sympathetic to religion often refer to it as if it were merely a useful fiction rather than the expression of God's relationship with humanity. Republicans like Bob Dole and Dan Quayle, linked in the media with the nefarious forces of the Christian Right, praise religion as a helpful force in subjugating the evil impulse of their fellow citizens, but in public they rarely speak of God Himself as a Living Being. Even the Christian Right itself has been secularized, its legislative priorities consisting mainly of practical issues like tax reform and school vouchers.

If our Father in heaven does indeed live, then this is not a natural situation, any more than it is natural for a child to be out of contact with his mortal parents. Freud wrote of the tendency of repressed instincts to express themselves under the cloak of a disguise. Just as my interest in knowing something about my birth mother could not be suppressed forever, neither can the spiritual hunger of men and women be denied without some consequence. For the past few years feature reporters in newspapers and magazines have reported, half in wonder and half in horror, the stirrings of a religious revival in the United States; and though this revival remains inchoate, mixing elements of traditional faith with flakier New Age notions, it would be hard to deny that it is under way. What's less certain is that the desire to know God only recently began to move itself in American hearts. More likely the spiritual instinct has been stirring among secularized Americans for decades. Possibly it has been doing so in the form of the movement toward heritage and authenticity.

———

HERE IS ANOTHER REASON to link the past with God. Most of us sense that reliable knowledge about the transcendent force in the universe cannot be arrived at in our spare time by speculation or meditation. Rabbi Abraham Joshua Heschel drew a distinction between mystical knowledge of God and prophetic knowledge. In one, knowledge of God is sought by man; in the other, God seeks out man. In the Jewish tradition there is an ancient belief in knowledge through mystical practices. These are said to have been passed down from the first human, Adam, who received them from God. Two thousand years ago in Palestine and a thousand years later in Babylon, Jewish scholars employed the system called "Chariot" mysticism to experience an ascent through the seven palaces of heaven. In thirteenth-century Spain the practice was to enter a darkened room lit only by candles, don tefillin and tallit, and contemplate the letters in the esoteric Name of God. If the disciple was worthy, he could experience the Divine Light, and mysteries of God and His Kingdom would reveal themselves.

Jews continue to practice mysticism and seek out firsthand knowledge of God. But so do a lot of other people, as they have for millennia, and the awkward thing about mystical knowledge is that mystics have discovered widely divergent spiritual "facts" about God. Nothing, for instance, could be farther from Judaism than New Age mystical pantheism, with its belief that divinity is in everything except maybe in God.

If reliable knowledge of Him is what we want, then we must look elsewhere, and as Heschel argued, the prophetic tradition is the only conceivable source. In prophecy, God made it his custom to descend suddenly on the soul of a man, unexpected and unsought after, in a moment of terror and anguish, and communicate through him to the rest of humanity. Beginning with Moses at Sinai, that tradition speaks in one voice. Or rather the tradition *spoke,* for Jews and Christians agree that it has ceased temporarily. Prophecy is of the past. The prophet Malachi assures us that God will eventually send the prophet Elijah "before the coming of the great and dreadful day of the Lord," when prophecy will resume. Meanwhile it should come as no surprise if in our era the repressed longing for God roused itself and sought expression, disguised as a longing for the past.

That is, I believe, what lay behind my own preoccupation with old things and my new interest in knowing about my birth mother. The first preoccupation I mentioned in this chapter, my hypochondria, tends to confirms that.

The first time I feared mortal illness was in the middle of my mother's sickness. It was halfway through my senior year at Miraleste when I suddenly found it difficult to walk. My legs felt stiff all the time, and I worried that my mother's bone cancer had leaped across the house into my own bones. A few years later, at Brown, I began to worry about throat cancer. For a while I worried about brain tumors. Then came my heart and the concern that it wasn't working right.

I have forgotten my several psychotherapists' explanations of this, the relation they posited between my health fears and my mother's illness and death. But a rabbi's explanation stuck with me. I was visiting Rabbi Daniel Lapin at his home near Seattle in 1996, and one morning we got onto the subject of hypochondria. He opened a Bible to Deuteronomy, in which (7:12–15) Moses prophesies about the blessings the Israelites will receive if they hearken to the Torah and its commandments. One blessing is bodily health: "The Lord will remove from you every illness; and all the evil maladies of Egypt that you knew. He will not set them upon you, but will set them upon your foes."

In fact Moses was speaking not of the world we live in today, but of the redeemed world we will inherit after Elijah returns. Even so, Rabbi Lapin explained, a connection exists between Torah in our time and the *perception* of health. He next opened the Talmud's tractate Eruvin to a puzzling statement from Rabbi Joshua ben Levi: "When a man fears [illness] because of [a pain in] his head, let him occupy himself with Torah. . . . When a man fears because of his throat, let him occupy himself with Torah. . . . When he fears because of his innards, let him occupy himself with Torah." This rabbi from the second century C.E. was not anticipating Christian Science, the view that bodily ills can be cured through faith alone. A better way to understand the teaching, said Rabbi Lapin, is this: If a man is sick, let him go to a doctor. But if he is merely *worried* about his head, *worried* about his throat, *worried* about his innards, *then* "let him occupy himself with Torah."

"If you were fixing a hole in your wall," said Rabbi Lapin, "you would call in some workmen. They would spend hours working on the problem, and they would create a huge mess in the meantime. You might wander into the room where the hole was, see the dollar signs flashing before your eyes, and wish you'd never hired them in the first place. You brought them into your home to fix a problem, and here they are, turning a little hole into an enormous mess! Spiritual growth works in much the same way."

When did you first begin to worry that you were going to die from some terrible disease? he asked. My senior year in high school, I said. And when did you "convert" yourself? (He knew that story.) Around the same time, I said.

At that moment the clouds parted a little for me. It was true that my hypochondria ran a course parallel to my growing interest in Judaism. Rabbi Joshua had anticipated not Christian Science, but rather my own peculiar symptoms and very likely the symptoms of a lot of other people. Spiritual growth, he was saying, brings with it what you might call growing pains.

The Torah is God's plan for the Jews. The realization that God has a plan for you, and that you do not know what it is, produces a kind of distress that can manifest itself in any number of ways, including somatic distress. What is the solution? "Occupy yourself with Torah."

Today I still don't know enough Torah. But I have some idea of how much I do not know. In 1988 I had no such idea. Like the many other seekers of authenticity and heritage, I had no sense of what it was that would satisfy the hunger I felt. I didn't know I was hungry for God. It would take a Christian to tell me that.

# Chapter 9

# AVE MARIA

his is a right-wing love story. Maria McFadden's father ran a collection of traditionalist Catholic and antiabortion periodicals out of the eighth floor of the *National Review* building. I had met Maria, who worked as the managing editor at a conservative religious journal, once or twice. We didn't have a real conversation, though, until June 1989 at a meeting of the Teachout Thing.

Terry Teachout, an editorial writer at the *Daily News*, held a monthly cocktail party for young conservatives in the parlor of an East Side brownstone mansion. He called it "the Vile Body," after the Evelyn Waugh novel about decadent prewar London socialites, but the group was less formally known as the Teachout Thing. I never intended to fall in love with Maria. I asked her out because I thought she was so pretty, with blond hair and big deep blue eyes, and for her combination of silliness and earnest intellectualism, the latter expressed in a prodigious appetite for gloomy novels by Joan Didion and Graham Greene.

For our first date, June 10, we took a cab down to a restaurant in Greenwich Village where I generally brought first dates. I figured that Maria must be quite a devout Catholic; but although this intrigued me more than the family stories she chattered away about throughout the meal, I kept quiet about religion. After we had made our way through a bottle of wine, I felt more free to share my feelings. We began walking and before long arrived at Wall Street in front of Trinity Church. At the time, before it was cleaned and its original alabaster color revealed, this neo-Gothic landmark was black with grime and seemed to loom like a Halloween decoration at the foot of the financial district. As we stood there at two in the morning, rats darting past us, I tried to explain to Maria my attraction to this church and could only come up with a goofy speech about the aesthetic appeal of the "sinister" quality of certain buildings. Maria was amused. I took her hand. On a bench next to the Municipal Building, I kissed her.

After I had dropped Maria off at her little apartment on East 88th Street, walking down to my own on East 74th, the date resumed the next day when we met at nearby Immanuel Lutheran Church. It was Sunday, and after mass she was to help move the props for the performance of a medieval German morality play. In black jeans and black turtleneck, she looked like a nice Catholic girl attempting to appear bohemian: in other words, adorable. I didn't like being in this church, a functioning one with a congregation rather than a tourist attraction like Trinity. It was more creepy to me than sinister. I was glad to get out.

We quickly developed customs: Saturday brunch at Cronie's, a restaurant around the corner from her apartment; brie cheese, crackers, and red wine in her apartment on Sunday afternoons. I think I fell in love with her the night we went to the bar at the top of the Beekman Tower Hotel, with its views over Manhattan and the East River. A lifelong New Yorker, Maria looked across the river toward Queens. "Wow," she exclaimed, "look how close New Jersey is!" On a trip to Maine with a friend, I decided that before long I was going to tell Maria that I loved her. When I got back, I did. She admitted she loved me, too.

When I think about that time and the reasons I adored Maria McFadden, I first of all think of a certain magic in her eyes, a quality you can't hope to find more than two or three times in a lifetime. When I looked into her eyes it lit me up inside. I think, as most men do when they recall their love for a woman, about her love for me. "My little girl," I called her, though Maria was actually four years older than I was. After that I think of her spiritual life, which she gave me the opportunity to enter. Yet her Catholicism was a subject we hardly touched on until one Sunday afternoon in August.

We were standing in front of her refrigerator. Someone's impending marriage had come up in conversation and she asked me the obvious question. "David, could you ever marry someone who wasn't Jewish?"

The true answer was, of course, yes. Without saying so explicitly, my mother had made clear to me that she would be disappointed if I married a gentile. So have many other secular, Reform, or Conservative Jewish mothers made this clear to their children. But for most of these same mothers, Judaism is mainly an ethnic designation with no relationship to ultimate truths about God and man. So the Jews are just an ethnic group, however special. So intermarriage threatens the existence of Jews as such. Why should their existence be allowed to stand in the way of a man and a woman who love each other? Liberal rabbis have proposed no convincing answer to that question, which is why the ones among them who perform intermarriages at least have philosophical coherence on their side.

On the other hand, I was twenty-three years old, none of my college friends had gotten married yet, and the implications of Maria's question alarmed me. "Gosh," I fibbed, "I've never thought about that before. I guess I'd have to say no. I don't think I could." She raised the subject again a couple of weeks later at an Indian restaurant, and I repeated my opinion. Women cry easily. We had to leave the restaurant.

"I hoped you'd get interested in Catholicism," she told me later. But Maria never had to press her faith on me, because it pervaded her life. We went to mass together, where I was amused and pretended to be shocked that one of the hymns was sung to the tune of *"Deutschland über Alles"* (from an old Lutheran hymn, she assured me). I had noticed all the Catholic books on her shelves, which were eclipsed by her father's collection. We often visited her parents in their apartment on Park Avenue, where the gruff but jovial J. P. McFadden puffed on a pipe and held forth on all subjects Catholic. We joked that, due to a genetic quirk, her father could not bend at the knees to sit down without launching into an anecdote, generally about his experiences as an antiabortion "propagandist," as he cheerfully described himself. Her parents would take us to Cronie's in the evening to sit out at one of the sidewalk tables. Mr. McFadden called me "old man" and kept my glass filled with wine. I liked all her many siblings and loved being in the home where Maria had grown up. Whatever opinions the McFadden family held, they did so emphatically—a fact reflected in the writing several of them did for Mr. McFadden's publications, in which the *frequent* use of italics played a *conspicuous* role. I was unused to being around people who believed in anything with such clarity and vigor, and charmed by it. In short, as I loved Maria, I also loved her Catholicism. "I wanted to give you a family," she said later, which made me want to cry.

But what appealed to me about her faith was not simply that it was hers. We are told in Deuteronomy, "Love the Lord your God with all your heart, and all your soul, and all your might." Maria loved God. She had that quality I once thought was ridiculous: a "relationship" with Him, the state of perceiving, cherishing, and engaging with God's presence in one's life. What made this obvious in Maria wasn't pious talk or any kind of weird joyfulness of the kind we tend to suspect of being manufactured for show. It was that from her conversation and actions, she made it clear, and without trying to do so, that God lived in her months, days, and hours. You could tell she took satisfaction from serving Him, in church, in prayer. He was her constant companion, and she subjected whatever she did to scrutiny based on the criterion, Does what I'm doing please God or not? I came to envy her.

———

THAT I MIGHT BECOME a Catholic entered our conversations for the first time that winter. A social worker named Arlena operated from the basement of the St. Jean Baptiste Church on Lexington Avenue, and Maria had sought her out for relationship counseling. The social worker prayed over Maria, hugged her, told her that she herself had dated a Jewish man, and at last stated her view that "if David really loved you, he would convert to Catholicism." Maria reported this news to me. Women cry easily. I urged her to stop seeing Arlena, and she eventually did; but the idea had been planted in both our heads.

It happened that Maria's mother was friendly with a nun at the Regina Laudis monastery in Bethlehem, Connecticut. The nun had once been approached by a Jew who wanted to be baptized. "He was a secular Jew, I guess," Maria told me later. "Anyway, Mother Whoever sent him away, and said that he should learn all he could about Judaism and then come back and speak to her." Though I had as yet expressed no interest in getting baptized, it occurred to Maria that possibly the sequence of events could be worked in reverse. If I learned about Judaism a little, that might awaken a desire in me to learn about Christianity. "David, I think you're confused about your relationship to Judaism," Maria said. "I mean, here you are dating a Catholic girl. And then there are the doubts you've had about whether you really are Jewish or not." I had explained those doubts to her. "Sweetie, maybe I'm crazy for saying this, but I think you should go talk to a rabbi about all this."

So the first person in my life to urge me to adopt a more serious attitude toward Judaism was a serious Catholic. But what rabbi could I approach? From the Teachout Thing I knew a young gentile woman, Jane Brooks, who had married a Jewish man. Independently of him, she had decided that she wanted to become a Jew. I knew that she attended a Conservative shul on the East Side led by a rabbi she admired, Louis Blumberg. She suggested that I talk to him about Maria and about my status as a Jew. It seemed like a good idea.

For three or four weeks I attended the Saturday morning service at Congregation B'nei Avraham. Like Jane, I was impressed by Rabbi Blumberg's brief comments about the week's Torah portion—though less so by the exchange of views that followed the reading. Conservative Judaism has gotten the idea into its head that laymen, no matter how ignorant, can contribute valuable "input" regarding the interpretation of sacred texts. Thus Rabbi Blumberg, a wise but perhaps overly modest person, declined to give sermons and allowed the congregation to endlessly air their opinions about whatever had been read. The group of prosperous Upper East Side New Yorkers didn't know much about the material at hand, but they knew what they liked. "I have a problem with this," was the most frequently heard comment, as in "I have a problem with the way Moses gets so ticked off here with the Golden Calf thing and breaks the tablets and all. I mean, he'd been up there on the mountain for forty days. They must've thought he was dead! No wonder they decided to resort to extreme measures."

I went to see Rabbi Blumberg at his office. He explained, "It's true that, from a technical perspective, you would be considered a gentile. But that can be corrected without too much difficulty. What you'd need to do is come before a religious court, state your intention to live as a Jew, have a symbolic circumcision in which a drop of blood is drawn from the tip of the penis, and be immersed in a *mikvah*, a ritual bath." He asked me a couple of questions about my level of Torah observance, to which I said it was minimal but that I wanted to be more observant in the future. That intention had not entered my mind before, but now it did and seemed entirely logical. Surely, I thought, getting myself converted to Judaism would inspire me to take God more seriously. The rabbi was satisfied. Just by showing up at the *mikvah* on West 78th Street, I could resolve any questions about my Jewishness. I requested an appointment for nine A.M., January 18.

For some reason I tended to make important announcements

while Maria and I were standing in front of her refrigerator. My impending conversion did not strike her as the simple resolution of a technicality, and once again I was reminded how easily women cry. But she did not try to talk me out of it, in part because a potentially still more troubling barrier seemed about to go up between us. I was moving to Washington. John Podhoretz, editor of the "Life" section at the *Washington Times*, had offered me a job as a movie and television reviewer for the *Times*.

The conversion went effortlessly. I arrived at the *mikvah* and met Rabbi Blumberg, another Conservative rabbi, and a Conservative *mohel*. They chatted with me about my current job and my new one, then asked a couple of questions. "You know that we Jews have historically been oppressed and persecuted," said Rabbi Blumberg. "Are you sure that you want to throw your lot in with the people Israel?" I said I was sure. It had never occurred to me that I could disassociate myself from the Jews, whatever my legal status. The second rabbi then inquired about my observance of the commandments, and I told him what I had told Rabbi Blumberg. That was it.

We went into another room, set up like my parents' bathroom in Palos Verdes—big mirror, big counter space, lots of drawers, hairdryers. The symbolic circumcision, like the immersion, needed to be accomplished before three witness. I felt a little funny, sitting exposed while the *mohel* sterilized the appointed spot, but the awkwardness vanished at the sensation of steel meeting skin. Whatever physical distress I felt lasted only a second or two, and then it was on to the bath. Now I stood entirely naked in front of three men in business suits. Again there was some awkwardness in this, but not much. The immersion was brief: three dunks in lukewarm water, each time over my head, in what might have been a nondescript Jacuzzi lined with rose-colored tiles. Afterward the three nice men shook my hand, and I walked over to Broadway to catch the subway to work. I was now a Jew.

Yet in my feelings, beliefs, and actions, nothing had changed. Maria got over it. The conversion didn't mean I intended to exit our relationship. She knew I loved her now more than ever. Becoming a Jew should be an awesome moment: the convert has undertaken to observe the 613 mitzvot revealed to the Jews in the wilderness, of which, minutes before, he had been obliged to observe none. He enters an entirely new relationship to God. But the only new relationship I entered in January 1990 was with the *Washington Times.*

---

ONE NIGHT that first winter in Washington, asleep in my apartment in Dupont Circle, I had a dream. I found myself crossing a river via a Gothic bridge like the Charles Bridge in Prague. I was following Harrison Ford. The atmosphere was dark until Ford reached an expansive and brightly lit public square. At its far end I saw an unnaturally huge, brooding Gothic cathedral. Other people besides Harrison Ford were walking toward the cathedral, tiny figures in the distance. Suddenly one of them was lifted up into air, then another, and another. Who knows what Harrison Ford felt about any of this, but I seemed to be gasping for breath as a scream built up inside me. Inevitably, since it was a dream, the same invisible force caught me by the chest and began lifting me. My legs and arms dangled below as if I were a marionette or, perhaps more to the point, like the Christ one sees in paintings of him after he has been taken down from the cross. I didn't scream, but with my heart galloping I bolted upright in my bed and woke from the dream.

I would think about that dream often in the months to come, with its sensation of powerlessness in the grip of an irresistible force that was drawing me toward it, whether for good or evil I didn't know.

Although Maria and I continued to see each other on weekends, I sensed an unnerving absence in myself that couldn't entirely be explained by the fact that she and I were separated by 250 miles. Through Maria's relationship with God, I had experienced a kind of surrogate spiritual life—the way a person watching his friend enjoy a meal can almost taste the food himself. Now I was cut off from that. Could solace be found, I wondered, in Judaism?

In any big American city there is likely to be one Conservative synagogue with a reputation for attracting young, intellectually and spiritually lively Jews. The institution like that in Washington was Congregation Adas Israel on Connecticut Avenue. But the Friday night that I visited Adas Israel, the puny audience, scattered through the cavernous sanctuary, was composed of Jews mainly over the age of fifty whose limp prayers accompanied the tinklings of an elderly pianist. At the evening's climax a man went to the podium and spent ten minutes elaborating on some awards received by the Men's Club ("Best Programming in the Country," "Most Money Raised for Jewish Charities"), after which he introduced a reporter from *U.S. News & World Report* to discuss the situation of Soviet Jewry. Very spiritual.

I also tried an Orthodox synagogue in Georgetown, Kesher Israel, where the unfamiliar setting made me nervous and the difficult liturgy rushed past me. The rest of Washington's synagogues were in the suburbs. In a week, I had run out of shuls.

When Maria spent the weekend in Washington, part of me longed to go with her as she went off on Sunday morning to the stately red-brick St. Matthew's Cathedral with its lovely green-copper dome. Continuing to attend Adas Israel was out of the question, so I stuck it out with Kesher Israel, where I would go every other Saturday morning or so. When Maria got back from St. Matthew's, she would tell me about the priest's homily and how it or some scriptural reading had comforted her about our difficulties or moved her to tears by its sheer beauty. Though I kept hoping for such an experience at Kesher Israel, the shul persisted in withholding one from me. The rabbi, Barry Freundel, delivered sermons with none of the lachrymose sentimentality that seemed to have been a requirement for ordination among many of his colleagues in all three denominations. As more rabbis should do, he consistently made Torah confront the world, explaining the relevance of the tradition to our personal lives as well as to current events. He rarely said anything that was less than fascinating. But what I really longed for—the burst of emotion, the clenching at the back of my throat that I had experienced many times at the conclusion of melodramatic movies, a love for God as strong as my still growing love for Maria—didn't come. She had sensations like that all the time in church. That disturbed me.

This is one reason why Maria never had to do any evangelizing. My own experiences, or lack of them, were doing the job for her. Occasionally I would picture myself making the decision to become a Catholic, though really, I see now, the chance of my suddenly being touched by Jesus was about as slim as the chance that Maria would suddenly feel uncontrollably drawn to Torah. Oh Maria, it was unlikely that you and I would ever have long-term contentment together. But the capacity of a man in love to fool himself is astonishing.

As I vaguely imagined it, my transformation into a Christian, should it come to that, would not be like my evolution from a liberal to a conservative. There was nothing terrifying about the latter. You must realize to what extent my self-understanding was founded on the legitimacy of Judaism as a statement both about God and about me: a statement that God's Covenant with the Jews remained in effect and that I was part of it. As I've said, the soul of every adoptee is affected by a certain tension, having to do with the seeming arbitrariness of his identity. Jewish thought has a phrase that captures this sensation of apparent randomness: "a little thing decided his fate." As Avivah Gottlieb Zornberg points out in her book *The Beginning of Desire: Reflections on Genesis,* the classic instance of it is found in Rashi's commentary on the death of Sarah. The first biblical matriarch is said to have died in a swoon of existential anguish at the following idea: that had God not stopped Abraham at the last moment on Mt. Moriah, her son Isaac would have been slaughtered. The knowledge that things might have gone very differently in a person's life but for some little thing, some unlikely intervention of fate, produces a sensation of dread—crystallized by Sartre in the word "contingency." "The knowledge of one's contingency," Mrs. Zornberg writes, "the vertigo of being, is expressed in the instability, the dizzying symmetry of equivalent possibilities. On this view, Sarah dies of radical doubt. She suffers an attack of vertigo." For those who aren't sure they believe in a fate assigned and assured to the individual soul by the Lord of the Universe, identity in the case of an adoptee appears to be the result of pure contingency. Everything I believed, or wanted to believe, about myself—that I was the son of my parents, that I was a Jew—looked from this perspective like a sentimental Just So story.

Now along came Maria. This lovely, blond, blue-eyed girl, who like Sheryl Spencer might well look like my birth mother, was inviting me to join a new family and worship a new god. To do so would have been half joy and half terror: joy because I had never loved a woman as I loved Maria, terror because joining her would not only constitute treason against the people who had raised me and loved me for twenty-five years—it might be treason against God. Most terrifying of all, perhaps, it would definitively reveal the sheer randomness of my beliefs and personality. We all want to think that we could not have been anyone other than who we are. But what if that's not true? If Judaism was defective in its grasp of the Truth, as Maria implied, then it could not be accurate to say I was a Jew. A conversion to Judaism assumes that the convert's change in existential status—from gentile to Jew—is ratified by God. If Maria was right about Judaism, God would hardly ratify a conversion to that faulty religion. If I was not a Jew and could never become one by correcting a minor technical problem, what was I? My parents had told me I was Jew. If they were wrong about something so fundamental, perhaps they were also wrong to call themselves my parents. If I was not a Jew, maybe I had no parents at all. An abyss was opening at my feet. I could feel Sarah's case of vertigo coming on.

One Saturday after shul I walked to the National Gallery and moped around the pretty little fountain room in the north wing. I looked at the art near the bench I sat on. Almost all of it was Christian, notably a marble Madonna and Child, which epitomized the sweetness I sensed in Maria's faith. I got up and walked through the nearby galleries of Renaissance paintings, with their tireless depictions of the Nativity, the Crucifixion, and the Resurrection. I went back and sat on the bench. The marble Mary seemed to be holding her child out to me. What did God want? The abyss under my feet had opened a little wider. I could hardly bear to look down, for fear of what I might see rising up from below to seize me.

That Sunday night Maria and I spoke, fought about which one of us was being more resistant than the other to religious compromise, and at last we decided to stop seeing each other. Dear Maria. Though she only wanted to love me and to be loved in return, by this point I had come to be slightly afraid of her and of what she could do to me.

———

WHENEVER FRIENDS OF MINE break up with their girlfriends, or when their girlfriends break up with them, I always counsel immediate action: in order to ease the pain and loneliness, immediately call another girl, or go to a bookstore and try to pick one up, or *something*. I had no interest in meeting another girl, but I knew I had to take some kind of action. The day before, when I rejected Mary's offer of the child in her arms, I would not have predicted that the next day would be the day I accepted the Jewish Sabbath.

Rabbi Haym Soloveitchik has offered an acute insight into the psychology of those who spontaneously take religious disciplines on themselves. He was writing about the phenomenon of ultra-Orthodoxy, in which the children of Orthodox Jews have in growing numbers decided that the restrictions imposed by traditional Torah Judaism are not enough and have embraced stringencies above and beyond the actual demands of Torah. In the journal *Tradition*, Rabbi Soloveitchik wondered what drives them to do this, and he proposed an answer: Secular culture invades even those Orthodox Jewish communities that try hardest to isolate themselves from modernity, with the result that "the perception of God as a *daily, natural* force is no longer present to a significant degree in any sector of modern Jewry, even the most religious." He exaggerates, but the undertaking of stringencies is indeed a way to bridge the distance that has opened in the past century between man and God. "Having lost the touch of His presence," ultra-Orthodox Jews "seek now solace in the pressure of His yoke."

Having lost the touch of Maria's presence, and thus my most vital link with God, I decided to seek the solace of His yoke. On Monday I told John Podhoretz that I would prefer not to work on the Jewish Sabbath—sunset on Friday till dark on Saturday. It would be impossible for a reporter of breaking national news to observe Shabbat. But movie and TV reviews can be juggled and swapped in advance with colleagues. And even if they couldn't, John proved to be a very sympathetic boss. "Good for you," he said. "Just make sure to let us know in advance when you'll be out for a holiday." (Jews who commit themselves to keeping Shabbat, especially ones like me who were told in their Reform Sunday schools that Sabbath observance is incompatible with modern life, are usually surprised to discover how little resistance they encounter on the job, and how much encouragement.) I planned to make the coming Friday my first real Shabbat, down to such details as precooking my food for the coming twenty-five hours and setting my electric lights on a timer. That way, in line with Halachah, I wouldn't have to turn them on or off myself.

The day of my decision to try observing Shabbat, I got a letter from Maria expressing her sadness, and mine, at the gulf that separated our religious lives and as a result separated us. In thinking about marriage, many religiously mixed couples discuss the idea that one of the partners might convert. But Maria loved the Catholic Church in a way I had not come to love Torah. "It is so wonderful to believe," she wrote to me, "and to feel the warmth and delight of belief, and to have those moments when your mind and your heart are sure that it is astonishing and mysterious but in a way it makes perfect sense and aren't we so lucky because of it." As much as she wanted to be with me, the idea of even nominally embracing Judaism "well, it takes God away from me, it makes him distant and seemingly unreachable. I do respect Judaism and I do believe religious Jews are blessed by God, but to practice Judaism as it was before Jesus still seems to me like a step backward, an emphasis on activities rather than belief, and a stubborn resistance to the Spirit. If I came to believe that Jesus was not the Messiah, a great light would go out in my heart."

That week I started having weird experiences in automobiles. Driving around Georgetown on the way to or from preview screenings of the movies I was to review, I would notice in the streets what seemed like an unusually high number of Catholic priests, presumably affiliated with Georgetown University. All of them struck me as impressively serene and dignified. One night I was picked up in a taxi by a black man who ranted confusingly. He insisted that I agree with him that there was no such thing as white people: "They all Anglo-Saxons! Lookit you! You ever look at yo'-self in a mirror? You ain't white!" As for "these so-called Jews," he continued, "they ain't Jews. The real Jews is black folks!"

I have always been superstitious. What in fact was God trying to suggest? Was he reminding me that I wasn't really a Jew, but a Swede or whatever, with therefore the freedom to choose another faith and thus to marry the girl I loved? Listening to the radio as I drove out across New York Avenue on my way from work one afternoon, I heard rock songs that could lend themselves to a Christian interpretation. "And here's to you, Mrs. Robinson. Jesus loves you more than you will know." "Here comes the sun! [son?]" People "lose their soul" and "never the glimpse the truth, then it's far too late, when they pass away." With each song my hands gripped the steering wheel tighter. Others contained phrases such as "born again" and "come to Jesus." It seemed unlikely to me that the Creator of the Universe would stoop to bad puns and the cruel joke of employing a car radio to inform a person that he was in danger of losing his soul—but not impossible. After all, the same Almighty Lord caused the gentile prophet Balaam to be addressed by a talking donkey.

Maria had lent me a copy of C. S. Lewis's work of apologetics, *Mere Christianity*. One night I opened it to a page she had marked with a prayer card. There, Lewis discussed non-Christians. "Here is another thing that used to puzzle me," he said. "Is it not frightfully unfair that this new life [after death] should be confined to people who have heard of Christ and been able to believe in Him? But the truth is God has not told us what His arrangements about the other people are. We do know that no man can be saved except through Christ; we do not know that only those who know Him can be saved through Him." This comforted me briefly. Then: "But in the meantime, if you are worried about the people outside, the most unreasonable thing you can do is to remain outside yourself." I went back to fretting.

This sent me to my copy of the Bible. St. Augustine had encountered divine communications to himself by opening his own copy of that book to a randomly chosen page, sticking his finger onto a random passage, and reading it. Warning: Do not try this at home. I did and came away more confused than when I started. First I would open to a psalm: "Sing unto to the Lord a new song!" Ah! New song, New Testament. A Christian message. Then I would open to the verses in Deuteronomy defining a false prophet, which reminded me of Jesus. Ah-hah! A Jewish message.

Lying in bed that night, I thought, But what if Christianity is true? Christians often talk about the danger in rejecting Christ. What if the Messiah really has come, and the fate of my soul depends on my willingness to recognize that fact? Christians say that faith comes only to those who first open themselves to Christ. I was on my back, eyes wide open, any possibility of sleep as far away as New York and Maria. These thoughts had entered my head before but never as menacingly as now. People who grew up in the Soviet Union and at any time considered betraying their parents to the secret police will have some sense of how I felt as I considered betraying my parents, my adoptive parents, and what they had told me about the God of their people—in return for the embrace of Maria's God, the God of my birth parents.

All right, I thought, I'll say the words and see if anything happens. This must seem painfully naive, but I was very much in earnest. Looking up at the ceiling of my apartment, I whispered to God, "I open myself to Jesus, if he is the Messiah."

I turned my eyes from the ceiling to the window and looked out across Corcoran Street, wondering if I would see him rising up past the Washington School of Psychiatry, arms held out to me.

No Jesus. Might I then perhaps find a cross formed by the folds in my bed sheets? No cross.

Maybe the sound of a still, small voice, whispering back to me, "Jesus loves you, Mr. Klinghoffer"? No voice.

All right, so this precise technique has probably never worked for anyone hoping to receive a message from God. All right, so it was never very likely that I would become a Christian, despite the incentive I had in Maria to do so. But I'm sure that other Jews in a similar predicament, faced with losing a beloved religious Christian they very much want to marry, have had what they perceived to be a genuine Christian rebirth and ended up at the baptismal font. It's easy to see why some Jewish parents worry when their children date Christians, despite the son or daughter's protestation that he or she will always remain a Jew no matter what.

I would guess, however, that not many Jews have tried to strike up a conversation with Jesus one night and a few nights later commenced observing the Jewish Sabbath for the first time in their lives. By a quirk of timing, that was, I thought the next day, pretty much what I was obliged to do. Since I had just told my editor that I intended to observe Shabbat, if only to avoid professional embarrassment I had to start doing so.

Torah affirms the value of performing mitzvot even if we have little or no understanding of what they mean. By the spring of 1990 I could, on request, supply a number of pious-sounding sentences about how the Sabbath gives "a foretaste of the World to Come," the redeemed world of peace that will follow the advent of the Messiah; how it is "an island in time"; how it teaches us to put our worldly concerns in proper perspective, setting them aside one day a week to focus on God: His worship, His rule, His creatorship. The Torah suggests two complementary meanings of the day, noted in the two slightly differing versions of the Ten Commandments given in Exodus and Deuteronomy. One version says we observe the Sabbath to commemorate the creation of Earth and its creatures, because on the day following that event God chose to rest from his work. To acknowledge that everything in the world owes its existence to Him, we abstain from all creative work and observe the way the world can get on perfectly well without our efforts. According to the other version, Jews observe Shabbat to mark their liberation from Egyptian bondage: to proclaim that when the Israelites left the Egyptian king's service they entered into the service of the King of Kings. And our Eternal Master gives us a day off each week. Rabbi Abraham Joshua Heschel expressed a similar idea in opposite terms. Rather than declaring man a servant, the Sabbath declares him a prince. Since his true Ruler is God, he in reality has no earthly ruler: "To celebrate the Sabbath is to experience one's ultimate independence of civilization and society, of achievement and anxiety."

No doubt Shabbat has innumerable layers of expressible meaning. But when we write them down or say them out loud, it becomes clear why liberal Jews have found it easy to disregard the actual observance of the day. Abstaining from work on Shabbat seems like a dreadful inconvenience: not only does it require us to stay home from the office, but we are forced to refrain from all creative actions—cooking, cleaning, driving, shopping, writing, using electric appliances, using fire, spending money, traveling, moving objects outside the home, talking or even (ideally) thinking about any of these things. If the meaning of Shabbat can be spelled out in a few sentences, why not just read the sentences, even memorize them, and get on with your life?

"To celebrate the Sabbath is to experience one's ultimate independence of civilization and society," writes Heschel. The word to notice there is "experience." The truths of the Sabbath, like most of the teaching given to the Jews, can be articulated in words. But to be understood as God intended, they must be experienced as deeds. One of the clichés used in speaking about religion is that God asks us to make "a leap of faith." As Rabbi Heschel puts it, God asks rather that we make a "leap of action," which can result in faith. "The gates of faith are not ajar," he writes, "but the mitzvah is a key. By living as Jews we may attain our faith as Jews. We do not have faith because of deeds; we may attain faith through sacred deeds."

I have heard the Sabbath described as a "meditation." This is just a pompous way of saying that it changes the interior life of the person who practices it. It does indeed put the rest of one's life "in proper perspective." I still care about my career, but I view it as a thing of relative instead of absolute importance. At the *Washington Times* some writers took pride in the fact that they worked eighty hours over the seven days of each week rather than the forty hours over five days they were paid for. Once I admired people like that. Now I feel sorry for them. When Shabbat arrives, I greet it as a liberation. When I began taking the day off, its twenty-five hours felt much longer than they do today. At the nineteenth or twentieth hour, I began sneaking glances at my watch and longing for the twenty-fifth. Six years later, the twenty-fifth hour feels like the nineteenth, and I pick up the havdalah candle—to be extinguished each Saturday night in its cup of wine, marking the conclusion of Shabbat—with reluctance.

———

THAT LONG, SAD SPRING without Maria, we exchanged letters. She set the tone for the correspondence. "I believe that there is Truth," she wrote, "and that the Truth has to do with Christ." She pointed out that Jews and Catholics marry each other all the time, and the religious difference need not hinder them: "The truth that Christ has everything to do with is the same truth as in Judaism. It's not a contradiction but a new development: the Messiah, not as men expected him, but as God meant him to be." This is essentially the line of reasoning pursued by Jews for Jesus and the many other Christian organizations, such as the nineteenth-century American Society for Meliorating the Condition of the Jews, that have gone before it in the effort to bring Jews to Christianity. Judaism, say these Christians, was not abolished but "completed" by Christianity. Thus Jews who accept baptism do not cease to be Jews. They become completed Jews.

The truth about God: it is a question that modern Jews and Christians tend to avoid. Most of us have a conception of the Lord, derived from some combination of what our parents told us about Him and what we would like to believe is true. It is not a modern habit to think critically about our notions of Him. But Maria had implicitly invited me to do just that.

When you are judging two competing lines of argument, it helps to begin by considering their common premises. Christian and Jewish religious thinking do indeed share a common premise, namely all the claims advanced in the Hebrew Bible about God and Israel. Professor Fritz Rothschild has put it as clearly as anyone else: "Only where the faith of Israel and its Holy Scriptures . . . are accepted as true and valid can the claim be made that in the life, death, and resurrection of Jesus of Nazareth, the promises of God have been fulfilled." Christianity requires the Hebrew prophets: it cannot be believed without their agreement. Anyone who chooses the Christian understanding of God's will over the Jewish understanding had better feel confident that the claims of Christianity do not contradict prophecy. Do they?

In a series of love letters whose pedantry—my pedantry—still surprises me, Maria and I debated that question. Eventually we started arguing by telephone.

Discussions with Christians on this subject inevitably circle back on a handful of lines in Isaiah and Jeremiah, and my arguments with Maria were no exception. Sometimes in a bullying way that made me feel, when we finished, as if I had slapped her, I argued that the prophets offer a pretty uncertain basis for identifying Jesus as the Messiah, much less as God. Certain passages from their works can be construed as pointing to him (as in Isaiah's Suffering Servant, "pierced for our transgressions"), but others really can't (all the lines in Isaiah, Jeremiah, and Amos insisting that the Messiah when he comes will rapidly bring about universal peace and knowledge of God, as well as a return of the Jews to Zion). I vehemently explained to Maria that, on the basis of prophecy, no ordinary Jew living at the time of Jesus could have been expected to guess that the Messiah would do what Christians say Jesus did: 1) die for the world's sins; 2) somehow be identical, or consubstantial, with God; 3) change the content or binding nature of Israel's Covenant with God as described in the Torah; and 4) die without establishing the Kingdom of God as an obvious reality, radically different from the chaos of the unredeemed world. Yet Christians traditionally have said that the eternal salvation of that ordinary Jew depended then, as it does now, on making exactly that identification. We are asked to see God as a sphinx, putting to the Jews an inscrutable riddle that they must answer correctly or face endless punishment.

There is also the related question of what, in light of Jesus' ministry, to make of Torah and its demands on Jews. From the Christian perspective, there are two possibilities.

1) Perhaps, as St. Paul interpreted the message of Jesus, the Messiah-God had abolished Torah and its commandments. However, at the time the Torah was given, God seemed pretty determined that it be obeyed no matter what the future brought; He included no apparent escape clause. Before abandoning Torah, you had better feel very confident that Paul's understanding of Jesus, who he was and what he taught, is right.

2) Perhaps as Jews for Jesus and "Messianic Jews" prefer to say, the Messiahship of Jesus leaves intact the eternal Covenant of the Torah. Thus these individuals observe some of the better-known commandments, holding Passover seders, lighting Hannukah candles, and so on. The problem here is that, as I've explained, written Torah makes no sense without oral Torah. You can't coherently accept one without the other. And on the identity and characteristics of the Messiah, oral Torah speaks in much greater and clearer detail than the prophets do. It excludes belief in Jesus. Messianic Jews might respond that oral Torah was rejigged here and there by rabbis seeking to score propaganda points against Christian opponents; but if so, again we enter the impossible territory in which an omnipotent God can't manage to keep his Revelation free of dangerous mistakes and lies.

For the gentile peoples of the world, Christianity has done incalculable good, bringing a hundred generations of souls close to God. But to a Jew, both versions of the Christian message display a furiously blinking red warning light: DANGER. DO NOT ENTER.

Maria argued back: "No other good, holy prophet said he would die and rise from the dead after three days and then actually did so," she pointed out. However, in one letter she said something of which I should have taken more careful notice. Textual arguments weren't at all what she would need in order to bring her to the point where she could reject Catholicism. "It would take a huge mystical experience, an act of God." And she wasn't too worried that such a thing would transpire. "Even if Christianity weren't true," she said frankly, "I wouldn't give it up."

I had failed entirely to help Maria understand Judaism. As she made clear, she imagined Torah as a burden requiring almost neurotic scrupulousness, impossible to fulfill, thus causing uncertainty and unhappines—a classic Christian view. Our rabbis speak of accepting the "yoke of the Kingdom of Heaven," but the work imposed by that yoke is always assumed to be joyful, and it is. King David summarized his feelings on the subject in Psalm 19: "The Torah of the Lord is perfect, restoring the soul; the testimony of the Lord is trustworthy, making the simple one wise. The orders of the Lord are upright, gladdening the heart; the command of the Lord is clear, enlightening the eyes." What I did not understand as a proselytizer is that converts and *ba'alei teshuvah* come to accept Torah not as the end point of a series of logical deductions, but by trying on the yoke and carrying it for a while. Maria, whom I never encouraged to experiment with performing mitzvot herself, could not help but feel about them as she did.

What is less obvious is why I continued to some extent to share Maria's understanding, to see the commandments from a Christian perspective. Our arguments, with me in the role of anti-Christian inquisitor, hid the fact or maybe were an expression of it: I was defending myself from the suspicion that Maria was actually right about everything. I lacked an essential conviction in the Jewish ideas that were assuming an increasingly central place in my life—the sort of conviction that seemed to fill Maria the way helium fills a balloon, expanding and lifting her.

In the codes of Torah law, you will find no commandment of belief in anything. Yet there would appear to be a paradox in rabbinic literature, in which our rabbis do not hesitate to consign Jews who arrogantly adopt heterodox opinions to punishment after death. Famously, in his commentary to the Mishnah, Maimonides formulated Thirteen Principles of Faith to which every Jew must assent.

It wasn't until several years later that Rabbi Daniel Lapin explained the paradox to me. What Judaism aims at is not *belief* in God and Torah, but *knowledge* of them: total conviction. At each of the three daily prayer services, in the concluding affirmation *Aleinu,* we pray for the time when "[a]ll the world's inhabitants will recognize and *know* that to You every knee should bend, every tongue should swear." We do not pray for "faith" or "belief." When in the Book of Exodus God wishes to portray a man who represents the total negation of Torah—Pharaoh, king of Egypt—He has him declare, "I do not *know* the Lord," not, "I do not believe in the Lord." And how is such knowledge to be achieved? Through action. If we perform the commandments in the correct manner and spirit, it comes naturally.

We can't know which commandment will be the turning point in our spiritual evolution. I was now observing Shabbat and attending Sabbath meals in the Georgetown community, laying tefillin regularly, and more irregularly saying the central prayer *Amidah* as prescribed, three times daily, morning, afternoon, and night. All these helped form me as a Jew. But I have a theory that the action God was waiting for me to undertake was a decision to limit my romantic relationships to Jewish women.

I heard the connection alluded to in Exodus during the Torah reading one Shabbat morning, while another Catholic girl (albeit lapsed) waited for me in her apartment: There is a tendency of Jews who fall in love with the daughters of gentiles to "go astray after their gods."

While Maria and I were apart, I had gotten into a relationship with this other young woman. She and I spent a few months together, at the end of which I took her to New York for a weekend. I went up by train ahead of her, in order to have lunch with Maria. By the end of the meal Maria and I had decided we loved each other too much not to think once more about getting married. This left me to perform the task of breaking up with my present girlfriend on the first day of what I had presented as a romantic weekend in Manhattan. I broke the news the next morning at a Chinese restaurant called Pig Heaven. She rightly thought I was a pig. It was hell.

———

THINGS MOVED QUICKLY after that, though Maria and I persisted in refusing to see in what direction. I told her I could accept the idea of her remaining a Catholic if she raised our children as Jews, and I agreed to go with her to see a priest—or rather, an almost priest. Previously a Lutheran minister, Richard Neuhaus had been accepted in the Catholic Church and was in the process of receiving Catholic priestly credentials. He agreed to see us as a spiritual counselor, the night after St. Patrick's Day at his apartment near Gramercy Park. Since he did not seem to rule out the possibility of Maria raising Jewish children, she felt encouraged by the meeting. It didn't have the same effect on me. We told him about our scriptural discussions, and he dismissed the idea that, on the basis of my arguments with her, Maria could be expected to form an opinion one way or the other about the divinity of Jesus. He meant only (and he was right) that proofs from biblical texts are not the way most people decide what they think about God. But I took his comment as a challenge to Maria's ability to be a sophisticated reader of holy texts and dashed to her defense.

"Just a minute," I said as heat rose to my cheeks. "Maria is an intelligent woman, and God gave her a mind so that she could use it. I don't see why she can't read the Bible and decide for herself what it means."

Whatever misgivings Maria and I might have had about marriage to each other, we had taken a concrete action—speaking with a clergyman—that people take when they are preparing to get engaged. We began to think of ourselves as a couple on its way to matrimony and took other actions accordingly. In my role as a feature writer on movies and television, I was scheduled to fly to Los Angeles for a junket, a weekend for journalists arranged by film studio publicists in which we would interview the stars and director of the film version of *The Bonfire of the Vanities*. By telling a publicist that Maria was my fiancée, I secured a free trip for both of us to Los Angeles. This would give me a chance to introduce her to my father and stepmother and meet with a Jewish clergyman: Rabbi Dinnerstein. Before leaving Washington, I also located an Orthodox synagogue near the hotel, the Bel Age in West Hollywood, that would serve as the location of the junket. As it happened, God had chosen this weekend to be a bonfire of my vanities.

I still hoped that I could interest Maria in Judaism and had decided to take her with me to the shul. We got into Los Angeles on a Friday, and I said the appropriate evening prayers by myself at the hotel. The next morning, March 23, 1991, we set off for Congregation Emunath Israel.

The shul was in Los Angeles and on a map didn't look farther than a half hour's walk from the Bel Age. Nobody walks in Los Angeles, as the song says, but we did. The map I had consulted turned out to have been inaccurately scaled. We arrived at the shul, an ugly squarish modern thing, two hours after leaving the hotel.

The sanctuary was filled to capacity, with men on one side of a partition and women on the other, while a bar mitzvah went on at the front. This is what happens in a synagogue on Shabbat morning, but something was wrong here. It was the noise.

No one I could see around me was praying or even pretending to do so. The sound of conversation was so loud that if I closed my eyes, I could have imagined I was sitting in a football stadium at halftime. Everyone was talking—about work, or sports, or their social lives—at a volume appropriate to a restaurant or supermarket. At the reading of the Torah, the bar mitzvah boy's tremulous voice was almost inaudible. The rabbi's sermon could just barely be heard. No one seemed to be trying to decipher his words over the din, which was just as well since he was delivering a diatribe against "the *guuyim*," as he pronounced the Yiddishized version of the Hebrew word for "gentiles." When he said this it came from the back of his throat as if he were about to hawk and spit the people of the world out onto his oblivious audience: "The *guuyim*," he declared, do such and such and so and so—and he named several disreputable practices. "But *we*," he said—and he listed a number of points to be admired about the Jews. Afterward the cantor stepped forward to lead this particular group of admirable Jews in the additional service that follows the morning service on Shabbat, but I saw no one praying. That would have required interrupting their conversation. With blood pounding in my temples, my face flushed with outrage and humiliation, I could hardly pray myself.

When the crowd pushed onto the street after the service, I met Maria on the sidewalk. She had found the women's chatting as outrageous as I had found the men's. She could not bear to sit in the sanctuary and escaped early.

I had brought Maria to shul that morning in the hope of attracting her to Judaism, but clearly God had something else in mind. Instead I had showed her the worst possible face of Orthodoxy, an astonishing desecration of God's Name. The look in her eyes combined sympathy for me, because she knew why I had brought her there, with a kind of disturbed, even fearful, wonder. I guessed she was thinking she might have misjudged me. We had fallen in love partly because each of us sensed in the other a spiritual awareness, a hunger for God. Now I had brought her to a house of worship where the people didn't worship God but contemptuously ignored Him. Was I, the man she had considered marrying, in reality as spiritually deadened as the Jews of Congregation Emunath Israel appeared to be?

As we trudged back to the hotel, an appalling idea struck me there on the empty sidewalk beneath dried-out palm trees: It could not be a coincidence that we had ended up at this synagogue on this day. Our rabbis have an expression for the idea that nothing happens by accident: "personal supervision." Perhaps in His personal supervision of me, God had brought us to this place in order to demonstrate that, after all, Maria was right and He wanted me to be a Christian.

We tried to hold hands, but the early afternoon heat made our palms sweat and we had to let go. The rest of the way we went side by side in silence.

Maria had a brother living in the San Fernando Valley, so after we got back to the hotel she left me alone to go visit him. Sitting with my legs crossed in the middle of a bed at the Bel Age Hotel, I felt a premonition take shape that something awful—whether in the sense of awe inspiring or simply dreadful—was about to happen.

A year earlier, in bed in my apartment Washington, I had expected an apparition of Jesus to appear in the window. Now I expected something less cinematic: a surge of feeling, perhaps, that would evidently be a message from God, like the single great heaving sob of emotion suddenly released I had sometimes experienced in dreams. We have all heard Christian testimonies of spiritual rebirth. In *The Varieties of Religious Experience*, William James begins his chapters on conversion with a typical instance: the first-person account of a man's sudden experience of the Holy Spirit. One night in November 1829, Stephen Bradley of Connecticut was lying in bed when his heart began to beat very rapidly. Within minutes he was overwhelmed by what he took to be the sensation of God's love and grace, causing his heart to feel "as if it would burst." He groaned so loudly that he woke his brother, sleeping in the next room, who knocked on the door and asked him "if I had got the toothache." Bradley sensed that angels were hovering over his bed.

Curiously, like Stephen Bradley, I felt particularly vulnerable to the possibility of such an experience when I was in or on a bed. Or maybe not so curiously: Jewish prayer refers to the bed as a place of trial, and not only because of the sensual temptations that we customarily succumb to there. The siddur includes an order of prayers to be read before going to sleep at night in which one asks for protection in the tribulatory experience of being "upon the bed" overnight. A line from Psalm 4 is repeated three times, as a kind of amulet: "Tremble and sin not. Reflect in your hearts while on your beds, and be utterly silent." In a typical twenty-four-hour period, bedtime is when we are most free to set the mind on ultimate questions. I have struggled more intensively with my soul while on my bed than I have in any synagogue.

In my hands was a Catholic apologetic book by François Mauriac that Maria had given me. I reflected in my heart. I was utterly silent. The dread of betrayal washed over me.

As I had on that night in Washington, I spoke to God. Balancing on the edge of treason, I whispered to Him: "Forgive me, Lord, forgive me. I don't know what you want. Do you want me to be a Christian? How can I learn Your Will? Christians say that their God reveals Himself only to those who open themselves to Him first. So forgive me if I'm wrong to say this: I open myself to Jesus. I open myself to Jesus."

Have you ever walked down a deserted city street at night and seen in the distance the shapes of strangers walking in your direction, too close to avoid but too far to identify as either marauders or harmless pedestrians? It was your fate approaching you then as it was my fate approaching me now. "I open myself to Jesus," I said again.

And nothing happened.

I continued to sit on the bed. Five minutes went by. Ten. Fifteen.

Still, nothing happened. My heart did not race. I was not filled with the sudden knowledge of God's grace and love. I did not sense that angels hovered over the bed.

Something, however, did change in me. I knew then, with more certainty than at any moment since Maria and I had begun discussing what God wanted of us, that I was going to remain a Jew. After a while, I got up off the bed. It was over.

————

AFTER NOTHING HAPPENED TO ME that afternoon, it became increasingly apparent that my time with Maria must draw to a close. The following day we visited my parents and paid a call to Rabbi Dinnerstein for premarriage counseling. He said he didn't himself perform intermarriages, but he recommended that we read a book written by a Jew and a Christian who had gotten married and felt that mixed matrimony could work very well. "So okay," said Rabbi Dinnerstein, cracking a wry grin, "you're both blond. You look alike. That helps!" Afterward we drove south to

Anaheim and spent the rest of the day at Disneyland. "We had a great time," Maria remembered later, "because there's no religion at Disneyland."

The final blow was delivered by a Jesuit at the Church of St. Ignatius Loyola on Park Avenue. We had misunderstood Richard Neuhaus. The Jesuit showed Maria a copy of the certificate she would have to sign to be married in the Catholic Church to a non-Catholic. The certificate was a contract in which the Catholic partner promises to baptize her children and make every effort to raise them as Catholics, something I had already told Maria I could never accept. Shortly afterward, we separated for the last time. Our despair at each other's thick-headedness was conveyed by our last conversation as a couple. I was in Los Angeles on another junket and called Maria from my hotel room, which was bleakly generic in the manner of so many Los Angeles interiors. Maria didn't even come close to crying. "I hope you find a Catholic husband to marry," I told her, "because that's mainly what it seems you want." After hanging up, I lay on my back and stared at the ceiling for a long while.

Within two years Maria fell in love again and was married to a sturdy, gentle-hearted Catholic man. At this writing she is the mother of two impossibly cute Catholic children, a baby named Anna and a toddler named James, with more surely to follow. By coincidence we work in the same building, and I see her and the children as they come and go. Now and then we drop by each other's offices and talk good-naturedly. When that happens, if I am honest, I have to admit that despite her wedding ring, my old feelings for Maria seem to float over the two of us like a ghost or an angel. I can see it; can she?

Just before Anna was born, Maria, James, and I had lunch in a kosher Chinese restaurant around the corner. James, half of whom could have been my son, plainly adores his mother and clings to her. I thought about how heartbroken he will be, displaced forever from his rightful spot at the center of Maria's sweet attention, when his little brother or sister arrives. James, I thought, I know how you feel.

# Chapter 10

# BACK TO BATH

There is a logic internal to Judaism of which many Jews are unaware. A friend told me recently about the progress he and his wife have made toward Torah observance. They eat a Sabbath evening meal together, avoid mixing milk with meat, on Saturday try not to do work relevant to their jobs, have found a Conservative shul they like, are learning to pray, and speak with growing certainty of their desire to keep a traditional home when they have children.

"But," Edward tells me confidently, "I'm sure we'll never be Orthodox. I like good nonkosher wine and nonkosher cheese too much for that!"

Of course, as I see it, whatever progress he makes is a wonderful thing. Still, when he says there is a limit to the progress he can make I have to bite my tongue. I am tempted to tell him what has become obvious to me after meeting many *ba'alei teshuvah* and converts: once a Jew has accepted the more basic premises of Torah, especially the fundamental idea that God imposes obligations on Jews who wish to come closer to Him, it is as if he has climbed onto the bottom step of an upward-bound escalator. The escalator proceeds at a gentle pace; but after a while, to get off it or reverse your direction requires more determination than to stay on and be led by the power of the unseen engine under your feet. I am pretty confident that within five or ten years, Edward will have decided kosher wine can be tasty enough and that he will have no unkosher cheese in his refrigerator. It's in the nature of the way a Jew is drawn to Torah—all of Torah.

Even the most seemingly archaic or (to the modern sensibility) offensive Torah commandments eventually come to seem logical and beautiful. Take, for instance, the law of "family purity," namely the prohibition against sexual intercourse during a woman's menstrual period and for a week afterward. This alarmed me when I first heard about it, since it means, in marriage, abstaining from sex for almost half of every month. It doesn't help matters that English translations of the biblical texts from which the relevant laws are extracted typically describe the menstruant as being "contaminated" or "unclean"—an affront to feminists and nonfeminists alike. Fortunately, though I'm still single, I hear from *ba'alei teshuvah* who are married that family purity is a gift to marriage, once you have come to understand it, as almost all succeed in doing. And it is worth understanding.

To begin with, the Hebrew term translated as "contaminated" or "unclean" (*t'mayah*) is in fact untranslatable. Those two English words may reflect misogyny, but if so, it is the misogyny of the translators, not of the Author of the Hebrew. The taboo itself has a primitive ring, but only when thought about outside of its biblical context. The Book of Leviticus deals extensively with ritual "contamination," and the concept affects men as well as women. When the Temple in Jerusalem stood, a man was rendered "unclean" and thus disqualified from entering the Temple if, for example, he had experienced a nocturnal emission. The point is not to stigmatize him, but to render a crucial distinction. The emission of blood in the case of a menstruant and of semen in the case of a man who has had a nocturnal emission indicates the loss of potential life: the woman's egg that passed out of her body, the man's sperm that met its fate on the inside of his pajama bottom. To put it as simply as possible, Torah wishes to draw a bright, hot line dividing life from death. In sex, man and woman join with God to create the potential of life. In the sacrificial services of the Temple, human life was sanctified and cleansed of sin by the taking of animal life (as I attempted to explain in chapter 7). When the potential for life has been negated, it is time to withdraw temporarily from the activities and places where life is created and sanctified. Mixing sex with death is one of the hallmarks of moral corruption, from which Torah seeks to protect us. (That in the 1980s and 1990s sex was so intimately associated with a deadly disease is surely a token that something in American sexual culture needed urgently to be reflected on, for the purpose of repentance.) The same mystical notion is expressed in the prohibition against mixing milk (the ultimate beverage of life) with meat (a dead animal).

At a more utilitarian level, married couples who practice family purity report that it does wonders for their sex lives. One of the curses of a long marriage is sexual boredom, and I can confirm myself that even in a relatively short sexual relationship outside of marriage the constant availability of one's partner eventually makes sex a bit humdrum. When a couple endures separation from each other for almost half of each month, they long for reunion, and the night they come together is like a honeymoon reenacted twelve times a year.

Yet all this makes the return of a Jew to Torah sound a lot easier than it is. An opinion diffused throughout our culture holds that formerly secular people accept this or that religious faith because it resolves all their dilemmas, providing simple answers to the disturbing questions posed by modern existence. Not in the case of Judaism, it doesn't. When a Jew or gentile embraces Torah, that's when some of his troubles really begin.

He will achieve clarity and peace later on. I wish, in the last days of my relationship with Maria and after, I had known that.

In the spring of 1991 I mainly, desperately, wanted to be soothed. I wanted to know that in breaking with Maria, I had made the right decision. And I wanted to know, now that I had turned my back on Christianity, what I should do next. I decided to seek out the help of rabbis.

At Passover, a storm complete with twisters bearing down on me from the north, I drove Interstate 95 to Richmond, Virginia, to see David Novak. A Conservative-ordained rabbi who had abandoned the movement to join a new, more traditional breakaway group, he wrote for some of the politically conservative magazines I read. So I felt he would understand me, and he did.

On the subject of intermarriage, Rabbi Novak confirmed what I already suspected: that Maria and I, as a Catholic and Jew, would probably never find a community of Jews who were serious about Judaism but who at the same time would accept and welcome us as they would a Jew married to a Jew. This is the reason that Jews serious about Judaism who marry Christians serious about Christianity rarely produce children who will persist in any real commitment to Judaism. It doesn't take a village, but it does take an authentic Jewish community, to raise a Jewish child.

However, what I really hoped Rabbi Novak could give me was a way to understand my lingering doubts about the manner in which Maria and I had tried to resolve our religious differences. It has been noted wryly that the only thing all American Jews unanimously believe is that Jesus wasn't the Messiah. To that article of negative faith I needed to add a structure of positive belief. I knew what idea did *not* follow organically from the statements of the Hebrew prophets; but what ideas *did* follow from them?

Over tea and leaven-free Passover cake, Rabbi Novak and I talked about all this. I was surprised and moved when he admitted that as a young man he himself had felt the pull of Christianity. He wondered if there might be something to its claims.

"How did you clear up your own questions about Judaism and Christianity?" I asked him.

"Have you read Abraham Joshua Heschel?" he said.

I hadn't.

"That's who you should read," said Rabbi Novak. "He wrote a lot of books, but the one you should start with is *God in Search of Man*. It's a statement of what he called his 'philosophy of Judaism.' I think that will help a lot."

I knew a little about Heschel, a worldly rabbi from a distinguished Hasidic family in Poland who ended up teaching philosophy and mysticism at the Jewish Theological Seminary. He had won fame in his later years for marching arm in arm with Martin Luther King. Despite the justice of the cause, I harbored a suspicion that rabbis tend to get involved in liberal politics to the extent they find themselves without anything compelling to say about Judaism. But I trusted David Novak's judgment.

Soon afterward I picked up *God in Search of Man* in a bookstore in Dupont Circle. I did not read it again until several years later. When I did, I discovered that a number of the ways I typically explain to nonbelievers what Judaism means to me, expressions and ideas I thought I had come up with on my own, are in fact to be found in Heschel. I had absorbed them in such a way that I forgot I ever absorbed them at all. I would ask secular Jews, and still do, "Do you have an intuition that God *wants* something from us? I don't mean that you know through intuition exactly what it is he wants. But you know that it's something, right?" The question, straight out of Heschel, is among the deepest insights in a book containing many of them. Allow me to present a brief description of this amazing book.

Here is another of its insights: There is no need to prove that God "exists." (The word itself is wrong, since what God does transcends mere existence.) "Beyond our reasoning and beyond our believing," Heschel writes, "there is a *preconceptual* faculty that senses the glory, the presence, of the Divine. We do not perceive it. We have no knowledge; we only have awareness." Our awareness of the Lord is brought to the surface in moments of awe. At such times we are aware, in a heightened way, of the *createdness* of the universe. Even the most cynical among us have had moments like that, on viewing, for instance, the Pacific Ocean or the Rocky Mountains. *"The beginning of awe is wonder,"* writes Heschel, *"and the beginning of wisdom is awe."* The Bible doesn't bother to try proving God's existence, any more than you and I would try to prove to each other that *we* exist. Biblical man sensed God all around him. We would, too, except that our faculty of sensing the Divine is suppressed by the education in secularism and doubt we receive as children.

Yet in our ignorance we still dimly perceive two facts: first, that God lives; and second, that He wants something from us: "The soul is endowed with a sense of indebtedness," says Heschel. "In spite of our pride, in spite of our acquisitiveness, we are driven by an awareness that something is asked of us; that we are asked to wonder, to revere, to think and to live in a way that is compatible with the grandeur and mystery of living. . . . The awareness of being asked is easily repressed, for it is an echo of the intimation that is small and still. It will not, however, remain forever subdued. The day comes when the still small intimation becomes 'like the wind and storm, fulfilling His word' (Psalm 148:8)."

The Bible informs us that our debt to God can be paid through the service of the heart, which is achieved through the service of our bodies. That is, through the performance of mitzvot. How are we to discover the true content of God's demands? Heschel regards as absurd the notion that He could form creatures capable of understanding His Will and yet not reveal it to them. Some modern men assert that all pertinent aspects of the Divine Will can be known by any individual through his own effort—via meditation or other types of deep thinking. Hence the phenomenon of people who say, in all seriousness, "I have my own religion."

God does reveal Himself to individuals, often at apparently mundane junctures in our lives (like on the bed of a hotel room). But what is revealed is almost always fragmentary, obscure, subject to misunderstanding. As Heschel writes, these "moments of insight are not experienced with sufficient intensity by all men. Those sparks are powerful enough to light up a soul, but not enough to illumine the world. . . . In moments of insight God addresses himself to a single soul. Has He never addressed the world, a people, or a community? Has He left Himself without a trace in history for those who do not have the strength to seek Him constantly?" To suppose that He never did speak to the world or to a people boggles the mind more than to suppose that He does regularly commune with individuals.

The Hebrew prophets, from Abraham through Moses onward, made the audacious claim that God had spoken through them. And Heschel makes a further claim, also audacious, which is that we must believe them. "It may seem easy," he says, "to play with the idea that the Bible is a book like many other books, or that the story of Sinai is a fairy tale," as enlightened opinion encourages us to do. "But consider what such denial implies. If Moses and Isaiah have failed to find out what the will of God is, who will? If God is not found in the Bible, where should we seek Him?"

Heschel was speaking directly to me here. I had sought the Lord myself in secular philosophy, in liberal and non-Jewish religions, and had failed to discover Him in any of those places. In the course of my own evolution as a Jew I argued with myself continually, employing reason to guide my faith, and tried to make certain at each stage that my thinking about God was at least more intellectually coherent than it had been at the stage I had most recently passed through. The fact that I developed faith in the Hebrew Bible may, to hard-core secularists, make me sound like a crazed premodern religious extremist. But I'm not premodern, and I don't think I'm crazy. Like them, I just wanted to know what was true.

And despite its mysteries, the faith offered by the Hebrew Bible has intellectual coherence on its side in ways that secularism does not. Secularists and religious people alike habitually speak of transcendent moral truths—ideas about what is right and wrong, which are true whether we want them to be or not. But truths like that require a basis that transcends human existence, and a secular worldview offers none. The Bible calls that basis "God." If there is no transcendent being in the universe to establish standards for our behavior, then, as Dostoyevsky's Ivan Karamazov observed, "everything is permitted."

Not only do we need God to save us from the chaos of "everything is permitted." We can know Him. And that is the real goal of Torah observance.

Three verses in the Bible, Heschel teaches, suggest three paths that lead to God. They are 1) worship: "Lift up your eyes on high and see, Who created these?" (Isaiah 40:26); 2) learning: "I am the Lord your God" (Exodus 20:2); and 3) action: "We shall do and we shall hear" (Exodus 24:7). But the three in fact "are one, and we must go all three ways to reach the one destination. For this is what Israel discovered: the God of nature is the God of history, and the way to know Him is to do His will."

The ultimate purpose of Torah observance is not, then—as has long been derisively said—to "buy" eternal salvation as one would buy a vacation in Acapulco. When I hear that old charge against Judaism, I think of Dave Tendler, a boy a year ahead of me at Miraleste High. Students there would take weekend trips to Baja California. One weekend Dave hit on what he took to be an ingenious commercial scheme. He would prowl the junk markets of Tijuana, load up his car with thirty-pound onyx chess sets of the kind found everywhere in that city's tourist areas, and sell them at a marked-up price back home. Unfortunately Dave found that the effort needed to lug the chess sets to Palos Verdes, then to bug his parents' friends into buying them from him, could never be compensated by the slim profit he earned. Similarly, it's hard to see what truly desirable afterlife could be purchased through a barter system of the kind attributed to Jews by some of their critics. Imagine a God who would concern Himself merely with selling salvation. One pictures Him chewing on a cigar stub and ringing up our deeds on a cosmic cash register. After a lifetime of fulfilling the commandments, it wouldn't be much of a reward to spend eternity with a God like that.

Yes, Maimonides regards it as a fundamental principle of Jewish faith that, depending on what we do on earth, we can expect reward or punishment, which God will administer in this life or the next. But that is not the end of the story. Rather, says Heschel, "God asks for the heart, and we must spell our answer in terms of deeds." In the Garden of Eden, He called out to the first humans:

"Where are you?" He calls out to us, too. "All of human history as described in the Bible may be summarized in one phrase: *God is in search of man.* Faith in God is a response to God's question. . . . To strengthen our alertness [to His call], to refine our appreciation of the mystery is the meaning of worship and observance."

Some Jews insist they can achieve this result by selectively performing the commandments, or shuffling and amending them, thus inventing a new regimen more in keeping with modern assumptions about spirituality, gender roles, contemporary lifestyles, and so on. But this is breathtaking self-confidence. If the mitzvot really do what they claim to do, allowing us to approach God, then we must assume 1) that they are not founded on a lie; 2) that therefore they are what they claim to be—a product of the Divine Spirit; and 3) that the directions God has given for their use are sound. Any human who says he can legitimately edit these directions says, in effect, that he knows better than God.

---

WHEN I HAD READ HESCHEL, the next step seemed obvious. In several of the respects that define the plainest minimum of what Orthodox Jews look for in recognizing another Jew as Orthodox—Sabbath and festival observance, keeping kosher, daily prayer, tefillin—I was already more or less Orthodox. One day after work I attended the evening service at the Georgetown Synagogue and asked Rabbi Freundel if I could talk to him privately. An imposing man with a goatee who avoids speaking more words than necessary, Barry Freundel didn't seem like an entirely user-friendly rabbi. But sitting upstairs in the main sanctuary, with several obviously and personally difficult subjects before us, he proved to be a very kind and sympathetic listener. The saga of Maria came out. So did my non-Jewish lineage and what I had done to make myself a Jew.

He told me that conversions performed by Conservative rabbis were not generally regarded as valid. Given the perfunctoriness of my own Conservative conversion, I had suspected that. The members of a rabbinic court must be valid legal witnesses, meaning

among other things that they must be observant of the commandments. Many Conservative rabbis are not. And the convert himself
must be committed in the long run to being fully observant, which
most new Conservative converts are not. I told Rabbi Freundel I
felt certain I wanted to be accepted unambiguously as a Jew.

He said he performed conversions with two colleagues at a *mikvah* in Silver Spring, just over the border between Washington and
Maryland. I asked what most of the converts he instructed were
like. "Oh," he said, "they come from all sorts of backgrounds.
Some grew up in a Jewish home, and their father was Jewish but
their mother wasn't. If I had to identify the sort of convert I encounter most frequently, it would be a woman who is the daughter
of a Christian clergyman, usually an evangelical minister. She's a
very religious person, but at some point the idea of Jesus as it's
taught in Christianity stopped making sense to her. She couldn't
buy the notion that Jesus was the Messiah and the Son of God."

He thought I was atypical in at least one way. "It sounds like
you've been searching for what you consider to be religious truth.
That's not the way it happens to most converts. For them—and
this goes for *ba'alei teshuvah* as well—it's more like what I would
call a 'paradigm shift.' One way or another they encounter Torah.
Sometimes it's through a Jewish boyfriend or girlfriend. They get
interested in the subject, start to do some reading, or attend synagogue services, out of curiosity. They find themselves attracted to
Judaism, at an emotional rather than an intellectual level. But
they ask themselves a question: 'How could I ever integrate the demands of this system, Torah, into my secular life, my secular commitments?' It's hard. It nags at them. Then time goes by, they
experiment with mitzvot. And before long, without realizing how
much they have changed, they find they are asking the exact
opposite question: 'To what extent can I integrate my secular commitments into my commitment to Torah?' Torah now takes prece-
dence. It's almost as if they woke up one morning and simply
found that the commitment was *there* where it had not been before. That's the paradigm shift."

He sent me away with a long list of books to study: Isidor Grun-

feld's *The Sabbath: A Guide to Its Understanding and Observance,*
Hayim Halevy Donin's *To Pray as a Jew,* A. Cohen's *Everyman's
Talmud,* Maurice Lamm's *The Jewish Way in Love and Marriage*
and *The Jewish Way in Death and Mourning,* Joseph Telushkin's
*Jewish Literacy,* Samson Raphael Hirsch's *Horeb: A Philosophy of
Jewish Laws and Observances,* and a few selected chapters of a
book called the *Kitzur Shulchan Aruch,* which is a code of Jewish
law for laymen by a nineteenth-century Hungarian rabbi named
Solomon Ganzfried.

Over the spring and summer I read books from the list and
added further details of Torah observance to my repertoire. I
made my kitchen kosher, which wasn't difficult since I had never
cooked or served meat of any kind in any of my pots or other uten-
sils. George Clay, a close friend who was a fellow convert, about a
year ahead of me in his progress as a Jew, had long been wearing
the fringed undershirt intended to allow a Jewish male to fulfill
the commandment of tzitzit, wearing fringes of precisely twisted
wool cord on a four-corned garment (Num. 15:37–41, Deut.
22:12). Their purpose is sublime: to remind the Jew of the invisible world of the Divine. A symbolic calculation of the meaning of
this odd-looking piece of underwear begins with adding the nu-
merological value of the Hebrew word *tzitzit,* 600, to the number
of knots and threads that dangle from its corners, 13—for a total
of 613, the number of commandmants. But as I saw the matter,
this garment plus a cotton T-shirt beneath it would add up to excessive sweating on Washington summer days. George promised
that I wouldn't sweat more than normal. When I started to wear
tzitzit that August I realized to my relief that he was right.

Among the many useful hints I received from George were
some pointers about what to expect just prior to my conversion and
on the day itself. His conversion had also been with Rabbi Freundel. He told me that shortly before the rabbi judged that George
was ready for the *mikvah,* he sat him down and posed a basic halachic question about the differences between work regulations
governing Shabbat and the festivals. (I knew the answer, which, to
put it as simply as possible, is that on festivals, such as Passover,

you can cook food and carry objects outside your home, whereas on Shabbat you can't.) George told me something else I was doubly grateful to know. When he had been in the *mikvah*, up to his chest in water, the rabbis had asked him to compose a paragraph on the spot articulating his belief in the truth and authority of the written and oral Torahs.

On October 29, a weekday morning after the morning service at Kesher Israel, I told Rabbi Freundel I was ready. "Good," he said. We sat down at a long table in the study hall downstairs from the sanctuary. Then, sounding casual, he said: "Let me ask you something. In terms of observance, what are the differences between Shabbat and Yom Tov [the festivals]?" I felt like the kid in fifth-period history class who's heard from his buddy in third period what the questions will be on today's pop quiz. We set the date of my conversion for December 10.

I had a month to think about how I would answer when Rabbi Freundel asked me to spontaneously compose a declaration of faith. My stomach clenched like a fist when I imagined myself in the ritual bath with the rabbis arranged before me: the idea of saying anything to them that I didn't really believe filled me with dread. In a sense, I would be standing before God. I thought I knew what Rabbi Freundel would want to hear me say. But I had taken aboard enough modern skepticism to doubt the equation of Torah with the exact expression of God's will.

I was troubled by those ideas in the tradition that I found alien, illogical, even brutal or cruel. Most obviously this would include the seemingly backward attitudes of the rabbis toward women and non-Jews. The sages, teaching in Palestine and Babylon two millennia ago, assume a complex of social relations deeply offensive to people who consider themselves modern and cosmopolitan. Men spent their evenings in the study hall. Women raised children at home. Young men were forbidden even to touch a young woman before marriage. Gentiles, with their strange religions, were kept at a safe distance by a high fence of cumbersome practices—starting with the regulations defining acceptable food, which discouraged table fellowship with those who don't drink kosher wine or eat kosher meat. I had agreed to follow these rules, to the best of my ability, since I had reached the opinion that the rabbis were part of a chain of transmitted revelation that really had begun at Mt. Sinai. But where the rabbis conflict with modern opinion, I was susceptible to the view that it was the rabbis who had to prove themselves right.

The Talmud also bulges with statements that are not merely anachronistic, but just flat-out bizarre. I encountered these in anthologies with titles like *Legends from the Talmud and Midrash.* In these books, the items of rabbinic wisdom were presented with little or no commentary, as if the subject matter could be evaluated like an article in *The New York Times.* A typical example: One tractate of the Talmud contains a section on the interpretation of dreams. In the course of the discussion, a fourth-century C.E. sage called Rabbi Ze'era pipes up with the opinion, "A man who has gone seven days without a dream is called evil." Why? He doesn't say. It turns out that there is a commonsense explanation. The rabbis associate rising late in the morning with a lack of zeal to do God's will. As anyone can confirm by experimentation, we are most likely to remember dreams if we get out of bed immediately upon waking up, rather than lying around and pushing the snooze button on the alarm clock every seven minutes. Thus failing to remember one's dreams reflects a certain indolence, which is indeed a form of evil. But to anybody without a rabbi to help him understand, Ze'era's comment will seem to be nonsense.

What, then, would I tell Rabbi Freundel when he asked me if the Torah was true? The response I came up with says as much about the progress I had made in my thinking as it did about the progress I had yet to make.

The day of my conversion arrived, a cloudy winter morning. I arrived at the building in Silver Spring, a plain little white house in a neighborhood of plain little white houses, this one distinguished only by a homely sign outside lettered in Hebrew.

Rabbi Freundel and two colleagues sat on folding bridge chairs in what had been the diminutive living room. I sat opposite them in another bridge chair. The other two rabbis, from communities in Maryland, smiled in a businesslike way. Rabbi Freundel suggested that I explain how I had come to want to be a Jew. One of the rabbis asked questions to probe my familiarity with the details of Torah observance—for instance, about how it is possible to serve warm food on Shabbat if you can't cook. (The answer is that precooked food can be left on the stove Friday afternoon for use on Shabbat.) Another rabbi asked how I would educate my children. Earlier we had been talking about the ideology of Conservative Judaism, which I think is why I said, "Well of course I would send them to a Conservative day school."

For a couple of seconds they looked at me.

"I suppose," said one of the rabbis, "you mean an *Orthodox* day school."

I blushed and stammered, "Yes, yes, of course, of course, right, right. That's what I meant to say. An *Orthodox* school."

The conversation went on for about forty-five minutes. Here was the main difference between an Orthodox conversion and a Conservative one. These rabbis truly believed that when I came out of the *mikvah* I would be obliged, forever, to follow the way of Torah in every respect. When an infant is converted, his parents know that he will receive, at his entrance into adulthood as a bar mitzvah, the opportunity to renounce his obligations as a Jew and revert to the status of a righteous gentile. An adult who is converted will never have that opportunity. At my Conservative conversion, the rabbis had no strong reasons to believe that I would live up to the obligations they said they were helping me undertake. You can only conclude either that many Conservative rabbis cynically regard conversion as a piece of legal mumbo-jumbo, often useful as a fig leaf for intermarriage, allowing the rabbi to marry a gentile to a Jew without fearing the wrath of his board of directors—or that they haven't thought through the ramifications of it with enough seriousness.

At the end of the interview, we stood up and went into an adjacent room. What followed I knew well by this point. It would be my fourth circumcision—a record, surely. The *mohel*, a man in a black suit and a gray beard, was waiting for us with a black bag of the kind of doctors once carried on house calls. He took out the now familiar implement he would use to draw a drop of blood from the correct location, a metal tablike thing with a sharpened end, in a sterilized plastic jacket—used by doctors to take a blood sample from the end of your thumb or forefinger. I directed my gaze to an impersonal object, the tip of my shoe. *"Baruch attah Hashem,"* the *mohel* said quietly, *"Elokenu Melech ha'olam, asher kidishanu b'mitzvosav, v'tzivanu al ha'milah."* It was the third time I had heard these words said, or said them myself, over my body. I felt the pinching sensation of the metal tab as it cut me, followed by a light pressure as the *mohel* extracted a drop of blood. He cleaned the tiny cut with an alcohol pad.

I was left alone in the room, where I undressed, showered, and walked through a door next to the shower. There was the *mikvah*—an almost photographic duplicate of the facilities on West 78th Street in Manhattan, with pale salmon-colored tiles and a few steps leading down into a pool the size of a Jacuzzi.

The water was lukewarm as I climbed in. A moment later the rabbis entered. They didn't waste time.

"I'm going to ask you a few questions," Rabbi Freundel said, "at the end of which you will immerse yourself in the water of the *mikvah*. Are you ready?"

"Yes," I said. This was not a situation that encouraged cool, intelligent responses to probing inquiries. But these moments in our lives, difficult ones we would not think ourselves capable of carrying off with grace or ease, tend to carry us themselves the way ocean waves carry a ship along their surface. I was being carried. My heart didn't pound. I was calm.

Converting to a religion has certain things in common with getting married. You are entering a relationship that didn't legally exist before. The relationship will be permanent. It carries responsibilities. It is characterized by the deepest love between the parties being joined, husband and wife or human being and God. It will change your entire life. At Orthodox weddings, people whoop and shout for joy. A moment before I was to become a Jew, I didn't sense any whoops or shouts welling up in my chest.

But that made sense. After all, if I was ever to be authentically a Jew, it would mean that my soul had stood at Sinai and that, therefore, I had always been a Jew. "Becoming a Jew" is like never having seen your birth certificate before and then receiving a copy of it in the mail from the Department of Vital Statistics. You knew that you had been born. Now here comes the State of California to tell you, in an official way, the same thing. Yet there is a certain awe in holding the document, with its photocopied image of the diminutive, inked impression of your infant footprint in one corner and in the other the signature of the obstetrician who, with that same hand, pulled you from your mother's womb.

"You know," Rabbi Freundel began, "that Jews the world over are subject to persecution and to anti-Semitism that sometimes can be violent. Why would you choose to subject yourself and your potential descendants to that sort of life?"

The answer came to me as if I had prepared it ahead of time. "Since I began to learn about Judaism," I said, "I've felt that there was a sort of momentum, independent of me, that was leading me to join the Jewish people. I've never really worried about being persecuted, partly because I don't happen to know any Jews who are being persecuted, but also because I don't feel like I've got a lot of choice in the matter. What I mean is that it's not so much that *I've* chosen to link my fate with the fate of the Jews, but that God has chosen that for me."

"You know," he continued, "that before you came here you were not obliged to follow the dictates of Halachah. Once you convert, that option is no longer open to you. How do you feel about accepting the laws of Torah with all its duties and restrictions?"

I wished I had a response for them that was different from the one I had given to his first question, but the answer that entered my mind was exactly the same. "Of course I'll miss some things about the way I used to live; but again I don't think I have a choice. I believe that God has chosen me to join the Jewish people."

Rabbi Freundel accepted this and moved on to his final question, the one George had told me to expect. "Please take a moment to compose a paragraph indicating your commitment to the God of Israel and to the Torah, both the written and the oral Torah, the Torah given to Moses and rabbinical law. After you've said that, gather your thoughts and immerse yourself under the waters of the *mikvah.*"

What should we make of the Torah's claims about itself? Where, exactly, does it come from? That is the problem that today, above all others, divides Jews into rival philosophical factions. Does the Torah come from God? From man? Or, like one of those supernatural beings in Greek mythology, born of a liaison between a god and a man or woman, is it partly divine and partly human? Is the Torah—oral and written—true, or not?

In his commentary on the passage from Deuteronomy I had read at my bar mitzvah, Rashi makes a profound comment that bears on this crucial subject. In God's name, Moses is commanding the Israelites that when they want to know what God would have them do in a given situation, one not explicitly addressed in the Torah, they should go "to the priests and Levites, and to the judge, that shall be in those days; and you shall inquire. . . . According to the law which they shall teach you, and according to the judgment which they shall tell you, you shall do; you shall not turn aside from the ruling which they shall declare to you, either to the right hand or to the left." We no longer have Levites or priests to guide us, but we do have rabbis, who draw on the tradition contained in the Mishnah, Talmud, and other rabbinic sources. We must obey the tradition, Rashi explains, even if the judge who parses it "tells you regarding the right that it is left, or regarding the left that it is right, and certainly so if he tells you regarding the right that it is right, and regarding the left that it is left."

But what if the judge or rabbi you have available to you does not seem to embody that tradition in the same way his predecessors might have done? It doesn't matter, Rashi says. He cites the Talmud: "Even if he is not like the other judges who were before him, you must listen to him." The reason is obvious when you think about it: "You have nothing but the judge who is in your days." However much a Jew may doubt the perfect authenticity of the religious authorities in his own time, and by extension the oral tradition that claims to interpret the Torah for us, and even the written Torah itself, he has no practical choice but to accept their authority. The alternative is sheer indeterminacy—a situation in which the individual, wishing to live in accordance with God's will but confronted with multiple and contradictory representations of that will, is left to his own devices in choosing among them. What happens in that situation is predicted in the third paragraph of the *Sh'ma:* the person who sets himself free of traditional authority will follow "after your heart and after your eyes after which you stray" (Numbers 15:39).

As I had prepared my response to the question I knew Rabbi Freundel would ask me, I reflected that Torah may not be *the* Truth, the whole Truth, about God's will. The oral Torah may include inauthentic material, along with the authentic understanding of the Pentateuch given to Moses by God at Sinai. The written Torah may include, but not be limited to, the document revealed at Sinai. On certain points, the rabbis could be wrong in their determinations of what God asks from us. But that tradition is all we have. It is all God has given us. It must be His will that we obey it.

With that in mind, I hit upon the word that would allow me to answer Rabbi Freundel's question truthfully, but in a way that would satisfy him. The word was "contain." The Torah tradition *contained* God's will, even if it wasn't on every point precisely identical with His will.

"I have come to believe," I told Rabbi Freundel and his colleagues that day, "that God wants something from the Jews, and that he wants the same thing from me. I believe that His will for us is contained in the written Torah, the oral Torah, and the rabbinic tradition. He chose the people Israel as the vehicle for His will."

I took a breath.

When you immerse yourself in a *mikvah*, the water must cover the whole surface of your body, just as a person's relationship with God should cover the entirety of his life, every aspect, no matter how trivial it seems. I ducked under the surface, spread my fingers wide to let the water in there, and lifted my feet from the tile floor, so as not to neglect their soles. For a moment I floated, my skin touched by nothing but the water.

Then I came up, a bit of *mikvah* water touching my lips and tongue. It tasted like the water from any bath you ever took. The rabbis were smiling warmly now. *"Mazel tov,"* they said. "Congratulations."

Once I had dried off, dressed, and met them in the living room of the little house, they congratulated me some more. I drove back to the newspaper, where I had a deadline to meet. I was satisfied and looked forward to beginning my life as an authenticated Jew. Because I was a Jew now.

Or was I?

# ALL IN THE FAMILY

few weeks after my appoint-
ment at the *mikvah* in Silver Spring I found in my mailbox a copy
of the conversion document. Rabbi Freundel and his colleagues
testified that "a gentile man, David Klinghoffer, came before us
and indicated his desire to accept the commandments and beliefs
of Israel, in the manner of converts who wish to enter beneath the
wings of God's presence." This gentile had been "circumcised and
entered a kosher *mikvah*, in our presence, for the sake of becoming
Jewish. . . . Therefore he is a son of Israel for all things and from
now on may his name be Dov Shalom son of Abraham our Father."

Dov Shalom was the Hebrew name my father and mother had
given me, in one of the few gestures they made to the fact that the
year I was born was in the middle of the hippie decade. *Shalom*
means "peace" while *Dov*, which means "Bear," was the name of
my mother's paternal grandfather. In translation I sound like an

activist with the American Indian movement: "Peace Bear." But the rabbis gave me a new patronymic, *ben Avraham Avinu*, or "son of Abraham our Father." That is the euphemism assigned to converts, whereas native-born Jews are called "son of" or "daughter of" whoever their actual father happens to be.

The designation is employed because in a sense the convert has no parents. Torah defines one's "father" and "mother" in strictly biological terms. Before joining the people Israel, someone like me will have had a gentile mother and father. However, once he becomes a Jew, his legal connections to that man and woman are permanently severed. Adoptive parents have a status closer to rabbis: guides and teachers to whom the child owes love, respect, and loyalty. Upon emerging from the *mikvah*, a convert becomes in effect an orphan, the child only of our Father Who is in Heaven.

This is difficult to write, for I will always feel that Paul and Carol Klinghoffer are my parents. Yet for a long while after converting to Judaism, I did indeed think of myself as a kind of orphan. And not just that: an outlander, an alien, and a stranger.

————

THERE IS A WIDESPREAD NOTION one hears repeated that getting religion makes life easier for the newly faithful because, among other things, it provides a warm nest of fellow believers with whom to take shelter, in unity and love, against the cold, isolating winds of secularism. It certainly does this for many people. For others it mainly creates sources of strife and resentment where they hadn't been before. For still others, it does both. I count myself in the last category.

A significant proportion of *ba'alei teshuvah* meet with resistance from the friends and family members with whom they had previously shared their secularism. Parents complain when their grown children visit and refuse to eat food prepared in a nonkosher kitchen. They are hurt when their sons and daughters, who want to take the seder seriously, refuse to spend Passover with their mother and father. An unsubtle message is delivered that the parents of *ba'alei teshuvah* somehow failed in their role as Jewish educators. (The message is unfair since most secular parents never received such an education themselves.)

My own father accepted my evolution toward Orthodoxy with good humor and compassion. The resistance I experienced was mainly from other Jews. Religiously speaking, most Jews believe that they have no special responsibilities beyond being a good person and performing the occasional ritual. Jews like me disturb the peace.

Not long after my conversion, I moved back to New York City to become the literary editor at *National Review*. My colleagues at the office, many of them Catholic, were mildly curious about the skullcap I now wore. I fielded their occasional inquiries about what Jews do on the Sabbath or why I ordered fruit or raw vegetables when we went out for lunch at Paone's. In general, however, they simply accepted my new religious views, always making accommodations so that I could take off work for Jewish festivals and leave the office in time for Shabbat.

My secular Jewish friends from Brown accepted my Orthodoxy less cheerfully. Alex Abrams, a lawyer, complained about kosher restaurants. When we ate out together, he wrinkled his nose at the food and noted that the prices seemed higher than what you would pay for comparable nonkosher food. "Okay," he would say with a sigh when the check arrived, "let's see what the rabbi tax comes out to here."

"Don't you think," he asked, "that you should consider what your motivations might be in taking all this stuff on? I mean, you say you think it's what God wants you to do, eat in these expensive restaurants where the food's not even good. But is that really what's driving you?" He suggested it might be helpful to discuss the matter with a psychotherapist.

Ross Levin, another classmate, visited my synagogue a couple of times and paid special attention to the clothing worn by the men. A partisan of traditional American tailoring, he asked: "Did you ever notice they all wear suits without a vent in the back? You know, that sort of faux European style. I look at them and say, 'That's disgusting!' Don't you?" We were jogging in Central Park when he brought this up, and he wouldn't let go of it until I asked him what *his* motivations were in objecting so forcefully to the style these men preferred in their suit jackets. "I just think it's repulsive," he said.

A gay friend, Matt Gilman, didn't bother to hide his unease behind complaints about food or clothing. One night he called me from Philadelphia, where he was a law student at Penn, and insisted that I defend the whole concept of "organized religion." One weekend I went down to Philadelphia for a wedding. It wasn't a kosher wedding, so I ate fruit for dinner along with too much Scotch. When I got back to Matt's apartment, he leapt at a remark I had made earlier about gay pop culture—that there is something sterile about it—and proceeded to tell me what *he* had been thinking about *me*. "I don't know why you hang out with me, David. You're so narrow-minded and intolerant. You don't have any compassion. Basically, I think you're a bad person." The next morning the combination of pineapple, melon, and whiskey caught up with me in a violent way. Matt compassionately studied his law books and ignored me as, on shaking legs, I made repeated trips to the bathroom. I thought I was surely about to meet the Lord Himself and find out what a bad person I really was. Matt had no Pepto-Bismol in the house and, on this iron-cold winter morning, didn't offer to go out and buy some. As soon as I thought I could stand the cab ride to the airport without throwing up, I left. We haven't spoken since.

Still, on the whole, the secular world makes it easy to be an Orthodox Jew. Except by my own evil impulse, I have never been kept from doing what Torah requires, or even seriously discouraged from it. I have been caused much more anxiety by Orthodoxy itself. By that I mean that I understood Judaism in two ways that it took me years to see were not true to the spirit of Torah.

One of them was introduced into my consciousness by a book I should never have read more of than Rabbi Freundel prescribed. The *Kitzur Shulchan Aruch,* or *Code of Jewish Law,* is a popular item in Judaica stores, frequently given to nonobservant bar mitzvah boys and bat mitzvah girls by religiously uneducated friends

and relatives. It is not to be confused with the authoritative sixteenth-century digest of Jewish observance, the *Shulchan Aruch.*
*Kitzur* means "short" or "brief," and this nineteenth-century
work, by Solomon Ganzfried, an ultra-Orthodox Hungarian rabbi,
seeks to lay out the obligations of a Jew in a manner understand-
able by a layman.

Rabbi Freundel recommended a couple of passages dealing
with the blessings we say before and after eating various kinds of
food. Unfortunately I read beyond these sections. There is a reason
that Judaism strongly advocates learning from a master or teacher
rather than from a book. That reason is summarized by an inspec-
tion of this book. It presents Judaism the way the Manhattan
White Pages presents New York City. In a phone book, the Metro-
politan Museum of Art can be found side by side with Metropoli-
tan Dry Cleaners, both important, but not equally so. In this
volume, with its phone book idea of Judaism, long before learning
about such matters as charity and avoiding gossip, the reader is
warned always to tie his left shoelace before his right; also that "a
man should be careful not to pass between two women, two dogs,
or two swine"; that "he who defers easing himself is guilty of vi-
olating a biblical commandment." "Moral Laws" get 1 chapter
out of 221, and so does "How to Shampoo the Hair" (for women
about to enter the *mikvah* after the monthly period of sexual separation). Rabbi Ganzfried gives no hints as to what obligations a
*ba'al teshuvah* should undertake before going on to more rarefied
ones, or what any of these tossed-together rules and regulations
actually *mean.* Many years later I heard an Orthodox rabbi say,
half in jest, that this book is suited to be used only as a doorstop.

Rabbi Ganzfried's work illustrates why it is incorrect (though
difficult to avoid) to translate the word "Halachah" as Jewish
"law." Everything in that book has been drawn, sometimes word
for word, from classic rabbinic literature. But Rashi's comment on
Exodus 21:1, "Now these are the ordinances which you shall set
before them," is pertinent. Says Rashi: "The Holy One Blessed Be
He said to Moses: 'It should not enter your mind to say "I shall
teach [the Israelites] the chapter or the law two or three times,"

until it will be fluent in their mouths as it is worded [verbatim]; but I shall not trouble myself to make them understand the reason of the thing and its explanation.' Therefore it is stated 'which you shall set before them'—like a table which is set and prepared for eating before a person." Just as it is improper to set unprepared food before a diner, however fine the raw ingredients, it is wrong to set out words of the rabbis—for instance, from the Talmud—as if they were the rules of the road in a pamphlet from the Department of Motor Vehicles. Some Jewish "law" is indeed meant to be followed strictly and literally by all Jews. Other aspects of it are meant to provide a model of the Torah's worldview. To know the difference, which is a matter of oral Torah, you need to ask a rabbi who received that tradition from his own teachers.

To illustrate what I mean, consider the petition most siddurim include to be said by travelers, the Wayfarer's Prayer. It includes the line "May You send blessing in every work of our hands." As I once heard a rabbi say, the strong implication is that when a Jew goes on the road, it should be only for the purpose of work, in other words, commerce. From this perspective, a Torah Jew has no business traveling for the purpose of mere sight-seeing. When I heard that, my heart sank. I love sight-seeing. But, continued the rabbi, who happens to be an ardent amateur sailor, the point is not that Torah forbids travel for leisure or education the same way it forbids us to eat pork. Rather, that at the highest spiritual levels more can be learned about, for instance, the Egyptian Pyramids or the Grand Canyon from Torah than from actually viewing those monuments. So traveling to see such things may be a wasteful diversion from Torah study. All knowledge of heaven and earth, to the extent man can ever possess it, is contained in Torah. But that doesn't mean every, or perhaps any, living Jew can discover all that knowledge unaided simply by opening the Talmud. The Wayfarer's Prayer teaches the centrality of Torah study, not that a Jew must never travel except on business.

All the crazy-sounding rules cited in the *Kitzur Shulchan Aruch* fit this pattern. Some are not meant to be discussed at all by unlearned laymen except in conversation with their rabbis. A proper explanation could take hours and, in the case of the several instances previously cited, is either beyond the scope of this book or beyond the range of my still very modest comprehension of Torah. The same goes for the more shocking commandments issued to the Jewish people in the Pentateuch—like stoning adulterers or the commandment to commit genocide against the wicked (and fortunately now extinct) people of Canaan when the Jews entered that land after escaping Egypt. The Five Books of Moses are intended to be studied with a teacher, not browsed through like an airplane novel. Any Jew who is not an outstanding Torah scholar and lets himself be drawn into a discussion of such matters by a skeptical inquisitor is a fool.

In short, if you asked me if I follow all the Torah's "rules," the answer would certainly be no, not yet, but then I don't consider Torah merely a listing of rules. I would say that I hope, more and more, with each year to improve my observance of Torah and the obligations it imposes: not as I would understand those obligations from a simple reading of randomly selected pages by Rabbi Ganzfried, but instead as my rabbi explains them to me, in the order he thinks appropriate to my spiritual development. Of course while Torah laws never become invalid or outdated, at the present time many simply cannot be observed since there is no Temple or Sanhedrin (high court composed of properly ordained sages). For example, it is impossible to perform the sacrifices described so minutely in the Pentateuch. Those circumstances will change, the prophets assure us, when the Messiah appears.

So you begin to see why it's a shame that so many children get the *Kitzur Shulchan Aruch* for a bar or bat mitzvah gift. In phone book Judaism, the concept of a loving relationship with God, developed through observance of the mitzvot, is barely acknowledged. In Orthodox neighborhoods like my own Upper West Side of Manhattan, you often meet phone book Jews. They discuss the rules endlessly, each wishing to be seen as stricter in his observance of them than any of his friends. As far as I can tell, they do their Jewish duty largely to avoid the wrath of an angry God. In this spirit, Rabbi Ganzfried will frequently suggest the punishment one may receive for erring even in small matters. Memory loss, for example, results from such disparate mistakes as putting on two articles of clothing at once or drying your hands on your shirt.

If this isn't enough to turn anyone away from Torah, Rabbi Ganzfried's book is notable for its joyless, fearful vision of sexuality. A rabbi in the Talmud who had intercourse with his wife "with such awe and terror that it appeared as if a demon was forcing him to do it" is proposed as a role model. (Such attitudes can be found in rabbinic literature; but asceticism hardly constitutes the mainstream outlook. The latter urges marriage as a requisite to human fulfillment and is summarized in Maimonides's statement that a man should make love to his wife "in their joy.")

This way of presenting Torah works well for certain people who are not beset by strong temptations. In Judaism there is a concept of an inclination in every heart to do good and a competing inclination to do evil. I know Orthodox Jews who complain that their evil inclination makes them long for delectations on the order of nonkosher pizza. "When I pass a nonkosher pizza place and smell the aroma," a man once confessed to me, "I just have this overpowering desire to go in and order a slice! Luckily I've been able to resist the temptation." "Lucky" is right. How fortunate he is to be troubled by nothing more powerful than the smell of baking mozzarella. Surrounded by all the world's pleasures, a soul that longs above all for pepperoni is likely to be satisfied by a stripped-down Judaism offering only rules and no reasons or passion, faith, love, or transcendence.

I wanted the peace of mind that phone book Jews seem to have; but it eluded me. For a few months after I was converted to Judaism, I had a respite from crazy health fears. But especially after I returned to New York, not a city famous for calming the mind, my hypochondria would come and go. Sometimes I hardly thought of it. Other times I thought of it quite a lot: sensing the hint of a pain in my left arm, which, I worried, could be a sign of developing heart disease; feeling an odd sensation of fullness in my forehead and wondering if it meant my blood pressure had risen precipitously; counting my pulse in the subway and feeling it speed up when the train unaccountably stopped in the middle of a black tunnel and sat there for long minutes.

My equanimity was also disturbed by temptations that good taste urges me not to specify with too much explicitness. I will just say this: Before my conversion, I had had some success with women. After it, oddly, I seemed to have only greater success. And sex is like money: the more you get, the more you want.

Not every man would regard that as a problem, nor even every Orthodox Jewish man. In his memoir *The Search for God at Harvard*, Ari Goldman attempts to justify his dalliances as a young, unmarried Orthodox Jew on the Upper West Side. He cites a by now completely hackneyed passage from the Talmud: "If a man cannot banish sexual thoughts from his mind, he should put on dark clothes, go to another town, find a woman, and satisfy his lust." The real meaning of that passage, say the classical commentators on the Talmud, is that if a man goes to all that trouble, he may "temper his lust and withdraw from so sinful an act." In fact, Judaism strictly forbids sexual relations outside marriage. It also forbids anything that might lead in that direction, starting with kissing and holding hands and including even being alone in an apartment with a woman you're not married to.

While I brought halachic control to most every other part of my life, here I was tormented by the fact that order refused to emerge from chaos. When you are lying on your bed on the day of fasting and mournful introspection called Tishah b'Av, a humid summer day, trying so very hard to figure out how you will resist the temptation when you see your girlfriend in a few hours, and you don't see how you can possibly do this—that's torment. How many times have I promised myself, and at Yom Kippur promised God, that I would discipline myself? I have failed in that resolution much more frequently than I have succeeded.

This is a dilemma every *ba'al teshuvah* with fully oxygenated blood must face. If you grew up Orthodox, and as an unmarried young man never experienced the satisfaction of your lustful inclination, then waiting for sex until marriage may be a challenge, but probably not an excruciating one. It helps, too, if you marry young, as traditional Jews tend to do. But at my conversion I was a twenty-six-year-old product of the secular culture of modern America. The thought of waiting till I got married before I again achieved sexual release filled me with dread. What if didn't marry until I was thirty-six? Or forty-six?

There is no getting around the sinfulness of sexuality expressed outside of marriage. Torah regards sex, in its holy form, as an act of unselfish giving in which the couple give to each other not just pleasure, but the potential of life. Sex between unmarried people (like masturbation), where procreation is ruled out from the start, is fundamentally selfish. But the anxiety I felt at my failure to control myself was increased, along with my fears of phantom illnesses, by the fact that there were profound truths about Torah that I had not fully assimilated. I had absorbed more of Rabbi Ganzfried than I realized.

The view that sees Torah as merely a long list of rules holds out a false hope: that if a Jew like me can just check off each item on that list, assuring himself that he is in compliance with all them, he will have peace. It's not so easy, though. There is always some way in which a person's actions will not measure up to his ideals. The Christian apostle Paul, a Jew himself, rejected Judaism because in his experience full compliance with Torah was impossible: "I do not do the good I want," he wrote, "but the evil I do not want is what I do." God, he felt, must have revealed the Torah to the Jews merely to prove to the world that a man can't win salvation by following even a divinely revealed code of behavior. Thus some other mechanism for salvation must be required. You might say that Paul is the most famous victim of the "Torah as phone book" mentality.

But Paul wasn't the first Jew to recognize the near impossibility of remaining free of sin. In the Book of Ecclesiastes, King Solomon made the point almost a thousand years before Paul was born: "There is a not a righteous man upon earth that does good, and sins not." According to an opinion in the Talmud, the only biblical figures who completed their time on earth without sinning were Jacob's son Benjamin, Moses' father Amram, King David's father Jesse, and David's son Kileab. As Rabbi Alan Schwartz of New York has pointed out, the quality those four men share is that while they did not sin, they didn't do much else with their lives. All relatively passive individuals, they became famous for their relationships to great men.

Sin can be resisted at the cost of locking yourself away in a monastic cell. But God prefers that we struggle. The Passover Haggadah teaches this. Perplexingly, the Haggadah stresses that the ancestors of the Jews were idolaters. The father of Abraham made his living as a merchant in the idol trade. Why must we be confronted with this uncomfortable fact on the very night that celebrates the creation of the Jews as a people in communion with the Lord? The Haggadah reminds us that God, for Whom time doesn't exist in the same linear way it does for us, is interested not in where we *are* spiritually at any moment, but in where we are *going*. Spiritual turmoil, in which the soul does battle with itself, is a sign that even from a very great distance, we are approaching God.

On this point, Genesis 37 begins with an apparently innocuous verse from which Rashi draws a deep lesson: "Now Jacob was settled in the land where his father had sojourned, the land of Canaan." At this point in the biblical narrative it is just prior to the onset of the dreams Jacob's son Joseph will have of himself ruling over his brothers and parents. The dreams will bring the resentment of the brothers toward Joseph to a climax, and they will sell him into Egyptian slavery. Rashi comments that "Jacob wished to settle in peace, [whereupon] there sprang on him the troubles of Joseph. The righteous desire to dwell in peace; [but] the Holy One Blessed be He said, 'Is it not enough for the righteous, what is prepared for them in the World to Come, that they seek to settle in peace in this world?" The desire for peace, in a sense, is an offense against God. We all struggle with sin, and we must always struggle.

———

BUT THAT IDEA is difficult to fully assimilate. I am still trying to do so, and I didn't really begin until I consulted a rabbi on the subject.

Even given that life is a struggle, I was struggling too much. I realized this one brutally hot August afternoon in Manhattan. I was headed to the West Side YMCA after work for a swim. On a crowded subway platform under Times Square, the foggy heat seemed to choke me, and my heart began to race. I felt short of breath. Eventually the train came, and in a short time I had arrived at the Y. I thought that a half hour in the cold pool would make me feel better. After swimming laps, I took a cool shower and met a date to see a movie. In the frigid air-conditioned theater I began to shiver—and panicked a second time, frightened that I had got a chill, and who knew what that could lead to?

The next day I spoke by phone with Rabbi Daniel Lapin, whom I've mentioned already. He is a South African who settled in the United States and started a popular synagogue in Venice, California. Later he founded an educational institute, Toward Tradition, to make the case that political conservatism is really the application of Torah principles to the governing of a gentile democratic nation. Though he and his family now live in Seattle, we had become friendly. As much as any rabbi I know, Rabbi Lapin sees Torah as a teaching with implications for every aspect of our lives. Our conversations often focused on hopes or worries I had about my life: my career and ambitions, my relationships with women. He spoke from a deep fund of Torah knowledge and practical experience. At his shul in Venice, he and his wife had made a specialty of introducing single men to single women. More than a hundred of their matches had led to marriage. He is that kind of rabbi. His advice is invariably on target.

So the day after my panic attacks under Times Square and in the movie theater, I called him from my office. "Am I crazy?" I asked. "Or is God trying to kill me with anxiety?"

He listened sympathetically and then drove to the heart of the matter: "Your problem, David, isn't psychological. It's spiritual. You think of God as an irritable police officer who is interested only in cataloging your sins. What you've got to aim at is to think of God as a loving father, which is what He is." It may have been the first time I heard a rabbi say that.

A few weeks later I visited with the Lapin family for Shabbat at their home on woodsy Mercer Island, near Seattle. On Saturday afternoon the rabbi and I sat down to look at a passage in the Talmud's tractate Berachot. He thought it would be relevant to me. It dealt with faith.

In a story related there, Rabbi Hillel the Elder is returning from a journey. Having reached his hometown, he hears screams. You might have expected him to panic; perhaps his wife and children were in danger. In fact Hillel's response is a compact model of faith: "I trust that this is not in my house," he says simply. The passage proceeds to apply to him a verse from Psalm 112, "He shall not be afraid of evil tidings; his heart is steadfast, trusting in the Lord." The verse, it is explained, can be read forward or backward as a kind of if-then statement. In other words: If a person does not fear bad news, then that means he trusts in God. But also, if a person trusts in God, then he has no need to fear bad news.

The Torah principle at work here is one I have already discussed: Feelings follow action. "If you want to be free of fear," Rabbi Lapin told me, "you have to work at *acting* as if you had nothing to fear. If you want to have faith in God as your loving Father, you have to act as if you already have it. Faith itself will follow."

What did I do at the time that reflected my fear and lack of faith? Well, for instance, there was my love affair with the sphygmomanometer. "You should take that device and throw it in the trash," said Rabbi Lapin. And there was the string of psychotherapists I had gone to in pursuit of inner peace. "You've got to give that up," he said. There were other practical things I could do: like concentrating on certain prayers, especially the one said at the conclusion of Shabbat with its line from Isaiah, "Behold, God is my salvation, I shall trust and not fear." Once I had begun to absorb this idea in my life, it came as a liberation. I quit therapy, threw out the sphygmomanometer, and never regretted either, though naturally that was only a start. I didn't begin using my copy of the *Kitzur Shulchan Aruch* as a doorstop, but I learned to think of it from a more appropriate perspective. Very gradually the hypochondria began to recede.

THE OTHER WAY that I had misunderstood Judaism was also crystallized for me in a book. However, I had come across that book much earlier in my life; and its lesson was reinforced by many other cultural and religious influences.

This book could generally be found on a coffee table in a room in the house where I grew up, the room with the big television. It was called *Meet the Mishpachah*, and it is not the only book of its kind. Another one, published recently, is called *The Jewish 100*. Each book lists famous Jews or alleged Jews who have changed world history: Jesus, Christopher Columbus, Marx, Freud, Trotsky, Einstein, and so on, plus lesser lights such as William Shatner and Leonard Nimoy. The Jewish reader is invited to take pride in his own membership in this high-achieving *mishpachah*, or family.

What's important about books like this is the idea they represent about what it means to be a Jew. It means belonging to a tribe: far-flung and diverse yet, despite the passage of centuries and the awesome physical expanse of the Diaspora, still one big cozy family, linked forever by blood.

This idea permeates Jewish culture. My mother's mother, Anna Bernstein, knew all the secret identities of the Hollywood celebrities with gentile names who were really Jews. A friend of mine who works at the secular Jewish newspaper *The Forward* is a particularly enthusiastic tribal Jew. "Whenever some famous person's name comes up," he says, "and I know he's Jewish, I automatically say, 'Jewish.' William Shatner? Jewish. Paula Abdul? Jewish. It's gotten to the point where when I hear 'Jesus Christ,' I say, 'Jewish.'" For the tribal Jew what matters most is the physical reality of Jewishness. It is, you might say, the Jewish body: William Shatner's body, Paula Abdul's. Judaism is about blood.

Not all tribal Jews are secular Jews. There are Orthodox Jews for whom God and His Torah are mainly tribal possessions of the Jewish people. These are Jews like the religiously observant girl I dated some years ago who couldn't understand why any gentile would convert to Judaism since "Jewishness is something that's in your blood. How could anyone expect to 'become' Jewish?"—or like the Orthodox rabbi I once heard refer proudly to God as "our own *Rebboino shel Oilom.*" He was employing the Yiddish pronunciation of a Hebrew phrase meaning "Master of the Universe," as if the Lord created all the Jews in His universe but did not create the Japanese, the Italians, or the Ethiopians.

I'm afraid that in making this point, I will needlessly hurt the feelings of other Orthodox Jews. So let me clarify. When I speak of "tribal Jews" in the Orthodox community it would be more accurate, though less concise, to say that there is a minority—I stress *minority*—among Orthodox Jews who to a greater or lesser extent have internalized the tribalist impulse.

In the Orthodox community, I have met Jews in whom the light of Torah burns as brightly as I can imagine it doing in a human being. I have met many kind, sweet, brilliant, soulful, generous, polite, engaging Jews whose personal qualities would make me ashamed of my own except that it is in their nature to make everyone they meet feel uplifted and happy, calmed and inspired by the encounter. And I have met many others who, while less transcendent, are still people I like, even love and admire, whose examples I will be very happy if I can ever succeed in imitating. I'm not writing about any of them now.

There also exists an Orthodox subculture in which Judaism is understood as an affirmation of mere ethnicity. This affirmation happens only secondarily to include references to a divine being, along with extensive customs governing food, dress, and synagogue ritual. For these Jews, ethnicity and the tribe define the borders of what truly counts in Judaism and in the universe. These borders are seen as basically arbitrary. Yet the old tribal distinctions are guarded as fiercely and mindlessly as any African tribe ever defended the borders of its own scrap of savannah. Whether they reside in Borough Park, Brooklyn, or the Upper West Side of Manhattan, tribal Orthodox Jews in fact inhabit a large though physically discontinuous shtetl. They rarely venture outside.

The contingent of Orthodox Jews who inhabit this ethnic enclave seem entirely unaware of it. In the old European ghettos, the

Jews knew there was a world outside, because the world guarded the ghetto walls and kept the Jews in. Now that the capital of Orthodoxy is New York, in a country that makes life easier for its Jews than any country has done as long as the Jewish Diaspora has existed, we are free to ignore our gentile neighbors. Torah requires that a Jew seek the welfare of the country in which he resides. Yet far from showing an appropriate interest in the fate of our host nation, or much gratitude toward the country to which many of their refugee parents or grandparents owe their lives, the kind of Orthodox Jews I am describing think and act as if they didn't live in America at all. It's not happenstance that the two principal Orthodox organizations, the Orthodox Union and Agudath Israel, hold their conventions on Thanksgiving Day, as if there were no need to set aside a day to thank God for the privilege of living in America.

Often the kind of Jews I am writing about speak as if they were citizens not of the United States, but of Israel. Israeli politics is a preoccupation for them. When arguing about what the Israeli government should do in its ongoing confrontation with the Palestinians, they lapse into the first-person plural. "We," they will typically insist, must never give up this or that West Bank city or plot of land to the Palestinian Authority (though if "we" turn out to be wrong in "our" strategic calculations, Israelis will be the ones who die for the mistake, while American Jews read about it in newspapers).

The tribalist impulse encourages a uniformity of appearance, even outside the tribalist minority. You can spot some young modern-Orthodox men a block away. It is something about the choice of clothes—neat, preppy in a generic sort of way, often with small oval eyeglasses—and maybe even the expression on their faces that tip off the experienced observer. I will be on Broadway, see a youngish man approaching me, guess that he's wearing a yarmulke, most likely (in the "cool" modern-Orthodox style) with his name printed on it ("JOSHIE"). When he passes and I turn and look at the back of his head, 90 percent of the time I'm right.

Everyone in the tribe knows everyone else. At how many Shab-

bat tables have I sat with a group of tribalists, outraged by boredom, blood pressure inching upward, as a tableful of FFBs (*"Frum*
[religious] from Birth") endlessly updated each other on the latest
news about other FFB friends along the Atlantic seaboard? This
can go on for hours: "Yeah, Yitzie got his accounting degree. He's
doing very nicely." "Hey, Shimie and Faigie had a baby! They're
naming him Moishie!" This activity is called "Jewish geography."

For some, the importance of the tribe is so great that it eclipses
God. I have heard Jews, raised *frum* and still observant, say they
don't believe in God at all. Some claim to have reflected on the
Holocaust and reached the conclusion that no perfectly righteous
Lord of the Universe could have allowed that mass murder to take
place. Mainly, however, their unbelief is due to complacency. They
have simply quit thinking about God as a living Being. In their
hearts they have substituted, for the consciousness of Him, the
outward forms of Jewish observance.

Why do unbelieving *frum* Jews obey the Torah to the extent
they do? "Because I love the culture," they say. Or: "Because I love
the lifestyle." The "lifestyle" centers on socializing with other
members of the tribe, whether at shul or around the Shabbat table.
The synagogue in Los Angeles that I visited with Maria McFadden is not unique among Orthodox synagogues. Though it's the
noisiest shul I ever entered, it has competitors. For such people,
talking in shul and feasting on Shabbat and the festivals create a
cycle of schmoozing and gorging that for them is the whole meaning of the Jewish calendar.

A tribe is a group defined by a certain culture and a certain
bloodline. In the case of tribal-Orthodox Judaism, it is the *frum-
mie* culture of Long Island or Brooklyn accents, certain character-
istic *frum* grammatical errors (such as substituting "by" for "at"
as in "I spent Shabbas by Malkie's family"), adults called by
names affixed with the Yiddish diminutive "ie" (Moishie, Yitzie,
Dovie), yarmulkes with those names stitched into them, and talking rather than praying in shul—combined with the fact that all
these people are related by blood, or seem to be.

All Jews who return to Torah Judaism must face the challenge of reconciling themselves to Orthodox culture—to the fact that some Orthodox Jews cling to certain aggravating folkways, having nothing to do with Torah, from which they have no thought of departing. But I, sharing neither the culture nor the blood of the tribe, was burdened with an additional dilemma. You can join a culture if you want to. You can't dissolve blood.

I could tell myself that the fact I had become a convert meant, in some mystical sense, that my soul had been present at Mt. Sinai—and therefore, in that same mystical way I was a Jew as much as any tribal Jew. Yet Torah defines the Jewish people as a spiritual entity with a definite blood component. The Talmud uses a formulation that says a lot about how deeply that attitude runs. It is found in a passage in the tractate Sanhedrin on a topic whose importance you might think was purely academic: the question of which version of the text of the Pentateuch is authoritative for deciding issues of Halachah. Hebrew can be written with or without vowels. Is the authoritative text the one found in a Torah scroll, *without* vowels (called *masoret* in Hebrew), or is it the text as it is traditionally pronounced when read aloud, *with* vowels (called *mikra*)? Often a word can be read differently depending on which form is considered authentic—that is, in accordance with the meaning intended by God. In the passage, it is finally decided that *yesh em la'mikra:* literally, the *mikra* has an *em,* a mother. The *mikra* is authentic. In other words, authenticity is linked with the authentic entity having a mother.

From that perspective an orphaned Jew like me, without a mother, a Jewish mother, isn't really an authentic Jew. That definition of Jewishness can be transcended through the rituals of *mikvah* and circumcision, but blood remains at the foundation of Jewish peoplehood.

I was always aware of my blood. Perhaps when I felt compelled to measure the pace of my heartbeats or, via the sphygmomanometer, the pressure they exerted on the walls of my arteries, what I was really doing was measuring the power of the gentile blood that flowed in my body.

When I entered a synagogue on Friday night or Saturday morning, I felt a hundred pairs of eyes following me to my seat, noting the blondish color of my hair, the un-Jewish line of my nose, the shape of my face as a whole, which, when I looked at myself in the mirror, seemed to say nothing so clearly as "gentile." When I patronized a kosher restaurant it was the same, if not more so. At least at a synagogue people would be distracted by their prayers or by their conversations. At kosher restaurants the patrons seemed to be less interested in their food than, I thought, in observing that vaguely Scandinavian-looking stranger who obviously didn't belong in this setting. The knowledge that I was foreign stayed either just below or just above the level of my conscious awareness. At certain Shabbat tables, at the umpteenth round of Jewish geography, I found myself staring at a point on the opposite wall and thinking, What am I doing here? Having undergone four circumcisions in twenty-seven years, I was now, surely, definitely a Jew under the strictest definition of Halachah. But if Judaism was a tribe, I was still a foreigner, a gentile.

Or so I thought—until one night in 1993, in my Manhattan apartment, when I had a peculiar dream that put an idea in my head that hadn't been there before. And which commences the last, or anyway latest, phase of my evolution as a Jew.

# Chapter 12

# MOTHER LOVE AND THE LAW

*O*nce, before I gave up on psychotherapy, I consulted a therapist who had a fondness for making oracular pronouncements. At the end of our first session he told me that he felt just then the presence of a ghost. It was dark outside the huge windows of his SoHo office, and I had got through relating the little I knew about my birth parents. Dr. Lipschutz pointed his beard at me and said in a vaguely mystical voice, "David, I have to tell you I feel that your birth mother is in this room. She's with us now. I have a very strong feeling about that."

He didn't mean that he saw a vaporous lady in a white dress sitting on the edge of the antique red velvet analysis couch. He meant, and he was right, that I carried her in my soul the way I carried my adoptive parents, though in her case I wasn't aware of it. Dr. Lipschutz sensed that she was approaching the border of my awareness. Soon she would break out into real flesh-and-blood life.

A few months later I was asleep in my apartment when an image came to my dreaming mind. It was the man and woman who had conceived me. No one told me they were my birth parents, but in the manner of dreams that was just who they seemed to be. In reality it certainly was not them. They seemed be a couple of Russian peasants, old and heavyset. The woman had a dull-colored scarf on her head and a straw broom in her hand. The man wore ragged clothing and a cap suggestive of a nineteenth-century London chimney sweeper. They looked tired and oppressed.

The following afternoon I had an appointment with Dr. Lipschutz. As I lay on the red velvet couch and described the dream, I was struck by a realization. It came to me in a flash, and instantly I wanted nothing so much as to cut the session short and dash to a telephone. The realization was this: There was no reason I should not do a little detective work and find out who my birth mother really was. I could locate the woman who had given me her genes and satisfy a curiosity that had lain dormant for twenty-seven years but was now erupting like a volcano. As soon as I got off the couch, into the subway, and back to West End Avenue I would begin to do whatever it took. In becoming an Orthodox Jew, I had found my Creator. Now I would find my creator: Harriet Lund.

I wanted to avoid involving my father in the search, so I first tried several official routes. The law, however, is not on the side of adoptees searching for their birth parents. In its Vital Statistics Section, the California Department of Health Services had on file the version of my birth certificate showing the names of my birth parents. But for most purposes my home state regards such documents as permanently sealed. Other government and private institutions were equally unhelpful. The Kennedy Child Study Center, lately renamed the St. John's Child Study Center, could find no Harriet Lund in its employment records. A man at the Swedish consulate was surprised that I thought he might have a list of names and addresses of Swedish natives living in the Los Angeles area. My father had told me that Harriet had a master's degree in child psychology. Perhaps she had earned her degree at a local university. But the alumni offices at UCLA and USC had never heard of her. Maybe, then, she had gotten married to someone in California or been naturalized as a citizen. But applying to the Los Angeles County Clerk or the Immigration and Naturalization Service for a record of her hypothetical marriage or naturalization would take weeks. I had no patience for that.

So there was no choice but to involve my father. I broached the subject the way it is always smart to broach delicate subjects with one's father: as if the matter were only of vague or academic interest, no big deal. I called from the office and we spoke about this and that: his upcoming trip to Mexico, the air conditioner I intended to buy. Then I said, "By the way, Dad, I thought I might try looking for Harriet Lund. Just out of curiosity. Who knows, maybe she's got a medical problem I should know about. What did you say the name of that lawyer was who arranged the adoption?"

I got the reply I had hoped for. His seemingly unsurprised reaction was mild and helpful: "Hmm, I'm pretty sure his name was Tony Carsola. That's interesting. Let me know if you find anything out." He paused. "By the way, I remember one more thing about Harriet. She had a roommate, named Mary Jane Dearing, who I'm pretty sure was Carsola's secretary."

When you are conducting an inquiry like this, stray facts often turn out to be of key importance. The name Mary Jane Dearing was such a fact.

Anthony Carsola, whose office I found, thanks to directory assistance, on South Beverly Drive in Beverly Hills, was and is in the business of introducing unmarried pregnant women to likely adoptive parents. However, he is not in the business of arranging reunions between adoptees and birth mothers twenty-seven years later. He got on the phone to affirm that he didn't remember Harriet Lund and had no records he would be willing to search for free. But, he said, Mary Jane Dearing had indeed been his secretary. He provided the name of the law firm she had gone to work for after leaving his office.

Mary Jane Dearing didn't work there anymore, either, I soon learned, but directory assistance listed her in Playa Del Rey, a beach town south of Santa Monica.

I saw no advantage in playing coy with her. When she picked up the telephone, I said I was the son, born in 1965, of a woman named Harriet Lund. There was the sound of breath being sharply taken in. "Oh, my goodness! Oh, my goodness! Harriet's son!" Again I heard breath being taken in. "Oh, my Lord, my Lord! Harriet! Harriet's son!" Mary Jane Dearing was given to exclamations. When she had recovered from the shock, she told me that when Harriet first visited Anthony Carsola's office, Mary Jane overheard her saying she lived in a grim district of downtown Los Angeles. Likewise a single young woman (and still unmarried), Mary Jane spontaneously offered her a place in her own apartment in the civilized neighborhood around the L.A. Mormon Temple. "Oh," Mary Jane said, "Harriet was dear to me!"

The two had not lost track of each other until the early seventies, so Mary Jane's memories of Harriet were more ample than my father's. There is a particular sensation when you are listening to a gifted rabbi as he explains a passage of Torah, laying bare the information about God and man hidden in its squarish black letters. The sensation is of ancient doors being unlocked, revealing secrets that had been there, waiting patiently to be uncoded for millennia. It was that awesome sensation that I felt as Mary Jane told me—with many interruptions as she exclaimed out of her own sense of awe, "Oh! Oh! Harriet's son!"—what she knew.

"She was about twenty-eight years old when you were born. She had come to America from Stockholm, let's see, about four years earlier. She looked like Grace Kelly. She was a romantic type, but steadfast, a very poised and intelligent person. She read a lot. When she was pregnant with you, I remember she was reading some of Graham Greene's novels. I think her mother tried to get her to keep you, but we really didn't talk about it too much. I never met your birth father, but I think they worked together. She lived with me until you were born. I remember that day so very well. She said, 'Oh Mary, my water just broke!' As quickly as I could, I drove her to Santa Monica Hospital.

"That was October 1965, of course. In December Harriet went home to Sweden to live with her mother. Back then I had a little dog called Homer, and the three of us went to the airport together. Such a cute little dog. Oh, Homer and I missed Harriet. But she came back a year later and we spoke to each other occasionally after that, you know, exchanged Christmas cards. Harriet was a social worker, and eventually she married another social worker. His first name was Don, but I can't remember the last name. She had gone to work for him at Big Brothers here in Los Angeles, then they moved up north, I think, to San Jose or maybe Fresno. I haven't talked with her in, oh, it must be twenty years. Maybe she's still there, up north."

That night I couldn't bring myself to go to sleep until past two in the morning. According to directory assistance there was no one named Lund in either San Jose or Fresno, towns in northern and central California, respectively. In her address book, Mary Jane had found Harriet's mother's name, Karin Lund, and address in Stockholm. At five A.M. I got out of bed and called directory assistance for Stockholm. There was indeed a Karin Lund on Norr Mälarstrand, the name of the street Mary Jane had given me.

An American operator helped me place the call to—would it really be my biological grandmother? Karin Lund, I learned later, is among the most common of Swedish women's names. After a fruitless dialogue between herself and the elderly, unilingual Swedish woman who answered the phone, my operator was becoming frustrated. She complained to a Swedish counterpart who came on the line, "We're trying to make a phone call to Stockholm, but the family is speakin' Swedish," as if this were somehow a contradiction. "The name," my operator explained gruffly, "is L-U-N-D. D as in dog." After some two-way translating, it became clear that the elderly woman had no daughter named "Harriet," nor did she know anyone in America.

I then turned my attention back to California. The trick was to locate employees of the Big Brothers offices in San Jose and Fresno who had been with the group for twenty years. But I learned that in social work, job turnover is fairly rapid. No one at either Big Brothers location had been there more than ten years. Suddenly the trail went cold.

The notion of hiring a private detective crossed my mind. That would be expensive, but why be deterred by cost? After all, what was at stake was the opportunity to meet my own mother. My desire to find Harriet had become increasingly urgent. In spare moments I calculated how much money I would be willing to spend to do so: $500? Yes. $1,000? Sure. More? If necessary.

I didn't need to hire a detective, though, because it occurred to me a day or so later that *somebody* with Big Brothers must surely know someone else who worked elsewhere or was retired but who had worked at Big Brothers twenty years earlier. A couple of false leads led me, at last, to a name.

A woman at the Fresno branch told me that another woman called Donna Harper had once worked there. She had been with Big Brothers from the early seventies until the late eighties. My informant thought she now worked for the Council on Children and Youths in Oakhurst, California. A call to that organization was answered by someone who said Donna Harper had gone to work for the Madeira Unified School District. That turned out to be untrue, but in Madeira there was a listing for Donna Harper. That night I called and at last found a person who knew Harriet and was still in contact with her.

Donna Harper sounded mistrustful. "Yes, I knew Harriet when she worked for Big Brothers. I spoke to her a few months ago, actually. But who are you?" I told her everything. Though I wanted to protect Harriet's privacy, there didn't seem to be any other way to overcome Donna Harper's skepticism. "Well," she said, "Harriet lives in El Cajon, near San Diego, with her husband. He was the director of Big Brothers in Fresno when I was there. His name's Don Wilson. I think the best thing would be for me to call her, tell her you want to make contact with her, and give her your phone number. Then she can take it from there, if she wants to." I asked Donna Harper if Harriet and Don had any children together. They did not, she said.

When I feel that something momentous has just happened to me or is about to happen, I have a tendency to shiver across my chest. Sitting there with the telephone in my hand, I was shivering uncontrollably.

That was a Thursday in June 1993. The next day at the office, I got no work done as I waited at my desk for Harriet to call. She didn't.

Shabbat came in and I made no plans to eat Sabbath meals with anyone. If Harriet called, though I couldn't pick up the phone, I would hear her voice on the answering machine: my mother's voice, I thought in astonishment, in my ears for the first time since I was a fetus in her womb. I didn't even go to shul but prayed by myself in my living room. The twenty-five hours of Shabbat went by. Harriet didn't call.

Saturday night I made myself leave the apartment to see a Whoopi Goldberg film. It was about a young black woman who discovers that her mother, played by Miss Goldberg, became pregnant with her through an anonymous sperm donation from a white man. The young woman's birth father turns out to be Ted Danson.

Harriet didn't call Sunday, either. Finally, Monday night around ten o'clock, the phone rang. The woman who spoke on the other end had a noticeable Swedish accent and the quiet, sniffly voice of someone who has been crying. "David," she said, "this is Harriet Wilson." It was a good thing to be surprised by her call. If I had been the one placing the call, or if I had been expecting it at a certain time, my heart would have been beating so fast, I would barely have been able to speak. This way, Harriet was the one who sounded terrified.

What do you say the first time you speak to your mother? We are not prepared for such encounters when they come. She didn't seem to want to lead the conversation. In a friendly way I asked how she was, as if she were an aunt or cousin I hadn't talked to in a few years.

"I'm fine," she said. "I'm surprised, and very glad, to hear from you." Quickly it became clear that I was going to have to dispense with banalities and get down to asking her questions. I asked why she had given me up. Who my birth father was. What their relationship had been.

Her voice quavered as she enlarged on the story Mary Jane had told me. She had come to the United States, from Stockholm where she grew up, in 1963. Some of the facts I had heard about her from my father turned out to be imprecise. With a degree in social work from the University of Stockholm, she had found work not at the Kennedy Child Study Center, but at something called the Exceptional Children's Foundation. The latter trained "exceptional"—that is, retarded—teenagers to perform menial jobs. There she had briefly dated a stoic Kansan called Andrew H. Jones (she invariably included the middle initial), her supervisor on the job. An unprotected procreative act had resulted in—me.

An unmarried Swedish girlfriend of hers had got pregnant around the same time and gone back, in these pre–*Roe* v. *Wade* days, to Sweden, where they had ways of dealing with such situations. But, said Harriet, "I couldn't do that. I couldn't have an abortion. I just couldn't." She was twenty-seven years old, no helpless young girl, but the idea of raising a baby by herself seemed implausible. "I wasn't ready to be a mother. I felt that I would be incompetent. How could I take care of you?" When she told Andrew she was pregnant, initially he denied he was the father. When he at last admitted he was biologically responsible, he refused to accept any moral responsibility and would henceforth have nothing to do with Harriet. "He gave me the silent treatment. He wouldn't even take my calls." At that point Harriet contacted Anthony Carsola, who strong-armed Andrew into paying for her medical bills and arranged for Harriet to interview prospective birth parents. Thus she had met Paul and Carol Klinghoffer.

That all seemed straightforward enough, but certain angles on the story began to emerge immediately in this, which would turn out to be only our first of many, many conversations.

I assumed, for instance, that adoption itself was a fairly obvious, easy choice for a woman in Harriet's predicament. With a woman I dated years before this, I had a conversation of the type where the boyfriend tries to convince his girlfriend that even if, despite all precautions, she does get pregnant, everything will still be fine. "We'll just put the baby up for adoption," I said. When she countered that she could hardly imagine giving away her own baby, for a moment I could think of nothing to say. To me, adoption seemed painless. "After all," I reminded her, "I was adopted, and look how well things turned out."

Adoption was not easy for Harriet. It came out, gradually, that her terror had begun more or less as soon as she discovered that she was pregnant, with no man in her life she could turn to for love and protection. She was alone in a foreign land. The riots in Watts broke out during her pregnancy. At their height she first hid under a bed, then drove out to Lake Arrowhead with a scarf around her head. "I thought I would get shot on the freeway because of my blond hair," she said. As the pregnancy progressed, the idea that she was about to "desert" her own child grew increasingly large in her mind. On the way to filing adoption papers with a state office in Long Beach she stopped at an overpass on the San Diego Freeway. She got out of the car and considered throwing herself into the traffic below.

After my birth, Harriet slipped quietly back to Stockholm. "Staying in America was too painful for me," she said. "I thought, *I must vanish.* After I returned it was something I thought about every day." In those days, births to unwed mothers were seen as problematic and definitely not, unlike today, as appropriate subject matter for television sitcoms. Back home, her mother wanted to know, "Harriet, how could you abandon your son?"

A year after fleeing Los Angeles, Harriet returned, fleeing her mother. She found a job with Big Brothers in Los Angeles and married Don Wilson, her supervisor there. Together they moved to Fresno, where they stayed until 1986, when they transplanted to El Cajon. Harriet knew my name, and in the twenty-seven years between my birth and the night we first spoke, hardly a day went by that she didn't worry about what had become of me. The question became an obsession, reflected in the jobs she took.

At Big Brothers in Los Angeles, she interviewed volunteers. This involved watching out for men who said they wanted to befriend little boys without fathers, but who really had more sinister motives. In Fresno she worked as an inspector of foster homes for retarded children. In San Diego she got a job with a county agency devoted to rooting out child abuse. When the cops would storm the house of a suspected abuser, Harriet followed them inside, looking for the children, to whom she offered ice cream and safety.

In her personal life, she could not forget the one child to whose future she felt she had not attended. It had been a recurring daydream of hers that I would appear at her door one day. It had been a recurring terror, though, that I would walk through that door and demand an answer: "Mother, why did you desert me?" For years she would wake up in the middle of the night with a dismal feeling floating over her head. In the morning, as she set her feet on the floor, she would sense the weight of guilt she carried with her.

The Torah relates the story of a parent who gave up a child, or at least thought he would have to. In their extreme old age, Abraham and Sarah, the first Jews, had a child, Isaac, who they expected would follow them in teaching what had been revealed of Torah in the pre-Sinai world. When Isaac was still young, God asked Abraham to take Isaac to the top of Mt. Moriah and sacrifice him. Abraham grieved and withheld the news from Sarah. An old man with an old wife, he would never have another child. There would be no Jews after him, it seemed. But he knew something important was at stake even if he did not know what. So he took his son and laid him out on a rock. The knife was in his hand. At that moment an angel appeared. The angel told Abraham that because he had done right, the sacrifice was canceled. The father got his son back.

Harriet, too, had done right; and she, too, after twenty-seven years of grieving, got her son back. That first night we spoke, I reassured her that she could not have chosen better parents for me than she did; that I never blamed her for giving me up. But it is part of the bargain of adoption that, for twenty-seven years, Harriet, unlike Abraham, had no angel to tell her she had done right, that her decision would have consequences for the good that she could hardly anticipate.

The most obvious of these was that we ended up reunited after all. And not merely reunited in the sense of each of us coming to know that the other exists, at what address and in what state of the Union.

As soon as I got off the phone with Harriet after our first conversation, I sent her a fat envelope of pictures of myself, baby pictures, school pictures, and more recent ones. She sent a package of her own to me, with a note declaring that she did "not believe there are adequate words to describe the joy I felt in my heart when I heard your voice last night. I felt the missing pieces in the puzzle of my life were finally in place."

In her photos I saw that as a young woman, she had been astonishingly beautiful. At fifty-five she was still lovely. Mary Jane had said she looked like Grace Kelly. I would say more like a blond Audrey Hepburn. In one photograph she was perched, glamorous and carefree, on a railing, cigarette in hand, with a beach in the background, identified on the back as "Riccione, Italian Riviera, 1961." A later photo, dated at "Los Angeles, October '65," the month I was born, was striking in a different way. Bright blond hair piled on her head in a bun, Harriet was pictured in profile, looking as careworn as she had been carefree four years earlier.

As soon as I received those pictures in the mail I knew I couldn't be satisfied with photographic representations. A few months later I was flying from Kennedy Airport to LAX, then driving down Interstate 5 toward San Diego. We had arranged that Don would meet me at a Denny's restaurant near the freeway exit closest to their home. He was a small but strong-looking man with bristly gray hair, eight years older than Harriet. A veteran of the Canadian military, he impressed me somehow as very much the ex-Canadian military type. El Cajon is basically built on desert. I followed him in his pickup truck to their split-level, ranch-style house on the side of a desert hill.

Harriet was crying when I came through the door. I had half

expected that I would break down and sob myself, but I didn't. The three of us sat in the living room, drinking coffee out of tiny Swedish cups. The impact of the meeting, like thunder that you see before you hear it, didn't make itself felt until later.

There was much to separate Harriet from me. Strangers, we shared nothing apart from DNA. Also, she is a foreigner. I am a native Californian. Since moving to America, she had lived mainly in provincial cities: Fresno, an overbuilt agricultural town, and outermost suburban San Diego, where at night you can hear coyotes chase and eat wayward house pets. I graduated from an Ivy League university and live in Manhattan. Most mystifying to her was my religion.

The biographical details did not predict instant bonding. But over two weeks I visited Harriet four times and each time returned to tell friends about her in spiralingly enthusiastic terms. The movie star smile in those photographs from the sixties had turned cherubic. The kindness of the smile, it seemed to me, was no less than the reflection of her soul. Then there were the charming, small hand gestures, as if she held the reins of a tiny horse and was urging it on. There was the touching eagerness to understand and sympathize with all the surprising crotchets I, her son, came equipped with. On the phone, I sputteringly tried to communicate all this to a friend in New York. "You're in love with your mother," he said with a chuckle. Well, aren't all boys?

Seeking to explain what it was that made her feel so guilty about her decision to give me up, Harriet had said about adoption, "It's so unnatural." What impressed me about our meetings was the *super*natural quality of the almost instant relationship we developed. It was as if my soul had sleeping within it a need to be connected to her soul. That need could be awakened, or, like a person whose alarm clock has failed to go off, it could go on sleeping.

---

HARRIET VIEWED OUR SEPARATION as pure disruption. But I was beginning to see it as something else: the working out of a supernatural plan.

Toward the end of my first trip to California to meet Harriet, she and I were sitting on the whitewashed wall of a planter outside the old Mission San Diego de Alcala, a few miles west of Harriet's house. She had prepared a picnic, neatly arranged, in the tidy manner of all Swedes, in a little red Igloo cooler. We were talking about her cancer.

In all the calls and letters we had exchanged, Harriet hadn't mentioned that the previous winter she had discovered a centimeter-wide lump in her breast, that it had been removed, and that she had been receiving chemotherapy. She revealed this item of medical history the day after I arrived in California. Her prognosis, when her doctor finally gave it to her, had been as good as you could hope. As I write this she is in excellent health. But sitting outside the mission, we were talking about the weeks before she had received her prognosis.

Some months after finding the lump, she had a biopsy performed. A week and a half went by, then the doctor called, asking her to visit him at his office. Something about cancer was mentioned, but nothing about the hopefulness of her situation. "For two days," Harriet said, "I really thought I would die. I was so scared. And then you called!"

We agreed that this was an interesting coincidence. "It was like you had come to rescue me," she said.

Yet as I thought about it at that moment, "interesting" came to seem not quite the right word. I asked her again for the dates involved. The biopsy had taken place May 18. This, I remembered, was the day after I had suddenly decided to go looking for Harriet. Something about that dream, I recalled now, had made me think my mother needed rescuing: perhaps from loneliness, maybe a bad marriage. Cancer had not occurred to me, but in an instant the hard-to-explain timing of my precipitate decision made sense.

Now I do not go in for hocus-pocus, but in the warm Southern California air I was shivering across my chest and upper arms. Maybe it was the coffee we had drunk. But the more I shivered, the more I thought. And the more I thought about the circumstances of our parting in 1965, our reunion, and what had happened in between, the stranger it all seemed.

Was my adoption and our reunion twenty-seven years later intended to work out the way it did so that I could rescue Harriet from fear—the fear that she would die of cancer, never having met her son? Harriet and I were coming to think so. I wouldn't blame you if you scoffed at hocus-pocus like that. But it gets spookier.

Psalm 91 speaks of God charging His angels to carry us on the palms of their hands. Jews read that psalm at the close of the Sabbath as we prepare to begin the work week, a time when God's providence, as compared to the Sabbath, is less in evidence. Usually we are unaware of the way He guides our lives, but at other times the angels leave palm prints. Something else occurred to me as Harriet and I sat outside the mission—something about what my biological origin meant. Faintly, I thought I saw palm prints on my mother and me.

---

AS I'VE SAID, growing up as an adopted child meant that everything about me—especially the fact that I was a Jew—seemed a kind of pose. It's not pleasant to think of yourself as a poseur. So when I began to learn actual *facts* about my biological history, I found that I had an appetite for it that grew increasingly ravenous. After I found Harriet, I thought I could let Andrew H. Jones alone and rest contented. I was wrong.

Among the photos Harriet had sent me, I found one of Andrew. It is impossible to nail down exactly what she saw in him. The picture is a yellowed clipping from the *Torrance Press-Herald,* a local newspaper, about the opening of a workshop for the occupational training of retarded people. The grinning mayor of Gardena, a little city southwest of Los Angeles, is clipping a red ribbon. Next to him is Harriet, in a smock and odd cat-woman glasses. To the other side, identified by a caption, is Andrew Jones. In a dark suit, stringy black tie, and half-frame horn-rimmed glasses, with a jutting chin and fleeing hairline, my birth father looks like a smug accountant. In the picture, dated March 28, 1965, Harriet is two months pregnant.

"What did I see in him?" Harriet asked musingly. "I think we both wanted companionship—both needful, I guess. It was romantic in the beginning. But life has a way of changing courses." He drove a 1964 turquoise Thunderbird, had big hands and a sturdy build, smoked Parliaments, and ate Danishes. "That was all I ever saw him eat," Harriet told me. He didn't talk a lot. Once they were driving in the Thunderbird and a Peter, Paul & Mary song came on the radio. The song was "Lemon Tree," and the lyrics Harriet remembers are to the effect that "the lemon flower is sweet / but the fruit of the lemon is impossible to eat."

"That's what I think of love," said a grimacing Andrew, who obviously knew how to charm a girl. He said that he had once been married, but, typically for Andrew, he didn't elaborate.

Somehow Harriet drew the conclusion that he was a "family man" at heart. One night, February 12, to be exact, after drinks at the Cocoanut Grove in Los Angeles, they drove the short distance to his apartment on Gramercy Drive. "I thought it was a safe time of the month," Harriet recalled. Like countless unmarried women, she believed that if anything unexpected happened and a life began to grow in her body, the father of the child would take care of her.

Twenty-nine years later Harriet and I looked up the address in an old phone book at the L.A. Public Library and visited the building where I was conceived. It was newly built at the time, and Harriet recalled it as a swank kind of pad for a sixties bachelor, with floodlights in the sidewalk illuminating its apricot-colored walls by night. In fact it is a four-story chunk of concrete, blank faced and ugly, typical L.A. architecture for its era. Vietnamese immigrants live there now.

I found Andrew a year after I found Harriet. Basically I used the same method that had worked for me earlier, tracing him forward in time from job to job. I'm closing in on you, I thought to myself shortly before locating his address in June 1994, "you son of a bitch."

He turned out to be retired in Los Gatos, California, near San Jose, after a career in rehabilitation. He is married but, apart from me, never had children.

I sent him a Federal Express package including a letter explaining who I was, a photo of me that looked remarkably like him, and an article I had written for *Commentary* magazine about searching for Harriet. Our only conversation went like this:

"I hope I'm not calling you at a bad time."

"Actually it's the worst time in decades." His voice wasn't angry. It was simply the kind of voice that says: I want to get off the phone as soon as possible. "Exactly what is it you want to know?"

"Well, I just want to know about you. I mean, who you are, what you're like. Uh, how are you?"

"Oh, just about as bad as I've ever been. Why is it that you're pressing so hard right now?"

"I can try you again in a few days, if that's better for you."

"Actually, we've got guests and we're in the middle of renovating the house. It's a bad time. These guests just arrived. They must be sitting outside right now, wondering where I am." He said something in a muffled voice that I didn't understand.

"I beg your pardon?"

"Never mind. We're going on vacation for a couple of months as soon as they leave. I'd prefer to talk to you then."

I called him a few months later, but it was still "a bad time." Not long afterward, he changed his phone number and unlisted the new one. A real charmer.

I had just been resoundingly rejected by no less a person in my life than my birth father, but instead of feeling devastated I decided to take a sort of revenge. It would be to defy his obvious wish that I know nothing about him and that I know nothing about myself to the extent that I share a heritage of blood with him. A Jew is not supposed to take revenge (Leviticus 19:18), but I don't imagine any rabbi would have forbidden me this. Anyway, I didn't ask a rabbi.

From government documents available to the public, you can

learn a lot about a person who doesn't want anything known about himself. To adoptees with uncooperative birth parents, I recommend the book *Get the Facts on Anyone* by a reporter called Dennis King. Voter registration information makes a good start. You first want to know your subject's birthday. Los Gatos, California, is in Santa Clara County. A helpful lady at the Santa Clara County elections office faxed me the pertinent data. Andrew was born January 25, 1927, in Kansas. As a Republican, I was glad to hear he was registered as a Democrat. With this information I was able to hire a professional researcher whose name had been provided to me by the Kansas State Historical Society. For $10 per hour plus $.50 per page for photocopies, the cheerful Rowena Horr, of Topeka, told me we should try to obtain Andrew's birth certificate. That would include the name of the place where he had been born. In Kansas, apart from the concerned individual himself, only a child or other close relation of someone can request a copy of that document from the Bureau of Vital Statistics. With a letter from a lawyer friend of mine giving Mrs. Horr power of attorney for the purpose, she obtained a copy of Andrew's birth certificate in one afternoon.

"Hello, David," she called out across the telephone lines, "this is Rowena in Topeka. I got it! He was born in Shallow Water, Kansas. That's over in the western part of the state, in Scott County, a really tiny town, not far from the Colorado line. You might say it's desert country, pretty desolate." On a map I noted that Shallow Water sat amid miles of empty semiarid wheat fields to which the nearest town of any consequence was Garden City, made notorious by Truman Capote's *In Cold Blood.*

The birth certificate showed that my paternal grandparents were called Morton Claude Jones and Zelda Blanche Trimmer Jones, both thirty-four years old when Andrew was born. They had three other children at the time.

The next step was to find the names of Andrew's siblings. But how? Dennis King had a fine idea: probate court records. If Claude (as he was called) and Zelda died in Kansas, the local county probate records would list anyone named in their wills as inheritors. A few calls revealed that Claude had died in Pawnee County, a couple of counties east of Scott County, on May 3, 1965. A clerk with the Pawnee County probate court disinterestedly read out to me the names and addresses of my two birth aunts and one birth uncle, living, as of 1968, in Kansas, Hawaii, and California, respectively.

My experience with Andrew made me apprehensive about picking up a phone and calling these strangers. But when you're in a situation where you are faced with doing something that's awkward for you but that offers a potentially large reward, you should think to yourself: What are the chances that, having done this, even if it doesn't result in anything positive, I will regret having done it? The chances are usually slim.

The morning I called Amanda Jones Severn of Kailua, Hawaii, I had already gotten used to introducing myself to strangers who were closely related to me. I had it down to a routine: "Mrs. Severn, my name is David Klinghoffer. You don't know me, but we are related. I was adopted as a baby in 1965 and recently discovered that my birth father was your brother Andrew." There followed a silence, after which Mrs. Severn said in the tone of voice you might use with a telephone solicitor, "Who are you?" I repeated the story and elaborated a little. She registered neither surprise nor interest. "I haven't spoken to Andrew in years," she informed me. "And what's more, I have nothing to tell you about him. As far as I'm concerned, I'm obstinate enough to think this is Andrew's business. He can handle it as he wants."

"But," I tried to explain, "I'm not asking you to get involved, just to tell me something about your brother, about your family."

"Like what?" I didn't think she was primed to answer any personal questions, so I opted for the safe route of inquiring about genealogy.

"Well, for instance, where does your family come from originally? I mean, what is their ethnicity?"

She allowed that Jones was originally a Welsh name (not Irish or German). "I used to say I was English, Irish, and Pennsylvania Dutch. Then my mother said, 'How could you be when your father's Welsh!'" She refused to provide further details: "In our family, we don't get excited about these things. I know who I am."

I told her, "I think it's wrong of you to withhold this information from me."

"You're entitled to your opinion," said Mrs. Severn, and we hung up.

What I eventually found out about Andrew and his forefathers isn't glorious, but it is my history as much as his. I found it in a twelfth-floor office in Greenwich Village. Most big American cities have a branch of the National Archives, each housing the microfilmed results of every national census taken in the United States. As a source of concentrated information, none of the wonders of the Internet beats a visit to your local archives.

The earliest Jones ancestor of mine I could identify was born, probably before 1820, in Virginia. I don't know his Christian name, but he was my great-great-great-grandfather. He married a woman from Kentucky, and they settled in Tennessee. There in 1842, my great-great-grandfather, Reuben Jones, was born. He may or may not have served as a private in the Third Tennessee Mounted Infantry, in which capacity he may or may not have been wounded fighting Union troops at Staunton, Virginia; the records are unclear. Turning up in northern Missouri near the end of the war, he became a farmer, but—judging from the value of his personal estate and real estate holdings, listed in the census at $430 and $200, respectively—not a wealthy one. His son Andrew sired my grandfather, Morton Claude Jones. In 1901 the family crossed Kansas by prairie wagon and settled in Shallow Water. The 1925 Kansas State Census gives Claude's trade as "banker." The Jones story was a classic American one. Through two centuries the family had moved west as the country expanded, from Virginia to Tennessee and on to Missouri, Kansas, and finally California.

What more could I find out about my birth father himself? Harriet had said she remembered him telling her he had been married once. Presumably the marriage and divorce had taken place in Kansas. Maybe, I thought, his ex-wife would talk to me. I became very eager to find her.

Rowena Horr was still game for anything. I asked her how difficult it would be to find Andrew's marriage certificate. "Not too hard, I should think," said Rowena. "I'll just go on over to the Division of Vital Statistics." The next afternoon she faxed it to me at the office.

Andrew, I read, was married on November 23, 1954, age twenty-seven, to Florence Baldwin, age twenty-six. The wedding took place at Leonardville, in northeast Kansas, at the Leonardville Methodist Church. So the question became, Where is Florence Baldwin today, forty years later? Florence Baldwin, it turned out, wasn't.

I called the church, and the pastor gave me the name of its unofficial historian, Phyllis Swanson. A warm, grandmotherly lady, Mrs. Swanson sympathized instantly when I told her I was the birth son of the man who had married Florence Baldwin. She remembered her all right. Florence's mother, Ada, had been the minister of the church. "It was a poor little church in a poor little town," she told me. "The Reverend Baldwin had two daughters and a son, as I recall. Now just let me think a moment. . . . Yes, I believe one of the girls committed suicide, and it may have been Florence. As I recall, she took poison." A week later a letter arrived from Leonardville. Mrs. Swanson had found Florence's newspaper obituary, dated August 23, 1968. She had been right about the way Florence died, a fact confirmed by the obituary's classic euphemism. "Florence (Baldwin) Jones," it stated, "became ill suddenly" the previous Wednesday afternoon.

That his divorced wife had poisoned herself could not be an incidental point about Andrew Jones. Mrs. Swanson also gave me the phone number of Florence's sister, Emily Hasselbacher, in Lima, Ohio. In a pattern I was getting used to, Mrs. Hasselbacher didn't sound particularly surprised to hear from me. She first assured me that my birth father had been "very personable," an evaluation quickly refuted by everything else she told me. "When he got acquainted with my sister, he was working toward a Ph.D. in psychology at the University of Kansas over in Lawrence. After he graduated, he and Florence lived in Topeka. He worked at the Menninger Clinic, which is a very expensive hospital for the mentally ill. They were divorced in 1963." Mrs. Hasselbacher sighed. "Well, they had wanted children badly, I remember. Once, Florence thought she was pregnant, but she wasn't after all. That hurt them very much. Then he started going with a 'fast' crowd. His friends were very educated, and I think Andrew wanted to seem sophisticated. He was unhappy with Florence because he thought she wasn't broad-minded enough."

"In what way?" I asked.

"Well, for instance, my sister didn't drink. They would go to parties and Andrew would get a little bit exasperated with her because of that. I think you could say he had a drinking problem. There were times that Andrew gave my sister the cold and silent treatment"—just as he did to Harriet, I thought. "It got to be too much, and she initiated the divorce. He remarried rather quickly after that." I didn't have the heart to press her for the circumstances in Florence's life that immediately preceded the afternoon of August 23, 1968. They could easily be imagined.

My father had a way with women—not a very attractive way. I liked some of what I had learned about his past, the part of it before he was born. As for Andrew himself, I felt tempted to erase him from the personal history I had uncovered, the way an archaeologist might discard some of the less interesting pottery fragments he finds in the dust and bring back to the museum only the more beautiful specimens.

But I realized that would be a mistake. The philosopher Karl Popper formulated the Law of Unintended Effect, which has some relevance to Andrew Jones. It means that unintended bad effects can come from efforts motivated by noble, praiseworthy hopes and desires—such as efforts at social and economic reform—while unintended good results can come from truly despicable deeds. Long before Popper, Torah encapsulated this idea in a phrase used in the Book of Exodus. Before being called on by God to lead the Jewish people, Moses served as a chamberlain in Pharaoh's palace. One day, however, intervening in a fight between a certain "Egyptian man" (2:11), a merciless taskmaster, and an Israelite slave, he killed the Egyptian and was forced to flee for his own life. He fled to Midian, where he intervened in another conflict between oppressors and innocents. This one involved the daughters of the local priest, Jethro, and some ruffian shepherds. The latter had forcibly driven the women away from a well where they watered their sheep, and Moses drove off the shepherds. When Jethro asked his daughters who had saved them, they replied that it was an "Egyptian man" (2:19). Moses would eventually marry one of Jethro's daughters. So who was the "Egyptian man" in 2:19? Seemingly it was Moses. But, explains Rabbi Jacob Schacter, it can also be understood as referring to the slave driver in 2:11. The decision of that Egyptian to brutalize a Hebrew slave led to Moses' fleeing Egypt, which led to his saving Jethro's daughters from the shepherds, which led to his meeting his wife: the Law of Unintended Effect crystallized in two Hebrew words.

Andrew, a certain "Kansan man," had treated Florence Baldwin so badly that she divorced him, which led to his flight from Kansas to California, which led to his meeting Harriet, which led to his cold-hearted treatment of her, which led to Harriet's decision to seek out adoptive parents for me, which led to the fact that I came into contact with Torah, which led to my becoming a Jew.

But there is a mystery here, a missing link in this chain of unintended effects, bad and good. It seems doubtful that I ever would have become a Jew had my birth mother chosen as my adoptive parents not Paul and Carol Klinghoffer, but rather, and far more logically, a couple of Scandinavian Americans. That she did choose them has to do with another chain of consequences, which unfolded not in Kansas but in Sweden. I had found out as much as I could about Andrew's family. What of Harriet's?

---

WITHOUT A DOUBT, as Harriet tells the story, the more colorful of her parents was her father. Born in 1885, Oscar August Constantin Lund came from a theatrical family. His father, Carl Ludvig Lund, owned a popular, groundling-type theater, the Folk Teatern on Stockholm's Östermalm Square. For an adoptee, one of the astonishing things about finding your birth parents is that you get to meet or see photographs of relatives who actually resemble you physically. In the one photograph I have seen of him, from about 1890, Carl Lund looked remarkably like me—more so than any person I have ever laid eyes on. Oscar seems to have been a restless young man. In 1901 he sailed for New York. He evidently had a theatrical imagination and told Harriet stories of his youth in America, which she believes to have been literally true: stories of delivering mail in Alaska by dogsled, attending Yale or Princeton, and riding with a gang of notorious outlaws in New Mexico. After 1906 he arrived in San Francisco. One of the odds and ends he left Harriet, and which she passed on to me, is a battered brass shoe horn he found in the ruins of building that had burned down in the 1906 earthquake. There he embarked on the career that would occupy him for the next twenty years.

Beginning in 1910, Oscar produced, wrote, or acted in a total of eighty-eight silent films. Harriet doesn't know how her father got his start in the film industry. The first picture he produced, in 1910, was a short called *On the Firing Line* for the Great Western Film Company. The next year he transplanted himself to New York. Five years later he was producing and writing films for Louis B. Mayer's Metro Pictures Corporation, Carl Laemmle's Universal Film Manufacturing Company, and the Fox Film Corporation. The epicenter of the film industry had already moved from New York to Los Angeles, but Oscar stayed on in New York. In 1922 he organized the Lund Production Company, which produced five movies in four years from an office at 116 West 39th Street. He lived in Harlem when that neighborhood was still fashionable, in a boxy red-brick apartment building on Riverside Drive.

When I began to learn about Oscar Lund's life and work, I was amazed at the way his experiences in the teens and twenties foreshadowed his daughter Harriet's forty years later. He appears in numerous entries in the *American Film Institute Catalog* of fea-

ture films. Like a lot of other filmmakers at the time, he specialized in melodrama. A typical storyline for an Oscar Lund film,
summarized in the catalog, begins, "A hunchback plots revenge
against a beautiful American woman who, while vacationing in
Egypt, scorned him." Most of Oscar's plots are so crammed with
marriages, births, illnesses, swordfights, suicides, murders, and
other dramatic happenings that, from their summaries, they can
be figured out only with some difficulty. Helpfully, the catalog lists
the main themes for each film it describes. As I paged through
the entries for Lund productions like *The Butterfly* (Schubert Film
Corp., 1915), *The Debt of Honor* (Fox Film Corp., 1918), and
*Mother Love and the Law* (Crystal Photoplays Corp., 1917), I
was struck by the themes: "orphans," "foundlings," "adoption,"
"wards and guardians," "motherhood," "infants," "lost relatives."
Adoption came up more than once. This may have had something
to do with a melodrama that was unfolding in Oscar's own life.

In the apartment on Riverside Drive, he had taken up with a
young actress named Barbara Plum. In his scrapbook for those
years is a flyer advertising a film they made together in 1913,
*Lady Babbie,* "a gorgeous costume play . . . filled with thrilling
and romantic incidents . . . the Feature of the Year . . . Don't miss
it." In the oval-shaped photographs of the stars set in the corners
of the ad, Barbara is pretty, with a squarish, fleshy face and a slop-
ing bosom. She wears a big straw sun hat decorated with flowers
and has a slightly haunted look in her large eyes. Oscar is dashing
in a high-collared starched shirt and rimless oval glasses, his much
sharper features giving the impression of a Protestant clergyman
of the sort who would have made female parishioners swoon.

According to Harriet, around 1915 Barbara accidentally became
pregnant. Though Oscar pleaded with her to keep the child, she
refused. Evidently the movie industry was governed by relaxed
moral standards even then. When Barbara announced that she had
had an abortion, Oscar, deeply wounded, ended their relationship.

He then fell in love with a showgirl called Lilly Lucille, who
disappointed him, too. She moved in with him and they had a
child together, a girl. One day Oscar returned home at an unex-

pected hour and found Lilly in flagrante with another man, a certain John Stuhlmueller. Shortly afterward it developed that Lilly was pregnant. Oscar demanded that she vacate their home; and when this child, a boy, was born, Oscar saw to it that both children were adopted by a couple in upstate New York. Since Lilly didn't know who the baby's father was, she called him John Lund— "John" for John Stuhlmueller, "Lund" for Oscar.

By 1926 Oscar was living at 167 West 87th Street in a town house half a mile from the apartment I live in today. His apartment is a block north of the synagogue I attend, on West 86th Street, which Oscar no doubt walked past frequently. For a couple of years he settled in Hollywood; but judging from the clutch of rejection letters from a variety of movies studios that his wife kept after his death, his moviemaking career seems to have entered a period of decline from which it never recovered. In 1931 he returned to Sweden and seven years later married Harriet's mother. He spent the remaining years of his life dreaming of Hollywood. In his sixties Oscar would seize whatever opportunity he could to speak in English to anyone who would listen, proclaiming his love of America in a loud voice that sometimes embarrassed his teenage daughter. Swedes do not speak in loud voices, and for the most part they don't love America. Oscar Lund died, an American in Stockholm, in 1963.

His devotion to America inspired Harriet to move here herself. It is harder to understand Harriet's motivations in other respects. We come now to the missing link in the chain of unintended effects that led to the strange circumstance of a born gentile wishing to become an Orthodox Jew. As I've said, that circumstance very likely never would have come about if I had been adopted by non-Jews.

The first time we spoke, Harriet said that Anthony Carsola told her she could interview any number of potential parents who wished to adopt her child. Of those couples Harriet could have her choice. She remembers interviewing two would-be parents who were famous then and became still more so. One was Herb Alpert, leader of the Tijuana Brass band and founder of A&M Records.

Another was Alan Cranston, then California's state controller, later a longtime U.S. senator. His disgrace in the Keating Five scandal many years later was an event Harriet followed with great interest. But Harriet wanted to choose strictly middle-class parents for me. She wanted my father to be not a celebrity or a politician, but a professional man such as a dentist. And, she told me to my amazement the night of our first telephone conversation, she wanted my parents to be Jews. "To me," she said, "there was no question."

She could hardly explain why. "In Sweden," she said uncertainly, as if I had posed a question she had given little thought to before, "the Jewish people have a very good name. It's a status thing. They're supposed to be very stable, reliable folks."

I countered that Swedish Americans, of whom there is no shortage, have a reputation as straight arrows, too. Why not choose a couple of them for my parents?

"Well, you know," she told me, "my mother was Jewish."

I sat up, just then, very straight in my chair.

"Well, she wasn't *entirely* Jewish," Harriet continued, as if she had said nothing of any particular importance. "I did have a Jewish great-grandfather. My mother's maiden name, Goldkuhl, is a Jewish name. That played a part in my decision."

I couldn't believe what I was hearing. Or rather, the tribalist in me couldn't believe it. My mouth was open, my hand was quietly thumping the table in astonishment and excitement. If this were true, I was part Jewish by blood. But was it true?

The great-grandfather in question, she said, was August Edvard Goldkuhl, born in 1830, who had married a Christian woman, Ebba Maria Jerfving. Their son Gustaf Adolf was Harriet's mother's father. August Edvard had been the "town doctor," Harriet said, in Växjö, a little city in south Sweden. He died in 1904.

Of course, since this ancestor of mine was a grand*father*, that would have had no impact on my birth status as a non-Jew. He had married a gentile woman, so all his descendants were gentiles. My conversion had not been superfluous. Yet doing a quick calculation I realized that, to be precise, my blood was one-sixteenth Jewish. I could lay claim, however tenuously, to membership in the Jewish tribe.

For weeks and months afterward I would daydream, imagining the line of blood that connected me, the descendant of Missouri farmers and Stockholm theater owners, with the Jews who stood at Mt. Sinai. A direct ancestor of mine had been *there*. I wanted to shout that fact out my window onto West End Avenue. The tribe from which I had felt excluded because I thought I had no Jews in my blood's past was, suddenly—mine. The effects were immediate, though they may sound absurd: I could walk into a synagogue or a kosher restaurant and return the curious glances I felt on my face with an almost haughty counterglance: I really am one of you, I thought. You may not think so, but I am.

From the moment Harriet told me I had a Jewish great-great-grandfather, my interest in the rest of the birth ancestors I had acquired could not match my obsession with the Goldkuhl family, my blood link with the Nation of Israel. That obsession would eventually take me across the Atlantic Ocean, to Sweden. It was when I began to learn about this assimilated Swedish-Jewish family who were my not so distant ancestors that I saw, or thought I saw, the palm prints of angels in my life.

# Chapter 13

# PARHELION

*I*n an oddly homey-sounding book called *Table Talk*, Adolf Hitler offered the prediction that if ever five thousand Jews were to settle in Sweden, they would not assimilate but instead would quickly win all the most important political and cultural offices for themselves and establish Jewish racial dominion over the country. He was making two assumptions: that Sweden was a country without Jews; and that if Jews were ever introduced there, the combined Jewish will to power, on the one hand, and to preserve the Jewish tribe, on the other, was sufficiently powerful to conquer even the famous homogeneity of Sweden. For "blood purity," he explained in *Mein Kampf,* "is a thing the Jew preserves better than any other people on earth."

On both points Karin Goldkuhl's once Jewish family proved him wrong. Jews had settled in Sweden. And at least in the case of the Goldkuhls, it was the Swedes who swallowed the Jews, not the other way around.

Every time we talked on the phone, or when I visited her in California, I questioned Harriet about her mother's Jewish forebears. She knew only scraps of family history. This was frustrating. Nor could I turn to my birth grandmother, Karin Lund, for more information. Now in her early eighties, she lived in a ladies' retirement home on the grounds of a Polish Catholic convent in Stockholm. But Karin had suffered a couple of minor strokes and lost much of her ability to carry on an informative conversation. She and I spoke only once, by telephone, and it wasn't clear that she understood who I was.

Memories of things her mother had told her about the Goldkuhls would come back to Harriet unexpectedly. One day we were sitting in a car in her driveway. "I remember," she said, "that the Goldkuhls came to Sweden from Germany. It must have been the seventeenth century. They were in the fabric business. There were two brothers, and one of them burned down a church!"

"Why would they burn down a church?"

"I don't know, but I heard that when I was little girl. They were from a town in Germany called Osnabrück. Eventually the family settled in Växjö, in southern Sweden. That was where the Doctor lived." Harriet invariably referred to her great-grandfather as "the Doctor." "My mother was always very proud of her family. She used to say, 'The Goldkuhls have long been a professional family. My grandfather was the town doctor in Växjö!'" She showed me how to pronounce the name of the town the way her mother was taught—*Vek-fwuh*, which was how the local haute bourgeoisie said it, as opposed to the more pedestrian *Vek-shuh*.

When I asked how she knew the family had been Jewish, she said she couldn't recall when she'd first heard it. "I've known it for as long as I can remember. In our home we had a very old mortar and pestle that had belonged to the Goldkuhls, and someone once told me that back then every Jewish home had one of those." I had never heard that. Maybe it was a Swedish-Jewish thing.

"And," Harriet added almost triumphantly, "my mother was on a list!"

"What list? A list of Jews?"

"Yes! It was during World War Two. There was a small Swedish Nazi Party, and we knew a man, a very nasty man, who belonged to it. They were making a list of the Jews in Stockholm. If the Germans invaded, they would know who to round up. He put my mother and her sister Elsa on it, but not me or my two cousins because you had to be a certain part Jewish, I think it was one-quarter, to be put on the list." Harriet had been seven when the war ended, but fifty years later she still sounded alarmed at the prospect of being "rounded up." In return for the promise that it would not be invaded, neutral Sweden had granted Germany the right to move troops through its territory by rail and fly planes through Swedish airspace. "Sometimes we would see their planes over Stockholm, or you would be at a train crossing and there would be this trainload of Germans going by. Oh, we hated the Germans. It terrified my mother to see them."

Had her mother told her anything about Judaism? No. Nor about Christianity, for that matter. A typical Swede, Harriet had been raised in no religious tradition at all, though she had been baptized a Lutheran at the famous Hedvig Eleonora Church, where the minister was Ingmar Bergman's father.

Oscar Lund had a favorable impression of Jews. "My father would say the Jewish people in the film industry were good to work with," Harriet said. "They were honest with money. But my mother had more of a negative attitude. When we were shopping, she would always point out women she thought were Jewish. 'Oh there's a Jewish woman,' she would say. For instance, if there was a saleswoman who was particularly . . . sales-minded—"

"You mean pushy?"

"Well, I guess you could say that. If there was such a sales-woman, my mother would say, 'She's Jewish.' I would ask her, 'How do you know?' But she would just say, *'I know.'* I asked her once if she was Jewish and she said, very definitely, 'No.' She was really out to prove that she was not one of them."

One night we were sitting at Harriet's kitchen table with her husband, Don, talking about her decision to find Jewish parents for me. "As a girl," she said, "I thought the Jews were exotic, kind of neat. When I was about eight, I had a Jewish friend called Lillemor Heikenskjold. Of course, she was a small, dark girl. When I was twelve or thirteen, I had a couple of other Jewish friends, little Berit Sternholz, and Annika Lamm. Annika had long curly black hair. Jewish homes seemed to be bigger than most of the homes of my other girlfriends, with lots of toys. Just before I came to America I had a nice couple of dates with a Jewish guy. His name was Peter Haas. I remember he had a lot of respect for his father and his family, and I thought that was very admirable."

She cast her mind back to the first months of her pregnancy. She had been befriended by a young man called Hal Fisher, who was involved in an amateur theatrical group that had a large Jewish membership. "I paid close attention to who was Jewish and who wasn't. The Jewish ones had such nice homes, and they were so nice to me. I really liked them. Then there was Mary Jane, who had dated a boss of hers who was Jewish. She said, and she kept coming back to this, 'Your Jewish man is your best bet!'"

"Well, she obviously never met a Canadian," said Don.

Harriet ignored him. "So I was just very glad to find your parents. They were such nice Jewish people. I remember when they came to see me in the hospital, after I had given birth. They brought these brightly colored flowers, and they wanted me to sign a release form so you could have a"—she pronounced the unfamiliar word with care—"circumcision. The birth mother had to give her consent for that. Your parents were begging me to sign the document. '*You must sign this,*' the nurse said. 'It's so important.' Of course I signed it. They thought I might not, but I wanted you to be circumcised, because I knew it was a Jewish custom. They were surprised, but they shouldn't have been."

Shouldn't they? The whole business still failed to add up. In interviewing prospective parents, my birth mother had applied a religious criterion that could only be called eccentric. After all, Jews in her mind may have been pleasant, prosperous, honest folk, but they were hardly the only such people in Southern California. And she had observed at close hand the disadvantages of being identified as a Jew: the stereotypes Jews are sometimes subjected to and the fear it could produce even in non-Jews like Karin Lund. But I didn't press Harriet any further. It was clear that she had told me frankly what her thoughts were in the spring and summer of 1965. If there was a deeper layer of meaning in her search for a couple of childless Jews, she was unaware of it.

BACK, THEN, to the afternoon Harriet and I spent picnicking at the Mission San Diego de Alcala. I was thinking about what a coincidence it was that I had sensed that Harriet needed to be rescued and immediately set out to find her—within twenty-four hours of the biopsy that revealed the cancer in her breast. But there was something else that struck me with great force just then. Quite suddenly I knew what really had driven Harriet to do something as bizarre as to seek out Jewish parents for me.

As an Orthodox Jew, I believed that the Goldkuhls—if they really were Jewish—made a mistake in assimilating the way they did. But that was bizarre, too: that I, born a gentile and hardly driven to Orthodoxy by my Reform adoptive parents, should have chosen to embrace the religion the Goldkuhls must surely have felt relief in abandoning. I said earlier that I don't go in for hocus-pocus, but this seemed too real to brush off. As we sat outside the mission, it came to me that Harriet had not chosen Paul and Carol Klinghoffer to be my parents. Somehow she *had been chosen*, led, without her knowing it, to locate Jewish parents for her son.

There is a narrative line, I saw now, in the events of our lives. The progression, like a trip route traced on a faded road map, is there to be found. Certainly it could be found in my life. That was why Harriet could offer no compelling explanation of her desire to find Jewish parents. It had not really been *her* desire. It had been God's. He had sought to return the Goldkuhl family to their place in the tribes of Israel. The bloodline that should have linked the Goldkuhls to the Jewish people was now reconnected. Like a repaired pipe under the kitchen sink, they would resume pouring out Jews into the foreseeable future. God had intended that all along. My blood proved it.

Back in New York, that realization charged me as if I had been plugged into an electric outlet. It is one of the themes of the Book of Psalms that Jews must continually publicize the deeds of God to the rest of the world: "Relate His glory among the nations, His wonders among all peoples: that the Lord is great and exceedingly lauded, awesome is He above all heavenly powers." I was filled with an intense desire to do just that. I wrote magazine articles for *Commentary* and *National Review* about my search for Harriet, confidently explaining what God had been trying to achieve through us. My supernatural analysis struck many readers as entirely plausible. I received letters and e-mail from across the country. Strangers called me on the telephone to talk about God's involvement in their own lives.

One night in November 1994, Harriet called me at home. Her voice had the same quiet, sniffly quality I remembered from the night we first spoke. "My mother died yesterday," she said.

It was not simply her mother's passing that made her cry. Karin had lived to be eighty-two. Usually the death of an octogenarian can be accepted philosophically. But when an elderly parent dies without having resolved a grievous conflict with her child, the death can be extremely painful. The opportunity to effect a reconciliation, in the world of mortals, has been lost. When Karin died, Harriet still had not forgiven her mother, or her mother forgiven her, for the offense each felt the other had perpetrated. From 1965 until well into her late seventies, Karin berated Harriet for her decision, as Karin saw it, to abandon me in America. "You should have brought your son back to me," she would often say. "What a terrible mother you are. I would have raised him if you couldn't!" Karin always referred to me as "your son" or "the boy," because Harriet had never told her my name, which Harriet knew. Harriet would not give her mother the power to invoke a name against her. Even without it, Karin wounded Harriet. The issue between them—me—persisted, like a burn over which fresh skin has grown while the tender, unhealed flesh remains beneath.

A week after Karin's death, Harriet told me that before long she would have to travel to Stockholm. The nuns had stored Karin's belongings in an attic, including antique furniture, books, paintings, glass and china. Some of these items had to be thrown out, others sold to an auctioneer, and others shipped to America. "She was your grandmother," Harriet said. "There are things of hers I want you to have. There are family documents that would interest you, and lots of old photos. My mother had a beautiful desk that belonged to her grandmother, Ebba Maria, the Doctor's wife. I would like you to have that."

I was intrigued by nothing so much as the "family documents" Harriet had mentioned. What did she mean by that? "Oh, I don't know, papers and such."

For months I had been bragging to friends, and daydreaming, about my Jewish ancestors. What I didn't have was some tokens of their Jewishness. Among Karin's possessions there must be something: a Hebrew Bible, maybe, or the Doctor's tefillin. Harriet was delighted when I told her I wanted to go with her to Stockholm. The idea of sorting through her mother's possessions filled her with dismay, even fear. It would be like confronting Karin's ghost. I didn't want Harriet to do that alone. But my other motivation was greed—greed for history. I wanted physical evidence that would corroborate what I had realized about the way God and His angels led Harriet to my Jewish adoptive parents.

Harriet and I made travel plans for June 1995. We would be in Stockholm for two weeks, staying in guest rooms at the convent for $15 per night.

———

A COLLEGE FRIEND OF HARRIET'S met us at Arlanda Airport and dropped us off with the nuns. I noticed the name of their religious order, on a brass plaque outside the plane brick building: Serafim Sisters. Fortunately, in contrast with their fierce-sounding name, which in Hebrew means "those who burn" and refers to an order of angels said to be on fire with love for God, the sisters were an exceptionally sweet group of ladies.

I thought of the trip as a research mission. At that time of the year in Stockholm, the sun never really sets, except for briefly rubbing against the line of the horizon around three in the morning. For those accustomed to a period of darkness between one day and the next, the effect can be unnerving: visitors may feel as if they haven't been to bed in days, even if they actually have slept a regular eight hours each "night." I hoped that as much light would be shed on my Jewish ancestry.

I had done some reading about Sweden's Jewish community. The first officially tolerated Jews immigrated to Stockholm in 1774. Before that, they were allowed to live in the country only if they had been baptized as Christians—a state of affairs formally approved by a parliamentary act of 1727. This demanded that "Jews, drifters, and tinsmiths . . . be treated such as to be driven totally out of the nation and not be tolerated ever more therein." According to a history of Swedish Jewry by Hugo Valentin, *Judarnas Historia i Sverige*, the first documented baptism of Jews occurred in 1681 at the Tyska Kyrka, the so-called German church in Stockholm's old central district. The baptized Jews were two families from Holland. Referred to as the "Great Baptism," their conversion must have been celebrated as an important event in Stockholm because King Karl XI himself attended.

I made the Tyska Kyrka one of my first sight-seeing destinations. Forbidding and dark, the church's interior is dominated by a high black pulpit of ebony and alabaster in the center of which is carved the tetragrammaton, the ineffable four-letter Hebrew name of God. So it was that with two monarchs looking on, the Dutch Jewish families were called on to choose: between Karl XI and the King of Kings. It must have been an awesome moment for them, mixed with terror. What if they had made the wrong choice?

Visiting the library at the administration building of the Judiska Forsämling, Stockholm's official Jewish parish, as it is called, I discovered that the Great Baptism set the tone for the rest of

Swedish Jewish history. Jews disappear in Sweden. They aren't killed but are absorbed peacefully through intermarriage and conversion. The first practicing Jew to live in Stockholm, in 1774, was Aaron Isaac. A German merchant, he brought his family along with nine other Jewish men to serve as a quorum for prayer. From this minyan, the Jewish presence in Sweden grew to three thousand by 1879. Today the number is twenty thousand, but only thanks to periodic waves of refugees. Among descendants of the old Jewish families, just a handful in the entire country still consider themselves Jews. I've heard the number estimated at five. The progeny of the later immigrants are likewise assimilating, intermarrying, and disappearing as Jews.

Depressing as that may be, I felt comforted by it. If I had been entirely confident about the accuracy of Harriet's genealogical accounts, I might not have needed to come to Sweden in the first place. I saw now that the Goldkuhls fit the historical pattern, which reassured me.

So I wasn't surprised or terribly disappointed when Harriet and I drove down to Växjö. We saw the old Goldkuhl house, a long cream-colored building with a red tiled roof now serving as a sort of chamber of commerce, and the Doctor's grave. I had a vague hope that the latter would bear a Star of David or some other Jewish symbol. Of course it didn't. I had been silly to imagine that Edvard August, having married a non-Jew, would advertise his Jewishness from beyond the grave. On the jagged top of the black sandstone monument I left a small rock, a Jewish custom meant to signify that the grave has been visited.

I enjoyed the role of the Swedish Jew who has returned to the Old Country to set things right and revive the idea that there can be such a thing as a Swedish Jew. At the Judiska Forsämling I bought a severe-looking black siddur, with the Hebrew text on the left-hand pages and a Swedish translation on the right, and couldn't wait to get back to the convent to pray from it. One day I found the old Stockholm Jewish cemetery on Kungsholmen, or King's Island, not far from the address on Norr Malärstrand where Karin Lund once lived. Aaron Isaac and his minyan-men were buried here. There might have been Goldkuhls, too, but the Hebrew that covered the faces of the gravestones was too faint to read. I left more pebbles.

A few days into our trip we were visited at the convent by a first cousin of Harriet's. Gorel, called "Kick," was a Goldkuhl. After Harriet, she was the second blood relative I had ever met. This was less thrilling than it might have been because Kick, a large and confident woman, brought with her a deflating opinion.

When I mentioned the Goldkuhls and their religious background, Kick told me that her sister in south Sweden had somewhere around her house a copy of an old family chronicle. It traced the Goldkuhls back to the eighteenth century, when they had immigrated to Sweden from Germany. Conceivably I could visit this sister and look for the document, but Kick said I would be disappointed. "They weren't Jewish," she said matter-of-factly. "That was never true, as far as I know."

Harriet was as startled as I was. She countered that she had always understood that the Goldkuhls were Jewish and reminded Kick that the Swedish Nazis had put them on a list of Jews. As the two women enacted a scene of cousinly rivalry that had been a feature of their relationship since childhood, Kick remained unmovable. She asserted that a brutish acquaintance who was a Swedish Nazi had put the family on some list only because the name sounded Jewish. Harriet dismissed the argument. "Well," she said, "I'm pretty sure they were Jewish."

Pretty sure? It was, I thought, the first time I had heard Harriet speak about the Jewishness of the Goldkuhls in a tone of less than 100 percent certainty.

I discussed all this with Harriet as the mother superior led us up a staircase to the attic. All the retired ladies stored things here that could not be accommodated in their small rooms. The nun showed us a fenced-off area into which furniture and cardboard boxes had been closely fitted. Harriet looked stiff with apprehension, as if the lid of a coffin had been lifted up, revealing white bones to which some flesh still adhered. Once we had thrown ourselves into the task of sorting these bones, she relaxed.

In a corner was the desk that had belonged to Ebba Maria Gold-kuhl, a delicately carved walnut secretary with scratches made by Harriet when she was a little girl, seeking ways to avoid home-work. I am writing at that desk now. Among the material in the boxes we came across a pair of antique brass candlesticks passed down among the Goldkuhl women. For lighting on Shabbat? Maybe, I thought. Sabbath candles do indeed burn in them now each Friday night in my apartment. We also found perhaps two hundred photographs, including many of Karin Lund. A couple of these Harriet pointed to triumphantly.

"Doesn't she look Jewish here?" the daughter said of the mother. She was right. From generation to generation in a given family, faces recur, as Carl Lund's features did in me. The face that seemed to recur in early photos of Karin Lund, with her slightly bent aquiline nose and what appeared to be olive-colored skin, looked more Jewish than Swedish. We even turned up a photo of August Edvard Goldkuhl. I mentioned that Dr. Goldkuhl vaguely resembled Sigmund Freud. Harriet asked, "Well, *he* was Jewish, wasn't he?"

"That's right," I said, although the similarity in appearance had more to do with the goatee beard on the doctor's chin and his Victorian frock coat than with his face.

Just then, from a rustic old wooden chest, I drew a pair of homemade-looking documents. One, covered in a green hardback cover, was a tall, thin notebook of lined paper, with spidery an-tique Swedish handwriting inside. On the cover were printed gold letters, "Lachonius, 1580–1893." Lachonius, I knew, was the name of a family that had married into the Goldkuhls. Anna Au-gusta Lachonius's daughter Hildur Maria Johansson, born in 1880, had married a son of the Doctor, Gustaf Adolf Goldkuhl. Their daughter was Harriet's mother. The smell of aged paper rose from the open notebook. It was a family register, listing the names, oc-cupations, and other biographical facts about Lachonius ancestors extending back to a certain Hans Larsson, born in 1540: my great-great-great-great-great-great-great-great-great-grandfather. He was a *tolfman*, a sort of judge who sat on a local twelve-man tribunal. Hans Larsson's son, wanting a Latinate surname, called himself "Lachonius." *Lacus* means "lake" in Latin. Presumably the family lived near a lake.

Fascinating as this was, it couldn't compare with what I found in the second document. The latter was a series of legal-size papers, typed in 1946 (according to the cover date), between blue butcher-paper covers. No name was printed on the outside, but I knew what it was the moment I opened to the first page. It was a register of the family Harriet had been arguing about with Kick. I drew a breath, noticed that my heart was beating more quickly than usual, and examined the first page of the *"Register över Svenska Grenen af Släkten Goldkuhl och Dess Tyska Härstamning"*— the "Record of the Swedish Branch of the Goldkuhl Family and Its German Origin."

It went on for twenty-seven single-spaced pages and detailed the family's activities over 224 years. As Harriet had told me, they migrated to Sweden from Osnabrück, in northern Germany, in 1755 in the person of Friedrich Wilhelm Goldkuhl, then nineteen years old. With Harriet translating, a few points leapt out that seemed to support her thesis that they had been Jewish. My eye fell on the middle name of Friedrich Wilhelm's youngest brother: Gottlieb. That sounded Jewish. More significant, as I had read in Hugo Valentin's book, the first Jews in Sweden tended to be involved in the fabric trade. So was Friedrich Wilhelm. He came to Stockholm to work in the fabric-dyeing workshop of his uncle Henrik Wilhelm Zellen.

Harriet's stories had been accurate on other points, too. There was an account of a Goldkuhl burning down a church. Friedrich Wilhelm had been preceded in Stockholm by his older brother Johann Anton Wilhelm. According to the family record, this man started a fire in 1751 that destroyed not only Stockholm's St. Klara Church, but also "a good deal of the city." Around that time Johann Anton Wilhelm found it prudent to skip town. He went back to Osnabrück, leaving his younger brother behind.

This initial burst of encouraging information was, however, quickly rebutted. After Harriet first told me about the fire, I had

begun vaguely to imagine it as an act of sabotage somehow inspired by Jewish fervor. When we read the family register more
carefully, I learned that the episode was just bad luck, an accident
that started among the fabrics at the Zellen-Goldkuhl workshop.
Perhaps that was good news, at least absolving Uncle Johann of ill
motivations. But as I read on, my heart sank into my shoes, for not
a word could be construed as pointing in any real way to the family's Jewish origin. Much of it directly contradicted the idea. I noticed, for instance, that Friedrich had one sister called Maria and
another with the middle name Christina. Perhaps, as Kick said, it
was never true.

The drift of the evidence I had found so far was confirmed by a
trip I took one morning to Stockholm's City Archive. It had occurred to me that Friedrich might have been baptized as a Christian shortly after his arrival in Stockholm. If I could find a
reference to such an event, it would indicate that, at least in Germany, the family had been Jewish. Thanks to Swedish meticulous-
ness, since at least the seventeenth century almost every baptism
has been recorded in church logs, later to be saved on microfiche.
Amid the Swedish words committed to parchment two centuries
ago and now projected onto a dimly lit screen, I found no mention
of an adult baptism of anyone named Goldkuhl. I did come across
the record of Friedrich's burial in 1784, including the cause of his
death ("heart asthma"), the name of the minister who conducted
the funeral, the price of the ceremony, and the location of the
grave: the churchyard of St. Klara's. This didn't sound good.

That afternoon Harriet and I had a conversation in a coffee
shop. We were talking about her mother. Karin was a career
woman, preoccupied with her job as a translator of legal documents. She had little time to spend with her only child, a fact that
bothered Harriet. "I'm glad *your* mother was attentive to *you*,"
she said. "I think Jewish mothers are like that. They're very nur-
turing, aren't they?"

Something occurred to me, but I hesitated to say it out loud.
"Harriet," I asked, "you don't think, do you, that, I mean, you
might have looked for Jewish parents for me not because you had

a Jewish ancestor, but really just because you didn't want me to have a distant mother the way you did?"

Harriet cocked her head and looked thoughtful. "Yes," she said after a moment. "I think that could have had a lot to do with it."

Instantly the whole matter became clear. When Karin told Harriet she wasn't Jewish, the mother was not, as her daughter thought, in denial. Almost certainly, the "Jewish" great-grandfather was a fantasy imagined by a neglected girl who happened to know Jewish families in which the children were doted on as she was not. That the name "Goldkuhl" sounded Jewish to some Hitlerophile neighbors provided the seed for the fantasy. In all likelihood, no Jewish blood flowed in my veins. On the way out of the coffee shop I crumpled up my theory of unsubtle divine guidance and tossed it in the trash along with my paper napkin.

That realization struck me as a blow. I had convinced myself I was following a personal directive from God coded in my blood, and it now turned out that there was no code. Was God interested in my religious status after all?

This is the stuff that spiritual crises are made of. To take my mind off the subject, I did some more sight-seeing.

I saw churches, museums, department stores. The Goldkuhls, though, would not let themselves be pushed aside. Jewish or not, they were still related to me. And here I was in their homeland. If there was no archival record of their religious affiliations, there might be other, physical records they had left behind, testifying at least to the material circumstances of their lives: buildings, gravestones, the streets they had walked on. In the family register I had found the address of the fabric-dyeing workshop Friedrich had worked in and later inherited from his uncle. Then there was St. Klara Church and its graveyard. I decided to investigate.

I was in for more disappointments. According to a pamphlet set out in the vestibule, St. Klara's occupies the location of the church burned down in 1751, in the fire for which Johann Anton Wilhelm Goldkuhl was blamed. "The church," I read, "was ravaged . . . by fire which destroyed steeple and bells, roof and window, together with all fixtures and many movables." In the 1880s it was subjected to a restoration in which the tower was entombed in machine-made bricks, giving the impression of a small factory. I had hoped something might be left of the building my great-great-great-great-great-uncle burned down; but this church was very different from the one those first Swedish Goldkuhls knew. Nor could I find Friedrich Wilhelm's grave. A young man seated at a table in the church, assigned to answer questions from tourists, told me that most of the dead buried in the churchyard had been moved to a common vault and their gravestones disposed of, evidently in an attempt to tidy the place up—a Swedish touch.

As for the location of the Goldkuhl workshop—in the same part of town, called Klara in honor of the church—this had met with a similar fate. In the early seventies Stockholm razed most of the neighborhood and paved it over with cement, erecting a mammoth Soviet-style "cultural center" and banal shopping streets where the ancient buildings of Klara had stood. Today, at the address on Drottninggattan where the workshop had been, Building No. 30, there is a women's clothing store housed in a modern, steel-sided building intended to suggest the space age.

It seemed that every physical trace of the family in its early history had been destroyed. With no other Goldkuhl relatives to search for, I set out walking in the direction of Stadsholmen, the little island that was the original settlement that became Stockholm, with its peach-colored medieval houses and tightly packed streets.

As I walked, thoughts came to me unbidden. It's funny the way God suddenly helps us understand matters we had previously not understood. He likes to give us an experience, often a disappointing one, and let the meaning He wants to convey bubble up as if from dark waters.

I had come to Stockholm to find the link, traced in blood, between my body and the bodies of the Jewish people among whom I live today. The lesson of No. 30 Drottninggattan and of St. Klara Church concerns the tenuousness of all such physical connections. I realized now that even if I had discovered in some archive the precise date the Goldkuhls had accepted Christianity and begun to marry non-Jews, the line of blood I had been searching for would by now have dried up to the point of meaninglessness—just as the buildings those old Goldkuhls knew have been torn down, burned down, or transfigured beyond recognition. Of course in the system of Torah law, blood counts. But in practice blood guarantees nothing. It has not saved the successive generations of Jewish families who immigrated to Sweden, only to disappear as Jews when their children ceased to believe in Torah. Nor is it likely to save the Jewish families whose ancestors immigrated to America and whose children are now marrying gentiles at a rate of 52 percent.

It took a trip to Sweden to make me realize that this is the error at the heart of the tribal conception of Jewishness, an error I had shared in. It is the belief that blood will persevere in the absence of belief. That blood, by itself, means anything much at all. There may in fact be a message in my veins, as in those of every human being. Next time you get a paper cut, squeeze out a drop of blood and let it sit on a table for a few hours. See what happens. The message I received that day in Stockholm is that blood evaporates. Quickly.

Fortunately, as a saving mechanism for the Jewish people, there is an alternative to blood. Even if "Goldkuhl" really had been a Jewish name at some point, if it had turned out that the family underwent baptisms centuries ago in Germany, if they had remained Christians ever since, that would mean that my Jewish ancestors ceased to be Jewish for one reason: because they had ceased to believe, as Jews did and do, that Judaism is true. I, meanwhile, became a Jew for one reason: because I reached the conclusion that Judaism is true.

When I stood in the *mikvah* in Silver Spring, I had been able to affirm that Torah *contains* the Truth about God and His will, that Truth is a subset of Torah. That day in Stockholm I realized that was an inadequate way of understanding Judaism. Conservative Judaism states that Truth and Torah merely overlap. The summer I spent at the Jewish Theological Seminary I had sensed, without being able to state it in words, that Conservatism suffered from an inner affliction, a lack of *something*. As a result, it generally failed to ignite the souls even of Jews who identify themselves as Conservative. What it lacked was the conviction that Torah *is Truth.* Some Jews try to compensate for that lack by distracting themselves with tribal fantasies. That approach may work for certain individuals, but in the American Jewish community as a whole it is a formula for disaffection and boredom, leading to assimilation and intermarriage: in short, mass demographic suicide.

In Stockholm, much of what I had been thinking about Judaism for twenty years came sharply into focus. I could now see that the most fundamental question a Jew must ask himself is this: What happened at Mt. Sinai 3,300 years ago?

There are four possible answers. One is that, apart from some scorpions tottering around there over the centuries, nothing at all happened. In that case, aside from antiquarian interest, there is no reason to bother learning about or involving oneself in Judaism— or, for that matter, Christianity, which depends for internal coherence on the truth of the Torah. If nothing happened at Sinai, both religions are frauds.

The second possible answer is that one Torah is from God, the written one, but its oral counterpart is the work of human intelligence. I've already noted the problem with this theory. Much of the written Torah assumes a level of knowledge, of concepts and even words, that the two million escaped Egyptian slaves at Sinai could not possibly have had their disposal. What are tefillin? What is *melachah?* The text doesn't say. How is meat to be slaughtered "as I have commanded" if the Pentateuch elaborates on no such commandment? Either the written Torah was given at Sinai contemporaneously with some sort of oral explanation, or it was not. If not, it must have been composed after the legal structures it describes had already been instituted. But that contradicts the Torah's own account of its origin. Halachic jurisprudence rules that if the courtroom testimony of a witness contains a major discrepancy or self-contradiction, the testimony is dismissed. In this view, the testimony of the Torah contradicts itself on the key question of where the document comes from. It, along with Judaism, which means nothing without Torah, must therefore be rejected.

The third possible answer, offered by liberal rabbis, is that we don't know exactly what happened at Sinai. "I believe *something* happened there," is the formulation I've often heard. From this perspective, neither the Pentateuch nor the opinions of the rabbis can be entirely trusted. Some of the material reported to be from God—legal, ethical, philosophical, and mystical—really is from Him, but some is not. This had been my way of thinking.

However, if only parts of each Torah are true, how can we know which parts? Liberal rabbis are confident of their ability to distinguish true from false. But surely we can't share their confidence. After all, they disagree among themselves: Conservatives upholding much of Torah, Reformers very little. And it is suspicious how frequently, in rendering moral judgments, these rabbis find themselves in accord with the ruling godless ideology of modern times, approving abortion, intermarriage, and homosexuality, just to name the most obvious examples. If we deny the truth of Torah in any matter, again a contradiction in its testimony becomes apparent. We are asked to believe in an omnipotent God, but one who is impotent to keep his Revelation straight and intact for 3,300 years. This should be unacceptable to anyone who demands internal coherence in his faith.

The fourth possibility is that both Torahs are exactly what they claim to be: the documented will of God directed eternally to the Jewish people.

In other words, for us it is either Torah or a suddenly yawning emptiness where God had been. In Stockholm I opted, finally, to the extent my human intellect and weak will could do so, for Torah.

Let me insert a geography question here: The Torah was revealed at Mt. Sinai, but where is that? Christian and Moslem tradition locates it in the Sinai peninsula, which seems logical: a 7,500-foot-tall peak called in Arabic "Jabal Musa," the Mountain of Moses. Recently a pair of amateur archaeologists claimed to have discovered the true Sinai in the ancient land of Midian, now Saudi Arabia. This makes a kind of sense, too, since the Revelation took place immediately after Moses' meeting with Jethro, priest of

Midian, and therefore the Jews couldn't have traveled very far from that place. The Torah itself, however, is notably vague on the subject: Exodus relates that the Israelites "journeyed from Rephidim and arrived at the Wilderness of Sinai and encamped in the Wilderness; and Israel encamped there, opposite the mountain." This won't help you find the spot on any map.

I say that Mt. Sinai is in Stockholm. For me it is, at any rate. Torah has a very good reason for keeping quiet about where the event of Sinai took place: because it happened, and happens, everywhere. At this moment there is a real mountain in a blazing desert between Israel and the Egypt where, three millennia ago, the Israelite slaves fleeing Pharaoh accepted the Torah from God. If a Jew were to find it today and go there, his soul's part in the collective memory of the Jewish people might rumble under the surface of his consciousness. But the Mt. Sinai described in Exodus is really only the Mt. Sinai of the old Israelites who stood, body and soul, at its boundary on the day of the Revelation. Their acceptance of Torah was active: they immediately began implementing its teachings. The experience of the unborn Jews who also stood there was, however, passive: we heard the Voice but, as disembodied souls, couldn't do much about it. For all Jewish souls who have lived after the Exodus, Sinai is not a place; it is an experience. Our Mt. Sinai is wherever we happen to be when we realize about Torah what our earliest spiritual ancestors realized on the day that God's voice whispered to them amid smoke and fire: that Torah is entirely Truth, that it came from God, that it is His Presence in our lives.

There is a phenomenon in the Bible called "song," which isn't like a song you hear on the radio or even that you would sing in church or synagogue. We find ten songs in Scripture, most famously the ecstatic "Song by the Sea," which the Israelites sang at the Sea of Reeds after the Lord split it and drowned the Egyptian charioteers. A song occurs when very spiritually elevated humans receive a particularly clear vision of how God works in the world and then spontaneously break out in wildly enthusiastic meters of biblical poetry. We ordinary folk have a parallel, if far more modest, experience, when we suddenly, passingly, and dimly understand some aspect of God's reality that we had never understood before. This for me was a moment like that. I wasn't about to burst into song, but I could do the next best thing. A thrilling sense of clarity took hold of me. As I crossed tiny Holy Ghost Island, which sits between the main city and Stadsholmen, I stopped and took out a green stenograph notebook. I scribbled down what I had realized: that blood is only a hint. Torah is a statement by God about the universe and our place in it, a statement that He first entrusted to a group of people who were related by blood. However, Judaism is not about blood. Like Mt. Sinai, it is in our minds, our souls, not our bodies.

--------

FOR AN INDIVIDUAL, the consequences of that fact are obvious. Torah tells us how to order our lives in order to know God, and if it really is all and only His word, then its claim on us becomes all the more compelling. But there are consequences for the community of Jews as well. My own Sinai happens to cast some light on the debate, hot at the moment, about what can be done to assure the future of American Jewry.

The question has attracted the interest of some respected Jewish intellectuals of my father's and grandfather's generations. Not long ago in *The New York Times*, columnist William Safire looked around from his dateline of East Hampton, Long Island. He observed that in the past fifty years Jews as a portion of America's total population have declined from 4 percent to 2.3 percent. After considering some remedies, he hit on "religious study, with greater understanding of [Jewish] symbols and ritual," because religion has certain practical benefits including that it "(1) provides a sense of tribal belonging . . . , (2) satisfies an inescapable spiritual longing and (3) binds the family." In a similar vein, writing in *Commentary* under the title "Why Religion Is Good for the Jews," conservative critic Irving Kristol advocated a reemphasis on Jewish schooling as an antidote to intermarriage.

Any Jew who believes as a Jew can only thank William Safire

and Irving Kristol for their endorsement of religious education. Perhaps someday American Jewish leaders will reevaluate the priorities of the community and direct more Jewish money to Jewish learning. (Imagine if the fortune plunged into the U.S. Holocaust Memorial Museum in Washington—$194 million just to build the thing—had gone for scholarships to Jewish day schools.)

Yet these pragmatic authors have missed a step. Neither man hints at his opinion as to whether the religion of the people he wants to save is true or mainly a useful fiction. Their arguments treat Judaism as an instrument for the survival of the tribe. This has been the prevailing attitude among American Jews of generations previous to mine. The concern of our parents and grandparents was not for the Jewish soul, but for the Jewish body, Jewish blood. The leaders who set the tone of discussion in the American Jewish community suffer from the tribal fallacy. As a result the American Jewish community, or rather its liberal subdivisions, are disintegrating rapidly.

After all, Jews aren't stupid. We were once held together as a people through the force exerted on us by our surrounding hostile non-Jewish neighbors. But the neighbors aren't hostile anymore. Jews are now free to drift off, to join other faiths or to believe nothing, and think nothing, about God at all. They do so because their leaders signal to them that Judaism has no transcendent importance; that Torah isn't true; that it is merely a useful fiction. If so, why *not* marry a gentile? If Torah is not Truth, if the encounter between man and God at Sinai never happened as the Torah says it did, then the idea of a "Jewish people" amounts, as Will Herberg said, to "a persistent and rather malignant delusion." In that event, to worry about Jewish "continuity," about intermarriage and the threat it poses to the future of American Jews, is nothing better than sentimentality. It may be something worse. Many Jewish parents who reject Torah but insist that their children marry Jews can fairly be described as bigots.

Either we have a mission from God, fully and truthfully described in the Torah, or we do not. If we do have such a mission, the only hope we have of convincing our fellow Jews to join in it is to begin speaking about that mission, about God, explicitly and publicly, making Judaism itself the principal object of organized Jewish life. That will never happen under the present cohort of Jewish leaders. Those among them who have faith are mostly too shy to discuss it in public. Of the ones who do speak confidently of Judaism as Truth, mainly Orthodox Jews, not enough venture out of their self-imposed ghettos to confront the secular world and inspire the cosmopolitan young Jews who desperately need to hear about God and Torah—and who want to do so, as the *ba'al teshuvah* movement demonstrates. As the Jewish people enters the twenty-first century, the Truth of Torah and nothing else—Jewish belief, not Jewish blood—will guarantee our survival.

———

WANDERING EARLY THAT EVENING around Stadsholmen, I passed the Tyska Kyrka, and the Storkyrka, or Great Church, consecrated in 1306, where earlier that week Harriet and I had seen the famous Parhelion painting. In 1535 strange halos, called parhelic circles, appeared in the skies above Stockholm. Meteorologists tell us that such halos form when the sun's light is reflected through ice crystals suspended in the atmosphere, but the citizens of Stockholm opted for a supernatural explanation. Catholics said the Protestant Reformation then in progress under King Gustav Vasa was a crime against God. The Lord had created the halos to indicate His anger at the Lutherans. To defuse the Catholic interpretation, the nation's leading Protestant reformer commissioned a painting of the parhelic circles with Stockholm below, the oldest surviving picture of the town, and set it up in the Storkyrka itself. He meant to say that religious truth cannot be determined by examining the sky above our heads—or, one might add, the blood in our veins.

Maimonides had said much the same thing four centuries earlier. He wrote in his *Mishneh Torah* that the Israelites in the desert accepted Moses as their teacher not because of the miracles he performed—the splitting of the Sea of Reeds, the manna from heaven, the water from the rock—but because they had heard

God's voice at Sinai. "Whenever anyone's belief is based on wonders, he has misgivings, because it is possible to perform wonders through magic and sorcery."

The physical survival of the Jewish tribe through four millennia is often cited as a miracle. Tribalists regard it as a sufficient reason to take necessary steps to preserve the Jews as a people indefinitely into the future. In this view, the fact that Jews have existed for so long teaches us that we must continue to exist forever.

I had proclaimed Harriet's choice of Jewish parents for me, and my subsequent reconnecting of the Goldkuhls to the people Israel, as a small miracle. It proved, I thought, that God meant me to be a Jew.

The lesson of the Parhelion picture, anticipated by Maimonides, is that miracles tell us nothing. They may be beautiful, or useful, or inspiring. But from them we cannot draw conclusions about right and wrong, about what should or shouldn't be, in short about God's will. To know what He asks of us, we must listen to His voice as it emanates from Sinai. The defining Jewish criterion must be not blood, or culture, or nationhood, or any of the innumerable substitutes for Judaism that have been proposed by factions among our people—compassion, tolerance, freedom, socialism, Zionism, Holocaust veneration, Jewish self-defense, Jewish unity—but Truth alone.

In its tractate Berachot the Talmud prescribes an ancient custom. When a Jew reads the three paragraphs of the *Sh'ma* each morning and evening, he should immediately append a single word, *emet*, that isn't part of the scriptural passage that forms the prayer's final paragraph. "I am the Lord your God Who brought you out of the land of Egypt to be your God," he says. *"Ani Hashem Elokechem—emet."* "I am the Lord your God—it is true." Not only is it a pleasant, spiritual idea to say that the Lord is God, that he brought us out of Egypt to give us the Torah. It is also *true*.

A story is told of a certain Jew who could not accustom himself to the idea of Torah as Truth. This man, a secular intellectual, wanted to debate a rabbi in his town on the subject, to prove to the rabbi that, in observing the mitzvot, he was wasting his time. The secularist made an appointment and went to the rabbi's house. He found the rabbi in his library, pacing the wooden floor with his hands behind his back, apparently lost in contemplation. The rabbi didn't look up when the secularist entered the room. He continued to pace slowly around the room. After an extended period of time, the man was about to give up and leave. Then, still without having formally acknowledged the other's presence, the rabbi at last raised his head and looked into the eyes of the Jew who did not believe.

"But," said the rabbi, "what if it is true?"

# ACKNOWLEDGMENTS

Adam Bellow and Abigail Strubel, editors with The Free Press at the time, initiated the idea that became this book, which was shepherded to completion with unfailingly good literary sense by my editor, Bruce Nichols. Thank goodness for my agent, Mildred Marmur, who had faith that such a book was worth writing. Several editors kindly have published articles by me parts of which appear in modified form here, including Neal Kozodoy of *Commentary,* John O'Sullivan of *National Review,* and Katharine Washburn and John Thornton, whose volume *Dumbing Down: Essays on the Strip-mining of American Culture* was published by Norton. John O'Sullivan generous double thanks for giving me time off from my responsibilities at *NR* without which I would today still be working away at this book. Two rabbis have been of incalculable aid to me: Daniel Lapin, generous mentor and friend, whose ideas and formulations appear in so many places here that it would be impractical to cite him for every one, and Barry Freundel, who was my first exposure to Torah embodied in a man. If only the student were worthy of his teachers! Both read this book in an earlier version, as did Mark Charendoff, Milly Marmur, Bennett Schneir, Harriet Lund, and Maria McFadden. All pointed out errors and deficiencies which I have tried, surely without total success, to correct. Many thanks to them, and no less to Yvonne Cummins, Alex Abrams, Mark Miller, and of course to all my parents for their affectionate encouragement.

Certain other people and institutions have enlightened me, in ways described in this book, not necessarily by being good examples. Because they never asked to have their dealings with me written into the public record, I have changed some names and facts for the purpose of disguise.